Horizons 2000+
Career Studies

Judi Misener & **Susan Butler**

Vice Principal
West Hill Collegiate Institute
West Hill, Ontario

Career Education Consultant
Toronto, Ontario

Consultants

Richard Culverwell
Parry Sound High School
Parry Sound, Ontario

Melissa Nantais
St. Anne High School
Windsor, Ontario

Marie Gabriel
Durham District School Board
Whitby, Ontario

Maureen Prince
Waterloo Catholic District School Board
Waterloo, Ontario

Hal Humphries
Gravenhurst High School
Gravenhurst, Ontario

Gary Socholotuk
Beaver Brae Secondary School
Kenora, Ontario

McGraw-Hill Ryerson Limited

Toronto Montréal New York Burr Ridge Bangkok Bogotá Caracas
Lisbon London Madrid Mexico City Milan New Delhi
Seoul Singapore Sydney Taipei

McGraw-Hill
Ryerson Limited
A Subsidiary of The **McGraw·Hill** Companies

Horizons 2000+
Career Studies

ISBN 0-07-087411-5

http://www.mcgrawhill.ca

5 6 7 8 9 0 TRI 9 8 7 6 5

Printed and bound in Canada

Canadian Cataloguing in Publication Data

Misener, Judi, date
    Horizons 2000+: career studies

2nd ed.
First ed. published under title: Exploring your horizons
Includes index.
ISBN 0-07-087411-5

Vocational guidance – Juvenile literature. I. Butler, Susan (Dorothy Susan).
II. Title. III. Title: Exploring your horizons.

HF5382.5.C2M57 2000   331.702   C00-930976-4

PUBLISHER: Patty Pappas
ASSOCIATE EDITOR: Jocelyn Wilson
SUPERVISING EDITOR: Crystal Shortt
PERMISSIONS EDITOR: Jacqueline Donovan
PRODUCTION SUPERVISOR: Yolanda Pigden
COVER DESIGN: Sarah Coviello/ArtPlus Limited
INTERIOR DESIGN: ArtPlus Limited
ELECTRONIC PAGE MAKE-UP: Valerie Bateman/Brian Taft/ArtPlus Limited
PART AND CHAPTER ILLUSTRATIONS: Chum McLeod
ADDITIONAL ILLUSTRATIONS: Harvey Chan, Laurel Dewan, Stephen Hutchings, Sami Suomalainen, Nicholas Vitacco
COVER IMAGE: Bill Brooks/Masterfile

Contents

Acknowledgements

· ·

Since 1990 we have had the opportunity to develop together as friends and colleagues. We have shared many unique experiences. Positive responses from teachers across Canada to our books and our workshops have been energizing and very rewarding. We thank the many people at McGraw-Hill Ryerson Limited for their continued belief in the importance of career education. We could not have succeeded without the support of Patty Pappas and the wizardry of Jocelyn Wilson.

Special thanks are also extended to Kurtis Kitagawa for his endorsement of this book on behalf of the Conference Board of Canada.

Judi Misener and Susan Butler

Preface

· ·

Horizons 2000+ will help you learn more about yourself, your future possibilities, and your community. How often have you been asked "What courses are you taking?" or "What do you want to do when you graduate?" Have you ever asked yourself "Who am I? What can I do? What is ahead of me? Where do I begin?" *Horizons 2000+* is designed to help you answer these questions and more. You will gain knowledge that will start you in the direction that best suits your talents, abilities, skills, and interests. Employability Skills 2000+ will be the foundation for your future success.

Horizons 2000+ begins with an introduction to a Career Studies Portfolio— what it is, what you might want to put in it, and how you can use it for evaluation, volunteer placements, and job interviews. You will learn how to develop and maintain a portfolio using the Collect, Select, and Reflect model. As you work through the book, you will see a portfolio icon beside activities that are a possible selection for your portfolio.

Before you can start planning your future education and career choices, you must first discover as much about yourself as possible. In **Part 1, Discovering Your Strengths**, you will gather information about yourself from a variety of sources. Once the information is collected, you will analyze it to see what it says about you. Then you will be able to set some short-term personal goals and longer-term education and career goals.

Knowing what choices are available is necessary before deciding which direction you will take. **Part 2, Discovering Pathways**, informs you of possibilities and enables you to research what might suit you best. You will learn more about education—apprenticeships, college, technical schools, and university, as well as other forms of learning available to you after you graduate. You will examine the variety of career choices available to you when you leave school. You will begin to match who you are with the type of job you would like to have.

Recognizing how you fit into your community is the first step to being a contributing member. In **Part 3, Experiencing the Community**, you will meet people from your community and discover more about yourself by interacting with them. Discovering role models and connecting with mentors can help you determine what you want to be like when you are older. Networking in your community will also help you get the support you might need. Once you know what is available in your community and have learned more about the people who work there, your next step is to become actively involved.

In **Part 4, Working in the Community**, you will develop your employability skills based on the Conference Board of Canada's Employability Skills 2000+ recommendations. Improving your communication skills and developing effective job search tools will ease your transition into the workplace.

A Tour of the Text

To make *Horizons 2000+* visually appealing to you, the material is presented in an easy-to-read format. Photographs, illustrations, charts, diagrams, and cartoons have been included.

A chapter on **Developing a Career Studies Portfolio** appears at the beginning of the book to indroduce you to the purpose and method of creating and maintaining a portfolio throughout this course.

What You Will Learn appears at the beginning of each chapter and is a brief summary of what is to come.

Terms to Remember are key words that appear in boldface and are defined when they first appear in the text. They are compiled and alphabetized in the glossary at the back of the book.

Activities such as surveying, interviewing, role-playing, researching, and reading provide opportunities for individual and group work in each chapter.

Journal writing allows you to reflect on, and gain further insight into, who you are.

Portfolio activities relate to personal interests, talents, education, possible careers, community involvement, and other areas. There is one or more in each chapter. You will collect these items in your Career Studies Portfolio.

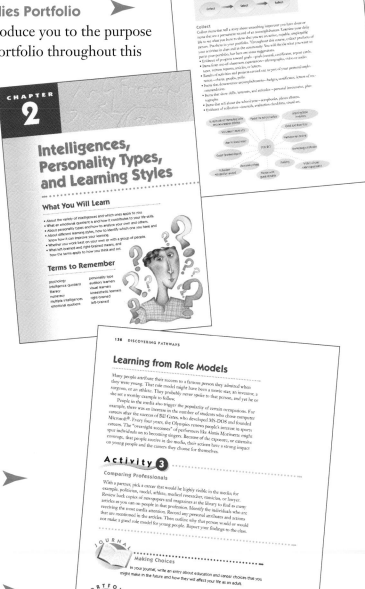

Profiles of famous Canadian or an interesting young person appear in most chapters. You can learn more about future possibilities for yourself through the lives of others. Questions relating to the content follow each profile.

In the News articles highlight people or news items relevant to the chapter content. They will provoke thought, discussion, and help you to set goals. At least one article appears in each chapter. It has pertinent questions following it.

Case Studies appear periodically throughout the text and feature people whose life experiences offer good models from which to learn. The questions that follow each Case Study allow you to compare your own experiences with those of the people featured.

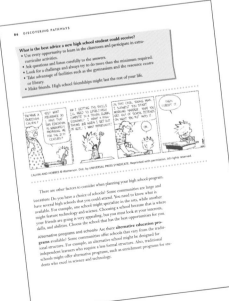

Cartoons selected for each chapter of this text will make you laugh and also learn! We believe that learning should always include humour.

◄ **Looking Back** sections at the end of every chapter feature questions that review and expand the chapter content.

◄ **Explorations** has activities that relate to the chapter content. They fall under the following headings:

Reflections offers an opportunity for journal writing, in which you record your feelings about an activity in the chapter.

Goals helps you set personal goals that relate to the chapter content.

Action! involves role-playing situations relevant to the chapter content.

In the **Featuring . . .** activities, you will be divided into groups to work on an edition of a magazine. For each chapter, your group will be given one of the following assignments.

Advice Column: Your team will create letters from readers asking for advice, and then write the answers.

Research: Using surveys, interviews, libraries, and the Internet, your team will research in greater depth a topic from the chapter, and then publish your findings.

Advertisement: Your team will create advertisements that relate to the content of the chapter. Be creative!

Editorial: Your team will write an editorial, which states an opinion and reasons for that opinion, on a given topic that relates to the chapter.

Personal Story/Interview: Your team will write a feature article on one person in the community whose story relates to the chapter.

Working through *Horizons 2000+*, your class will have created a number of editions of a magazine that cover all the topics. We recommend that a cover be designed and a unique name be given to your magazine.

A Note From the Conference Board of Canada

Horizons 2000+ builds on McGraw-Hill Ryerson's experience in developing and publishing career and personal planning resources for students in Grades 8–12. This new textbook addresses a key need in supporting high school students as they participate in co-operative or work experience programs and as they prepare to make more long-term transitions to the world of work.

McGraw-Hill Ryerson supports the work of The Conference Board of Canada's National Business and Education Centre in its action research networks, the Employability Skills Forum, and the Business and Education Forum on Science, Technology and Mathematics. *Horizons 2000+* provides many references to *Employability Skills 2000+*, which blends and updates the Conference Board's highly influential 1992 *Employability Skills Profile* and The Board's 1996 publication *Science Literacy for the World of Work*.

The authors of *Horizons 2000+* have been actively involved in co-operative education and work from its inception and prepared this textbook to meet curriculum requirements for career planning in high school. *Horizons 2000+* helps secondary students:

- get to know themselves;
- take stock of their interests and strengths;
- inquire into their values and career aspirations;
- explore careers related to their skills and interests;
- prepare career portfolios; and
- prepare for interviews.

Horizons 2000+ may be used in conjunction with The Conference Board's *Employability Skills Toolkit*, which is a set of practical tools to help learners and their coaches. By encouraging students to assess their skills, strengths, and career interests, *Horizons 2000+* is a valuable resource for all students.

Kurtis G. Kitagawa, Ph.D.
Research Associate and Manager
Employability Skills Forum
The Conference Board of Canada

Halifax, May 2000

Developing a Career Studies Portfolio

What You Will Learn

- The purpose of keeping a Career Studies Portfolio.
- How to select items for your portfolio.
- How to manage your portfolio.
- How to use your portfolio.

Terms to Remember

portfolio icon
inventory
assessment
evaluation
portfolio conference

What Is a Career Studies Portfolio?

A Career Studies Portfolio is a collection of purposefully selected items that you will gather during this course to illustrate your skills, values, abilities, and interests. These items will reflect the experiences you will have both in and out of school. Because your personal, academic, and interpersonal skills will be developed during your experiences, you can use these selected items as tangible reminders and evidence as you plan your career path. The Career Studies Portfolio will help you to clarify your interests, abilities, and aspirations. It will enable you to keep track of what you do well and to identify areas that need strengthening. In this way, the Career Studies Portfolio will assist you in establishing future goals and education and career plans. As well, you will be able to use items from the portfolio when applying for community placements, part-time jobs, and, in the future, when you apply for admission to specialty courses or other educational institutions.

Benefits of a Career Studies Portfolio

Although the Career Studies Portfolio is a collection of items that you select, it benefits not only you, the student, but also your teachers and community members. The following lists identify some of the purposes of a portfolio.

FOR THE STUDENT	FOR THE TEACHER	FOR THE COMMUNITY
• Contributes to the student's sense of accomplishment.	• Addresses the students' career planning needs.	• Identifies community members as part of the students' learning process.
• Provides materials to use in preparation for more education and/or a job.	• Provides documentation for every student.	• Increases community members' appreciation of the career planning process.
• Connects home, school, and community activities.	• Provides a framework for the students to direct their own learning in a number of directions.	• Allows community members an opportunity to be a partner in career development.
• Promotes personal accountability.		• Encourages community members' commitment to offer future career opportunities.
• Develops an awareness of the student's own knowledge, skills, and values through self-assessment.		

What Do I Put in My Portfolio?

The Collect, Select, Reflect Model will help you understand the process of preparing a portfolio. The following diagram represents this process.

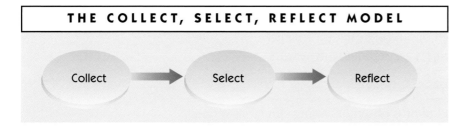

THE COLLECT, SELECT, REFLECT MODEL

Collect → Select → Reflect

Collect

Collect items that tell a story about something important you have done or items that are a permanent record of an accomplishment. Examine your daily life to see what you have to show that you are an active, capable, employable person. Put them in your portfolio. Throughout this course, collect products of your activities in class and in the community. You will decide what you want to put in your portfolio, but here are some suggestions.

• Evidence of progress toward goals—goals journal, certificates, report cards.
• Items from out-of-classroom experiences—photographs, video or audio tapes, written reports, articles, or letters.
• Results of activities and projects carried out as part of your personal exploration—charts, graphs, polls.
• Items that demonstrate accomplishments—badges, certificates, letters of recommendation.
• Items that show skills, interests, and attitudes—personal inventories, photographs.
• Items that tell about the school year—scrapbooks, photo albums.
• Evidence of reflection—journals, evaluation checklists, visual art.

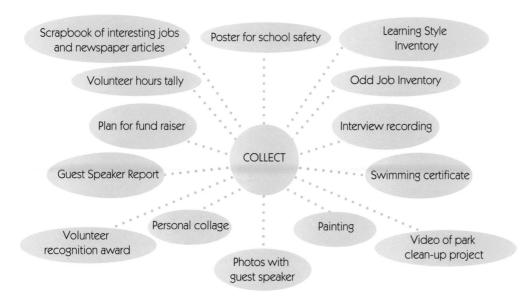

A Sample Career Studies Portfolio

Here is a list of items that one student gathered after participating in a Career Studies Course as well as volunteering in a community seniors centre for 20 hours.

- Résumé (up-to-date).
- Two letters of recommendation (one from a senior, one from a supervisor).
- List of daily responsibilities carried out during each centre visit.
- Audio tape of special interview project carried out with seniors.
- Safety Course Certificate.
- CPR Certificate.
- Personal collage done in class (and photos of seniors doing similar at seniors centre).
- Learning Style Questionnaire.
- Career Interest Inventory.
- Facts about the future of career choices in working with the elderly.
- Newspaper photo of recent family reunion and article written by student.

Select

Once you have collected a portfolio of items, you will be able to select those that will exhibit your capabilities for a specific reason. For example, if you are going to a job interview at an animal clinic, you might take:

- A résumé.
- A letter from your doctor saying that you are allergy-free.
- Evaluations from your volunteer placement at a seniors centre.
- A letter of recommendation from the supervisor at the seniors centre.

Or, if you are going to meet with a co-op teacher in an effort to get into the co-op course for recreation leadership, you might take:

- Your academic achievement record.
- A letter of recommendation from your physical education teacher.
- A letter of recommendation from the swimming instructor with whom you coached juniors each Saturday.
- First aid certificates.
- Recreational certification.
- Honour certificates or awards from your school.

Or, if you are going to meet with your community involvement supervisor and your guidance teacher for a discussion about your progress, you might take:

- A list of your goals.
- Your annual education plan.
- On-the-job reflections.
- A research report on available community services.

When you select items to show at a portfolio evaluation or to take to a placement or an interview, you think about what each one says about you. You also have to think of what the placement supervisor or employer is looking for. What special capabilities do you have?

The Portfolio Icon

Throughout Horizons 2000+, there are specific portfolio activities. The results of these should be included in your portfolio. There are also other activities that will result in items that are suitable for your portfolio. These activities are drawn to your attention by being highlighted with a **portfolio icon**, but the decision of whether or not to include it in your portfolio is yours.

Reflect

The Reflect part of the process allows you to ask yourself questions about the learning connected to the portfolio item. For example:

- What have I learned?
- What have I noticed?
- What would I do differently?
- What strengths and weaknesses are shown in this item?
- How does what I am doing affect my future choices?

Attaching this kind of information to each item in your portfolio before you put it away is important, so that you will have these notes as a reminder of your learning. When it comes time to prepare your portfolio for a conference, a volunteer or co-op position, or a job, you will have a record of your learning.

The following skills **inventory** lists areas of expertise and abilities. You can use this list to describe your own abilities when writing reflections for portfolio items.

Skills Inventory

COMMUNICATION

- Speak effectively
- Write factual material clearly and concisely
- Read with comprehension/speed
- Listen intently/ objectively
- Explain concepts well
- Express feelings appropriately

CREATIVE/INNOVATIVE

- Show imagination/curiosity
- Assume moderate risks
- Have a strong self-image
- Accept change as a challenge

INTERPERSONAL

- Withstand and resolve conflict
- Understand the feelings of others
- Motivate and encourage other people
- Appreciate/reward people's efforts

PROBLEM SOLVING

- Define problems
- Exhibit intellectual curiosity
- Distinguish between fact and opinion
- Propose and evaluate solutions

TECHNOLOGICAL

- Be familiar with major hardware components
- Use information to problem solve
- Make graphic presentations
- Access information from many sources
- Communicate using electronic means

LEADERSHIP

- Accept responsibility
- Understand followers and their needs
- Motivate others
- Accept and learn from criticism
- Behave confidently

Managing Your Portfolio

The portfolio of items that you will put together in this career studies course will be a model for similar collections that you will make in the future as your career experiences expand. Collecting only some of the items suggested on page 3 will result in an impressive selection and will be like a time capsule for your future. Choose a container for storing the items (a carton, an accordion file, a plastic file-box, a guitar case, a suitcase, a tool box, a computer file) and find an accessible place to keep it. File folders, computer disks, page protectors, a stapler, and paper clips would also be useful for keeping your collection in order. Most important is that all the items are kept together and organized.

You might want to organize your information by date (chronological), by topic, or perhaps by the topics related to what you will need for your résumé (Education, Work and Community Experience, Skills, and References).

It is essential to keep track of the items you add to your portfolio. Design a chart similar to the one following that you can add to every time you file an item. Allow space on the chart for a maximum number of items. Attach the list to your career portfolio.

Portfolio Tracking Sheet

DATE	DESCRIPTION		SOURCE	COMMENT
~~	~~~~~~~~~	~~~	~~~~~	~~~~~
~~	~~~~~~~~~	~~~	~~~~~	~~~~~
~~	~~~~~~~~~	~~~	~~~~~	~~~~~

Getting Started

Once you have selected a container for your portfolio items and have decided where to keep it, you may want to put a few fundamental items in it, such as a copy of your education plan, your personal information sheet or profile, your employment history or résumé (if you have done one), and your career plan. Samples of these appear below.

PERSONAL PROFILE

Name: _____   Date: _____

Grade: _____

- Academic Strengths _____
- School Activities (List clubs, teams, organizations.) _____
- Peer Help (List tutoring, reading partners, mentoring experiences.) _____
- Community Activities (List hobbies, volunteer work, sports.) _____
- Awards (List any form of recognition, awards, or citations for activities in and out of school.) _____
- Three words others would use to describe you are: _____
- Job Experience _____
- Co-op/Work-Experience Involvement (Take Our Kids to Work™, job shadowing) _____
- Other _____

CAREER PLAN UPDATE

Name: _____

1. If I could be anything I wanted, I would be:
2. One occupation I am seriously considering
3. The reasons I have chosen this occupation

4. To prepare for this occupation, I need:

Secondary School Credits/Courses

5. Activities and experiences that would he

6. Possible obstacles to overcome are: _____
_____

To continue my career planning, I will:
Research these occupations: A. _____   B. _____
C. _____

- ❏ Discuss my career options with a guidance counsellor or staff advisor.
- ❏ Complete an interest inventory.
- ❏ Enrol in a career planning program at my school or at a career centre.
- ❏ Enrol in a co-operative education course.
- ❏ Seek a volunteer, part-time, or summer job in potential fields of interest.
- ❏ Visit a college, technical school, or university.
- ❏ Use the career information materials in my school.
- ❏ Use the career information materials at a career centre.
- ❏ Job shadow.
- ❏ Interview a person in an occupation.
- ❏ Other: _____
I have discussed this Career Plan Update with:

Parent/Guardian: _____   Counsellor/Teacher: _____

EMPLOYMENT RECORD

Name: _____
Dates of Employment: _____
Address: _____   to _____
_____
Phone: _____
Responsibilities: _____   Fax: _____   E-mail: _____

Junior achievement of Toronto & York Region's *Career and Life Planning Portfolio* is quickly gaining recognition and support across Canada. It acts as a planner, diary, source file and "collector" of work to visually display the skills and talents of students. It is also a tool that students use to create a picture of themselves for any employer to see.

Portfolio Assessment

Portfolio assessment is . . . reflecting on the information you have gathered from a variety of sources about your growth and development.

Portfolio evaluation is . . . the judgement that is made based on what you have gathered.

When collecting items for your portfolio, remember . . . the more varied the assessments (number, types of items, point of view), the more accurate the evaluation.

As you go through *Horizons 2000+*, you may be asked to review some portfolio items. This is called portfolio assessment. What you are doing is deciding why an item is important and what it shows about you.

When you assess the items in your portfolio, consider these questions:
• What will it show about what I have learned?
• In what way(s) does it remind me of a lesson I learned or an event that changed my opinion or knowledge level?
• What does it have to do with my future choices?
• Which audience will be interested in this item? (teacher, parent, peer, community member, mentor . . .)

If you are selecting items from your portfolio to bring to a specific volunteer placement or job, consider these questions:
• What skill(s) does this item demonstrate?
• What skills would this particular employer be looking for? Which item will illustrate my competency?
• What would make this item better?
• Why do I want to show this item? What does it say about me?
• Are a wide variety of skills shown in the portfolio as a whole?

It is often valuable to obtain someone else's opinion on an item. Traditionally, the teacher evaluates your work. Before that evaluation, it is helpful to ask trusted people for their input.

Portfolio Assessment Team

❑ You
❑ Peer
❑ Teacher
❑ Parent/Guardian
❑ Staff Member at School

❑ Employer
❑ Coach
❑ Sibling
❑ Mentor

Preparing for a Portfolio Conference

When it is time to prepare for a **portfolio conference**, you will want to look through your portfolio items and sort them so they reflect your knowledge, skills, and attitudes. As you look through the items and try to decide what to select, you might want to ask yourself these questions:

• Why did I choose this?
• In what ways is it important to me?
• How does it illustrate my accomplishments?
• What would I say if I showed it to someone? What do I want that person to know?
• To whom would I like to show it?

Choosing Items for a Portfolio Conference

When preparing to share your portfolio contents in a conference, select a variety of items that illustrate:

• Creativity
• Progress
• Awareness
• Quality
• Diversity

• Knowledge
• Persistence
• Organization
• Accuracy
• Thoughtfulness

You will also want to prepare to speak about each portfolio item. To do this, you might want to complete sentence starters like the following:

• I have included this piece because . . .
• I want you to know that . . .
• When I did this I learned . . .
• I want to work on improving . . .

You might also want to rehearse your portfolio conference with a peer by presenting and discussing each portfolio item with him or her and getting feedback.

Setting Up a Portfolio Conference

In preparation for a conference, you might want to ask yourself questions like the following:

• What are the goals of the conference?
• Who will I invite?
• When can these people meet?
• How long will the conference take?
• What preparations will I have to make?

If you are inviting people to your portfolio conference, they may be more comfortable if you give them an outline to explain what will happen. For example:

• The time of the conference is _____ .
• This work covers the time period from _____ to _____ .
• The goals of this conference are . . .
• The purpose of my portfolio is . . .
• The contents of my portfolio will illustrate . . .
• You are welcome to ask questions about . . .

Portfolio Conference Checklist

❏ Items selected
❏ Participants invited
❏ Comfortable seating arranged
❏ Display area prepared
❏ Comment sheets ready

Reflecting on Your Portfolio Conference

Once your portfolio conference has taken place, it would be a good idea to reflect on the experience and record your thoughts and feelings in your journal or on a sheet of paper to be included in your portfolio. You might consider some of the following sentence starters to guide your reflections.

• Things went smoothly during the conference because . . .
• Things could have gone better if . . .
• One thing I wish I had shared but forgot to was . . .
• One thing I chose not to share but should have was . . .
• As I reflect on what I gained from being actively involved in my conference, I notice . . .
• Something I felt (*person's name*) gained from hearing things from my perspective was . . .

Having read this chapter on the Career Studies Portfolio, you should now be familiar with a portfolio's purpose, how to create and manage one, and what to put in it. You should also be aware of what a portfolio conference is, the different types there are, and how to prepare for one. This knowledge will enable you to have more control over your own learning, career, and lifestyle choices. In the meantime, you will learn more about yourself and be better prepared for the future.

Looking Back

1. Your portfolio contains a variety of items that reflect what you have learned. Make a list of materials and equipment you would require to create the ultimate portfolio. Cost is no object.

2. Now that you and your peers have participated in portfolio conferences, how would you explain the advantages to younger students?

3. Which article from your portfolio is your favourite? For what reasons?

4. Which item would you like to replace? Why?

5. Make a list of all the items in your portfolio. Categorize them by level of interest, importance, or difficulty.

EXPLORATIONS

Reflections

Complete the following sentence starters.

When I first started collecting items for my portfolio I thought . . .
Now I realize . . .
When my portfolio is complete, I will feel . . .
The time I am spending on career studies makes me realize . . .

Goals

When you discuss your own work and listen to the responses from your peers, teachers, and parents or guardians, you are learning about your learning and the achievement of your goals. What two long-term goals are now clear to you? What can you do in the next year to move toward them? What steps will you be taking soon to make them happen?

Action!

Create a series of monologues that reflect the following situations:
• What a student is thinking when choosing items for a portfolio conference.
• What a teacher is thinking during a conference.
• What a parent or guardian is thinking when he or she sees a number of portfolio items but cannot really understand their purpose.

Featuring. . .

Editorial: Write an editorial that offers your opinion on the value of portfolios for students, peers, teachers, and parents or guardians in measuring what was learned.

Advice Column: Create a ten-point checklist and guide to help other students in their creation of an excellent portfolio.

Advertisement: Create an illustrated advertisement for five different containers for portfolio items.

Personal Story/Interview: Develop five questions about the portfolio conference experience. Ask the same questions of the following participants: student, peer, teacher.

Research: Take a poll in the classroom to see which items students chose as most important in their portfolios. Illustrate your findings on a graph.

1

Discovering Your Strengths

Understanding yourself is the first step in educational and career planning. This understanding comes from collecting data, or information, about your likes and dislikes, your strengths and weaknesses. It comes from looking at past experiences. Your perception of self, or the way you see yourself, and the perception others have of you, assist you in answering the important question: "Who am I?" Once all the data is gathered, the second step is to examine it critically—what does it all mean? The final step is one of action—once you have a good understanding, what do you do with it? How can you make the most of your talents in the future?

Getting to Know Yourself

What You Will Learn

- How to collect and analyze data about yourself.
- Who you are in terms of values, attitudes, interests, aptitudes, and skills.
- How other people perceive who you are.
- How to identify your strengths and weaknesses.
- Which events in your life were important to you and helped shape who you are today.

Terms to Remember

profile	subjective
aptitudes	objective
skills	survey
values	questionnaire
attitudes	time line
journal	autobiography

Your interests, strengths, values, attitudes, and personal history all combine to make you who you are. In this chapter, you will gather and analyze information about yourself. You will look at how others see you to give you a more complete picture. Getting to know yourself is the first step on the path of determining what your future could be.

How You See Yourself

Filling in a chart is an organized way of developing your personal **profile**, or brief description of yourself. Following are two sample charts that will help you see how to explore your interests, aptitudes, skills, values, and attitudes. The charts do not describe a real person; they are samples only.

To begin, meet in small groups to discuss what you think the terms *interests*, *aptitudes*, *skills*, *values*, and *attitudes* mean. Have someone in the group record the ideas presented for each term. When you have reached a definition for each one, compare your ideas, as a class, to create final definitions. This will give you a clear idea of what you are describing when you fill in your own charts.

The first chart, Interests, Aptitudes, and Skills, is for recording activities and events in your life. **Aptitudes** refers to your natural talents and abilities, while **skills** means what you have learned to do well. Many of the categories in this chart relate to subjects studied in school. Remember that marks are important, but they are only one measurement. Your enjoyment and interest levels are important, too.

The second chart, Values and Attitudes, will help you explore your **values**, or what is important to you, and your **attitudes**, or how you view things.

FOR BETTER OR FOR WORSE © Lynn Johnston Prod., Inc. Reprinted with permission of UNIVERSAL PRESS SYNDICATE. All rights reserved.

Interests, Aptitudes, and Skills

CATEGORY	IN SCHOOL	OUT OF SCHOOL
Art	• It's okay • marks are average • like doing perspective	• design and silkscreen clothing • paint and decorate my room • create cartoon characters
Music	• like playing the drums • learning to read music is interesting • performing is exciting	• listen to music all the time • go to concerts • buy CDs of my favourite musicians
Sports	• like phys. ed. • am on intramural teams • swim a lot	• am on a hockey team • play baseball • am learning golf
Technology	• troubleshoot lab computer • participate in robotics competition	• create a new web page • build home robot • work on cars
Math	• have good marks in math • like the challenge • like applying math to real situations	• follow the stock markets • handle money at my job • am club treasurer
Science	• enjoy new topics • understand science easily • help to set up labs	• watch science shows on TV • raise tropical fish • subscribe to science magazines
Language Arts	• find spelling a challenge • love to read • enjoy group presentations	• am a member of a local drama group • keep a daily journal • frequent library and book stores
Media	• use a computer-generated slide presentation • enjoy making videos • enjoy reading newspapers	• go to movies often • keep photo albums • use digital camera and scanner extensively
History	• am taking senior credits • am a member of a history club	• am a museum member • read biographies and historical fiction
Jobs/Chores	• sell tickets • am on a stage crew • am a recycling monitor	• have a part-time job • have a summer job • am a volunteer

Values and Attitudes

CATEGORY	ACTIVITIES	BELIEFS
Friends	• group work is fun • talk a lot in class • talk on the phone	Friends should be: • honest • supportive • dependable • fun
Helping Others	• read to younger kids • help kids with special needs • take part in 4H Club community projects	• helping younger kids makes me feel good about myself • homeless people need our help • working at the food bank is important
Family/Culture	• eat together • keep up my cultural traditions	• my family means a lot to me • eating together keeps the family together • family traditions are important
Health/Fitness	• am very active • like being outside • love food	• eating good food is healthy • playing sports is good exercise • staying at home when you're sick stops germs from spreading
Attitudes	• work hard in school • am friendly • am optimistic	• doing well in school is important • helping others is good • being positive makes everything easier

Activity 1

Creating Your Personal Charts

Create an Interests, Aptitudes, and Skills chart like the one on page 16. On sheets of paper, make three columns with the headings *Category, In School,* and *Out of School.* Then write your subject names down the left side of the page under the heading *Category.* Beside each subject, give brief examples of your interests, aptitudes, and skills in that subject, both in and out of school. Refer to the sample to help you get started.

Then create a Values and Attitudes chart like the one on page 17, with three columns titled *Category, Activities,* and *Beliefs.* Write the category headings down the left side of the page. Fill in your chart, giving examples of activities and what you think of them, for each category.

Change or add to the categories in your charts, if necessary. Try to write at least three points for each category. Be honest and thorough. Use descriptive words. Describe what you are proud of, what you like, and what you do not like. Examine both what you do and what you *think* about what you do.

These charts will tell you a lot about yourself when you analyze them. You will learn what your strongest interests are, where your talents lie, and what your values and attitudes are. These facts will be very important to you when you develop your interests, skills, and social abilities in school, in the community, and, eventually, in your career.

1. Study your charts. Circle the categories that contain the most positive statements. Then choose either question 2 or 3 to complete.

2. Using your charts as a guide, write several paragraphs about yourself.

3. Write a poem or song about yourself, or draw a picture, describing what qualities or interests make you unique.

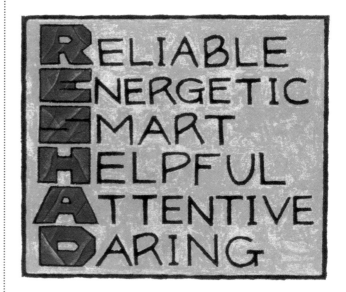

4. As a class, make lists of the qualities you expect from your friends, your teachers, and your parents. Underline the common items in the lists. How would you rate yourself for each quality? For example, if honesty is on your list, think about how honest *you* are. Are you always, sometimes, or never honest? Then create a list of the characteristics that describe you best.

 File your charts, paragraphs, poem, song, or drawing, and list in your portfolio.

Activity 2

Determining What You Value

From a cross-Canada study of people's values, a list of values important to teenagers was developed. These values are: friendship, freedom, privacy, being popular, recognition, excitement, being loved, success, a comfortable life, and family life.

On a sheet of paper, write these values in their order of importance to you. Then compare your list with the chart at right.

Teenagers' Values Across Canada

VALUE	PERCENT VIEWING AS "VERY IMPORTANT"
Friendship	91
Being Loved	87
Freedom	84
Success	78
A Comfortable Life	75
Privacy	68
Family Life	65
Excitement	58
Recognition	41
Being Popular	21

Activity 3

Identifying Family Influences

List ways your family has influenced your values and behaviour. Consider the rules you were taught at home, what things your family considers to be important, and the routines and daily habits, likes and dislikes, that come from your parents or guardians.

PORTFOLIO

Creating a Collage

Using photographs, drawings, objects, or pictures from magazines, create a collage that reflects who you are. Study your collage and think about yourself. Create a slogan, phrase, or title that describes you, and add it to your collage.

Recording Your Day

A **journal** is a record of events in a person's life and his or her thoughts and feelings about these events. A journal can be kept daily, weekly, or only occasionally. Each entry is dated so that, in the future, the person will know when the events took place. It is usually written in the past tense. Some people draw in their journals or include mementos, like ticket stubs to a special event. A journal can be a notebook, a diary, a computer file—anything you want to use that works for you. Read the sample journal entry at right.

Keep a journal for two weeks. At the end of each day, write about what you did and how you felt. Compare the ideas in your journal with those in your charts. Add to the charts if you learned more about yourself by keeping this journal.

SEPTEMBER 8, 20__

Back to school for another year. Where did the summer go? My classes are fine—got all the ones I wanted. Luckily, I know people in all my classes. What a change from this time last year. One new student looks really cool. Would like to know him better!! No homework tonight, but I'm sure that won't last long.

How Others See You

How you see yourself and how others perceive you are sometimes quite different. Your view of yourself is **subjective**. Your past experiences, your place in the family, your emotions, interests—many things influence how you see yourself. The way other people see you is **objective**. They are detached, or at least removed, from that first-hand knowledge. This enables them to see you as you are at that moment. They can observe your strong and your weak points. They might notice qualities about you that you were not aware of. They might see abilities that you do not even notice because you have had them for so long or because you do not see them as being unique. What they see might boost your self-confidence, surprise you, or, at least, be of interest to you. Learning how others see you can further develop your personal profile.

Activity 4

Taking a Survey

To obtain an objective viewpoint about something or someone, a **survey** is a useful tool. A number of people are asked the same set of questions. Their answers are compiled and the results are analyzed, either to get specific information or a general picture of a topic.

You will be taking a survey about yourself.

1. Create a **questionnaire** that asks direct and personal questions about how people see you. Study the following example to give you an idea of how it could look.

Sample Questionnaire

As part of a school assignment, I would like to know how you see me. Your opinions will be helpful as I learn more about myself. Please take the time to answer these questions.

1. My best qualities are. . .

2. In what area could I improve?

3. Give five words that describe me.

Thank you.

2. Select a close friend, a family member, a teacher, and one other person whom you trust. They will answer the questions about you.

3. To conduct your survey, ask each of the people the questions yourself and write down the answers, or hand out copies of your questionnaire for them to fill out. Use the following format to compile their answers. Record their names and the answers to each question beside the question number.

Survey Results

	(Friend)	(Family Member)	(Teacher)	(Other Person)
1. My best qualities are:	~~~ ~~~	~~~ ~~~	~~~ ~~~	~~~ ~~~
2. Area in which I could improve:	~~~	~~~	~~~	~~~
3. Five words that describe me:	~~~ ~~~	~~~ ~~~	~~~ ~~~	~~~ ~~~

4. After you have compiled your survey results, write down something from the survey that surprised you, something that pleased you, and something that you will try to improve.

Add any new information to the paragraphs you wrote about yourself earlier.

Attach the survey results to your paragraphs and file them in your portfolio.

Your Past Experiences

Looking back at previous experiences in your life provides other important puzzle pieces for understanding who you are. You can learn from your past triumphs and disappointments. Understanding the past and the present help you to plan your future.

PROFILE

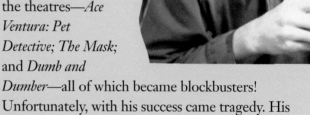

Jim Carrey—Alllrrighty Then

Born on January 17, 1962, in Newmarket, Ontario, Jim Carrey was the youngest of four children. Throughout his childhood, his father, Percy, suffered from manic depression and his mother, Kathleen, had kidney problems. The family's financial situation was like a roller coaster ride, going from middle-class comfort to poverty. Jim was put down by his peers because of his family circumstances. To overcome this, he developed funny routines to make them laugh so he would be accepted.

When Jim was 16 and in his first year of high school, his father lost his job as an accountant and could not find other work. The family became homeless, and Jim was forced to drop out of school to help earn money. After working as an office building cleaner with his family, he decided he had to do what he loved and had a talent for—comedy. Five years and several movies later, he became a successful stand-up comic.

In 1990, his character Fire Marshal Bill became a hit on the television series *In Living Colour*. Then he was in *Doing Time on Maple Drive*, a made-for-TV movie, which was nominated for an Emmy award. Unfortunately, before he became a big success, his mother died of kidney failure. He also ended his seven-year

marriage to Melissa Womer, with whom he had a daughter, Jane.

In 1994, Jim Carrey had three movies playing at the theatres—*Ace Ventura: Pet Detective; The Mask;* and *Dumb and Dumber*—all of which became blockbusters! Unfortunately, with his success came tragedy. His father, with whom Jim was close, died unexpectedly.

Since then, Jim has appeared in *Batman Forever; Ace Ventura: When Nature Calls; The Cable Guy;* and *Liar, Liar*. He received $20 million for the last film, the highest amount ever given to a comedian in a film. He has also been both host and guest on many talk shows. Besides having won numerous awards, Jim Carrey is immortalized on the Hollywood Walk of Fame.

1. Write about what reading this profile makes you realize about people.

2. Using information from the profile, create a time line like the following, recording the important dates and events in Jim Carrey's life.

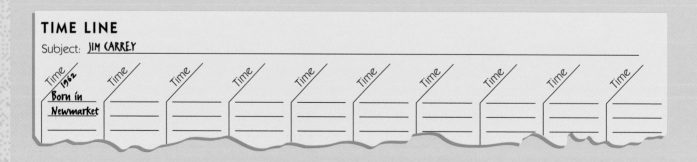

TIME LINE
Subject: JIM CARREY

Time 1962 Born in Newmarket   Time   Time   Time   Time   Time   Time   Time   Time   Time

Activity 5

Creating a Personal Time Line

Think about the major events in your life that changed both your life and you. If you consider these events for a while, you might start remembering things that you have not thought about for a long time. Now, draw a **time line** on a sheet of paper. List the important dates and events in the order they happened. When you have finished, share your time line with classmates, friends, and family members to see if they can add anything to it. Do you feel like you know yourself better now?

        You might wish to add your time line to your portfolio.

Activity 6

Representing Your Life

Write an **autobiography** or a song or draw a storyboard about your life. Include factual details, such as where you were born, where you have lived, who is in your family, and so on. Include three major events that had a big influence on you. Some examples are the birth of a sibling, a major accomplishment, the purchase of a pet, or something unfortunate, such as the death of a grandparent, or a family separation.

        You might wish to share your work with a teacher, parent/guardian, or friend and add it to your portfolio.

Activity 7

Creating a Box of Treasures

Create a box of treasures from your personal belongings. Include such things as a photograph of your favourite person, something you made, or something related to a hobby. Whatever you include should represent who you are. Put the box in a safe place. You might want to add new items to it periodically to update any changes in your life or create a new box to have different "time capsules" of yourself.

Activity 8

Assessing Your Past

Review your time line or autobiography, and then answer the following questions on a sheet of paper or in your journal.

1. What is your best memory? Why?

2. How have your past experiences affected who you are today?

3. Add any data from your past to the paragraphs you have already written about yourself.

IN THE NEWS

Living on Nothing But Music

By Jan Wong

At a time when government support of the arts is waning, Cheng Ma symbolizes the yearning of the human spirit to make music, no matter what the cost. At the Glenn Gould school in Toronto, faculty routinely leave food in a basement hamper for starving students. The conservatory is, after all, the place that produced one of the world's great sopranos, Teresa Stratas, who was so poor when she arrived in the late 1950s that her mother sewed her dresses from flour sacks.

Cheng, whose name means *galloping horse*, was five when she first heard a piano. She agitated daily for one of her own until her father, a postal worker and an amateur singer of Zhejiang opera, caved in. It cost a year's wages.

Cheng isn't one of China's seriously spoiled onlies. She has a brother, a graphic artist, six years older. That meant when she was born, the government fined her parents for having a second child. Her mother, a worker in a thermos factory, likes to joke: "As soon as you were born, you cost us money."

Her hometown of Zhaojiang is so tiny, Cheng says, "you can walk from one end to the other in 20 minutes." Within two years, she had learned everything Zhaojiang's one and only piano teacher could teach her.

So at the age of seven, desperately seeking a good piano teacher, she boarded a steam ship for Shanghai—by herself. "My father told one of the deckhands to look after me," she explains. "He was from our town." Cheng slept on a straw mat in the hold. Thirty-six hours later, an uncle met her at the docks, hoisted her onto the child carrier of his bike, and rode home. He had only a shoebox apartment for his wife and child, so he installed Cheng in an even tinier room one floor above. She ate with them, but was sent away each night to sleep alone with her rented piano. "I was afraid," she says. "I cried."

But Cheng didn't cry at school, even when her classmates mocked her as a bumpkin and threw stones at her. "I played to express my sadness. But I was also determined to be the best in the class. " She accomplished that, and became so popular she was elected class leader that year, and every subsequent year. She went home once a year, at Chinese New Year's. Even during summer vacation, she stayed in Shanghai to practise piano.

In Shanghai, Cheng, then a first-grader, charmed a famous piano teacher into accepting her. The teacher spent two years correcting her horrible technique. At 14 she heard a bassoon, and it was love at first sound. Never mind that many consider the bassoon the clown instrument of the orchestra. Never mind that in China, only boys play the *big pipe*, as it is called. Cheng found a teacher. Six months later, she aced the auditions at the prestigious Shanghai Conservatory, beating out five male applicants.

Her bassoon teacher there, Cheng says, encouraged her to study abroad. She searched the Internet and discovered Canada. Her classmates were leaving for Vienna, New York, Paris. "Everyone thought it was strange that I wanted to go to Canada. But I knew this was a country of immigrants where everyone got along."

1. **What obstacles did Cheng overcome to get to Canada?**

2. **Discuss what this article tells you about determination to fulfil a dream.**

Looking Back

1. How is knowing yourself helpful for your education and future career?

2. What is the benefit of knowing how others see you?

3. Why is being aware of your weaknesses as well as your strengths helpful?

EXPLORATIONS

Reflections

You have the opportunity to participate in an exchange program to another province. You will spend time with a student and his or her family in their home and the student will come to your home. It is important that a good match is made between you and the exchange student. You are, therefore, required to submit a description of yourself. Begin with the sentence "I am a person who . . ."

Action!

In groups, brainstorm a list of skills. Each member selects one skill at which he or she is competent. Imagine that you are together in a foreign city and have become lost. Develop a script about how you would combine your skills to find your way. Then role-play the scenario. Think of another problem that needs to be solved and role-play the outcome.

Featuring . . .

Advice Column: What advice would you give to teens who feel they do not fit in?

Research: Conduct a survey of teenagers' values using those listed in the Teenagers' Values Across Canada chart on page 19. Select whom you want to survey. For example, you might want to survey students and teachers and compare their responses. Compare the responses you get with the percentages in the chart.

Editorial: Write an editorial on the topic "Following the Crowd."

Personal Story/Interview: A mix of many cultures adds an interesting dimension to every classroom, school, and community. The differences in cultures are fascinating. Write a story about someone in your class, school, or community who is from a culture different from your own.

Advertisement: For the same exchange trip as mentioned in Reflections, you need to describe what you would like your exchange partner to be like. State your requirements in a "Wanted" poster or as an advertisement.

Intelligences, Personality Types, and Learning Styles

What You Will Learn

- About the variety of intelligences and which ones apply to you.
- What an emotional quotient is and how it contributes to your life skills.
- About personality types and how to analyze your own and others.
- About different learning styles, how to identify which one you have and know how it can improve your learning.
- Whether you work best on your own or with a group of people.
- What left-brained and right-brained means, and how the terms apply to how you think and act.

Terms to Remember

psychology	personality type
intelligence quotient	auditory learners
literacy	visual learners
numeracy	kinaesthetic learners
multiple intelligences	right-brained
emotional quotient	left-brained

In this chapter, you will continue to learn more about yourself by using methods that have been designed by specialists in the field of **psychology**. Psychology is the study of human nature. There are many theories, based on years of research, on how and why we behave the way we do. Some are featured in this chapter. You will discover many different ways to figure out who you are. When you know yourself, you can make choices and decisions that are right for you. You can make plans that fit who you are. You will also be able to compare yourself to others, and discover what characteristics you have in common and what your differences are.

Seven Ways to Be Smart

Have you heard of the term IQ? It is the short form for **intelligence quotient**. The quotient is a number that is determined from the results of a written test. The test focusses on ability in **literacy** (language) and **numeracy** (numbers). The higher the number, the greater the potential intelligence. The IQ test has been a standard for determining intelligence for decades. Average intelligence is a score of 100. But is it the only way to measure intelligence?

Psychologist Dr. Howard Gardner believes that the IQ test is too limiting and that humans are intelligent in many areas. After extensive research, he has identified seven kinds of intelligence, or **multiple intelligences**. Psychologist Dr. Thomas Armstrong uses the phrase "Seven Kinds of Smarts." Another way of thinking about how people are "smart" is to think about the many ways that people are talented.

Music Smart (Musical Intelligence)

This intelligence is based on how musical you are. People who respond to rhythm and beat, who perform either vocally or with an instrument, or who compose music have this kind of "smart."

Activity 1

Music-Smart Quiz

On a sheet of paper, write down the activity title and the statements that apply to you.

1. I have a pleasant singing voice.

2. I can tell when a musical note is off-key.

3. I frequently listen to music on the radio, cassettes, or CDs.

4. I play a musical instrument.

5. I often walk around with a song running through my mind.

6. I can easily keep time to a piece of music.

7. I know the tunes to many songs.

8. I often make tapping sounds or hum while studying or learning something new.

Body Smart (Bodily-Kinaesthetic Intelligence)

This intelligence relates to physical movement. Each person possesses a certain control over body movements, balance, agility, and grace.

Activity 2 ●

Body-Smart Quiz

On a sheet of paper, write down the activity title and the statements that apply to you.

1. I participate in at least one sport or physical activity on a regular basis.

2. I find it difficult to sit still for long periods of time.

3. I like working with my hands by doing activities such as sewing, carving, model building.

4. I frequently use hand gestures or other forms of bodily language when I am talking.

5. I need to touch things in order to learn more about them.

6. I enjoy daredevil amusement rides or similar thrilling physical experiences.

7. I think I am well co-ordinated.

8. I need to practise a new skill rather than read about it or watch a video describing it.

People Smart (Interpersonal Intelligence)

This intelligence is about person-to-person relationships. It is the ability to interact with others, understand them, and interpret their behaviour. It is how you notice contrasts in moods, and sense what people are thinking or feeling without them telling you.

Activity 3 ●

People-Smart Quiz

On a sheet of paper, write down the activity title and the statements that apply to you.

1. My friends come to me for advice.

2. I prefer team sports, such as basketball, instead of solo sports, such as diving.

3. When I have a problem, I usually talk to another person about it instead of working it out on my own.

4. I have three close friends.

5. I would rather play games like Monopoly with other people instead of watching television or playing computer games by myself.

6. I am comfortable in a crowd of people.

7. I am involved in extra-curricular activities at school or in my community.

8. I would rather spend time with my friends than stay at home.

Self Smart (Intrapersonal Intelligence)

This intelligence relates to how well you understand yourself. It is the ability to have insight into who you are, what you feel, and why you are the way you are. A strong intrapersonal intelligence can lead to high self-esteem and a strength of character that can be used to solve personal problems.

Activity 4 ·······································

Self-Smart Quiz

On a sheet of paper, write down the activity title and the statements that apply to you.

1. I like to spend time alone thinking and reflecting about my life.

2. I like to take quizzes that enable me to learn more about myself.

3. If I have a personal problem, I do not let it get me down. I solve it and get going.

4. I have goals for my life that I think about regularly.

5. I consider myself to be very independent.

6. I keep a personal diary or journal to record my thoughts about what happens to me.

7. I often prefer to be alone than with a large group of people.

8. I have a very clear idea of my strengths and weaknesses.

Picture Smart (Visual-Spatial Intelligence)

This intelligence, which relies on the sense of sight and the ability to visualize an object, includes the ability to create pictures in your head.

Activity 5 ···········

Picture-Smart Quiz

On a sheet of paper, write down the activity title and the statements that apply to you.

1. I often see clear images when I close my eyes.

2. I am good at co-ordinating colours.

3. I frequently use a camera or a video camera to record what I see around me.

4. I enjoy doing jigsaw puzzles, 3-D puzzles, and mazes.

5. I can generally find my way around unfamiliar territory.

6. I like to draw or doodle.

7. I can look at an object one way and imagine what it would look like from a different angle.

8. I prefer reading articles and books that have lots of diagrams and pictures.

Word Smart (Linguistic Intelligence)

This kind of intelligence relates to words and language, both written and spoken. People who are highly skilled writers, who have large vocabularies, and who speak many languages have this kind of intelligence.

Activity 6

Word-Smart Quiz

On a sheet of paper, write down the activity title and the statements that apply to you.

1. Books are very important to me.

2. I can hear words in my head before I read, speak, or write them down.

3. I get more out of listening to the radio than I do from watching television or videos.

4. I enjoy playing games that involve words.

5. I enjoy entertaining myself or others with tongue twisters or puns.

6. Other students sometimes stop and ask me to explain the meaning of a word I am using.

7. Language Arts, French, and history are easier for me than math and science.

8. I often write stories or poems in my spare time.

Logic Smart (Logical-Mathematical Intelligence)

This intelligence is the ability to solve logical problems and equations mentally. A person with this intelligence is good with numbers and doing calculations.

Activity 7

Logic-Smart Quiz

On a sheet of paper, write down the activity title and the statements that apply to you.

1. I can easily compute numbers in my head.

2. Math and science are among my favourite subjects in school.

3. I enjoy playing games or solving brain teasers that require logical thinking.

4. I am interested in new developments in science.

5. I am good with computers and enjoy working on them.

6. I like to do experiments and figure out how things work.

7. I can easily see numerical patterns.

8. I like to put things in order.

PROFILE

• •

World of Opportunities Await Bailey

by Randy Starkman

As a kid, Bailey always dreamed of soaring through the air, but even he never expected to reach such heights. He owns the 100-metre world track title, Olympic gold medal and world record, plus another Olympic Gold from anchoring Canada's 4 x 100-metre relay team's stirring win over the U.S.

"I never saw myself doing this at this level," he said. "I never dreamed it would be a worldwide thing. My brother and I were well-known athletes in Oakville, but I didn't think I'd be a household name worldwide. That's big. It doesn't get any bigger than that, I guess."

But even as he gets caught up in the whirlwind that comes with fame, Bailey has a firm grasp on where he's heading. His aspirations can't be confined to a track and field stadium. He was a serious businessperson before he was a serious sprinter. "I'm looking for new challenges other than track," Bailey says. "Track and field is definitely my tool to get where I want to go, to the successful podium. It's so wide-open right now. That's what I love the most."

Coming soon to a convention hall near you: Donovan Bailey, motivational speaker. Bailey is determined to improve himself in the area of public speaking. "I think it's one of my weaknesses, getting up and presenting my story and doing it fluently," Bailey said. "If it's one of my weaknesses, it can only be an asset if I continue to correct myself just as I do in track, so I can get to the point where I'm comfortable."

What has made Bailey so marketable besides the titles he's gained is that he's eloquent, forthright, and has the smile and charm sought by advertisers. He's impressed observers with his willingness to tackle tough issues head-on.

"One thing about Donovan is he's incredibly honest," says his coach, Dan Pfaff. "He'll look you in the eyes and tell you what's going on. The eyes generally don't lie and I think people recognize this instantly."

Bailey was on Wall Street on behalf of Bell Mobility when the company's stock went public. It gave him the chance to meet with some big financiers. "When I go out, the job I do can open doors for younger guys." It also enables Bailey to open the door toward his biggest goal— making a smooth transition from the track to the boardroom.

So the next step for Donovan Bailey is the motivational circuit. But what is left to motivate him? He speaks of running "the perfect race," but what appears to excite him most is a team goal—chasing the world record in the relay. With relay mainstays Glenroy Gilbert and Bruny Surin, whom he regards as good friends, he wants to keep beating the Americans and take their world record, too.

Bailey would like to lower the Canadian record of 20.17 seconds, set in 1991 by Atlee Mahorn, to a more respectable world level.

When asked what message he had for high school students, Donovan Bailey said, "Just pursue your dreams. Stay strong. You can do it. Whatever it is you want to do, just work at it. Stay positive."

Reprinted with permission—The Toronto Star Syndicate.

1. Identify the types of intelligences you think Donovan Bailey has.

2. List the careers Donovan has and will be involved in.

Activity 8

Identifying Your Strongest Intelligence

For each quiz you just completed, add up the number of statements you wrote. Each quiz has a possibility of eight. In which quiz did you have the most answers? The least? Which kind of "smarts" do you have? You probably had some answers in each quiz; you probably have more than one kind of intelligence, with some ability in all of them.

Each individual is born with a unique combination of talents. Most researchers believe there are more than those listed earlier in the chapter. The next two qualities are also considered to be forms of intelligence.

Humour Intelligence

Having a highly developed sense of humour and the ability to create humour is considered to be a form of intelligence. Writers, cartoonists, and comedians are in this category. How is your sense of homour?

Emotional Intelligence

According to a leading expert, Dr. Goleman, your **emotional quotient** (EQ) is your ability to handle your emotions. It refers to how you cope with demands and expectations, how you adapt to meet challenges. Dr. Goleman believes it is the most important form of intelligence. It includes your ability to manage your time and to finish what you start. Your EQ determines how successful and happy you will be and how long you will live. We can think of EQ in this way: Being smart does not matter if you do not know what to do with it!

Activity 9

Identifying a Person's Intelligence

On a sheet of paper, write the name of a person you know personally beside each question number. If you cannot think of someone who is right for the question, then give the name of a famous person.

1. If I ever get lost, I hope I am with —.

2. If I ever own a basketball team, I want — to be a player.

3. If I move to a new place and need to learn my way around, I hope I can be with —.

4. If we enter a poster contest, I want — on my team.

5. When my radio breaks, I hope — will be home so I can call for help.

6. If I work on an invention, I want — to help me.

7. I definitely want to have — on my debating team.

8. If I start a musical group, I sure hope I can get — to join.

9. For a fun time at my party, I will invite —.

10. When I need advice about a problem, I will always call on —.

11. We are going to try to get the school cafeteria to change its menu. I hope — will be our leader when we do this.

12. We are moving to a new community and I have to start at a new school. I hope — will stay in touch and help me adjust.

Personality Type

Determining your **personality type** can help you decide on the kind of career you might want. Just as experts have studied human intelligence, they have also studied human personality. There are numerous personality tests that can be taken. The results are scored and a person's personality type is defined. One of the most famous of these tests is called the Myers-Briggs Type Inventory, after the mother-and-daughter team that invented it. Their findings have been the basis of other forms of personality tests. A very popular and fun one to do is called True Colors.

Four colours—orange, blue, green, and gold—are used to represent the four different parts of your personality. Each personality part is represented by a different colour and refers to different personality characteristics. Just as some of you prefer to write with your right or left hand, you also have a preferred part of your personality that you like to use the most. Although you really have all four colours or parts in your personality, everyone has a favourite personality colour that is naturally like him or her. The colour that describes you the best is your dominant or strongest colour. Read the following descriptions. On a sheet of paper, write the names of the colours in the order *most like you* to *least like you*. Remember, all the personality colours are positive, and everyone has some of each of the personality colours.

Curious Green
Basic need is for mental power, or to be seen as smart.

Characteristics
• Analytical and conceptual (examines things carefully, thinks in terms of ideas or concepts)
• Independent, self-motivated, and logical
• Thinks a lot
• Values gaining and sharing knowledge

Strengths and Needs
- Possesses problem-solving skills
- Sees relationship of parts to whole
- Requires independence of thought and opportunity to work alone
- Needs to ask questions to satisfy curiosity

Adventurous Orange

Basic needs are for action, excitement, freedom, and to act on impulse.

Characteristics
- Playful and fun-loving
- Competitive and adventurous
- Likes to take risks

Strengths and Needs
- Exhibits high energy and zeal
- Seizes opportunities; is clever
- Needs hands-on approach
- Requires variety and flexibility
- Possesses a sense of humour

Responsible Gold

Basic needs are for structure, security, and to be of help to others.

Characteristics
- Organized and plans ahead
- Dependable, loyal, and responsible
- Follows the rules

Strengths and Needs
- Respects authority
- Needs order and sequence
- Responds well to a structured, stable environment

Harmonious Blue

Basic needs are for harmony and positive, close relationships.

Characteristics
- Friendly and sensitive
- Imaginative and communicative
- Wants to make the world a better place

Strengths and Needs
- Values the feelings of others
- Creates harmony
- Sees various sides of an issue
- Needs to feel emotionally connected with others
- Desires affirmation and encouragement from others

Activity 10

Determining Your Colour

From the previous descriptions, determine which colour is most like you. If you have difficulty deciding between two colours, ask a friend, a teacher, or a parent/guardian for his or her opinion. On a sheet of paper, write your colour as a heading, and list the characteristics, strengths, and needs for that colour. You might wish to file the description in your portfolio.

Activity 11

Discovering Your Colour Mates

Have each corner of the classroom represent one of the four colours. Go to the corner that represents your colour. Are you surprised by who is with you? With your group, discuss your colour's personality traits and give examples of how you have those traits. What are your values? What careers do you think suit your colour's characteristics?

Learning Styles

To learn, we depend on our senses to bring information to our brain. Most people tend to use one of their senses more than the others. Some people learn best by listening. They are called **auditory learners**. Other people learn best by reading or seeing pictures. They are **visual learners**. Still others learn best by touching and doing things. They are called **kinaesthetic learners**.

Scientists and psychologists do not know why people use one sense more than the others. Maybe the sense we use the most just works better for us. Knowing your learning style might help you learn better and more efficiently. It might also explain why some things are more difficult for you to learn.

It is not unusual to use different learning styles for different tasks. For instance, you might repeat your German lessons out loud to prepare for a test, but study your textbook to prepare for your math quiz. You might repeat some experiments you did in class to prepare for your science test. In these cases, you are using an auditory style to learn a language, a visual style to learn math, and a kinaesthetic style to learn science. Each one helps you learn what you need to know.

Another component of learning styles is whether you like to work in groups or by yourself.

Activity 12

Identifying Your Learning Style

For these questions, choose the first answer that comes to your mind. Do not spend too much time thinking about any question. Record your answers on a sheet of paper by listing the number of the question and the letter of your answer.

1. Which way would you rather learn how a computer works?
   a. watching a video about it
   b. listening to someone explain it
   c. taking the computer apart and trying to figure it out for yourself

2. When you are not sure how to spell a word, which of these are you most likely to do?
   a. write it out to see if it looks right
   b. sound it out
   c. write it out to sense how it feels

3. If you were at a party, what would you be most likely to remember the next day?
   a. the faces of the people there, but not the names
   b. the names but not the faces
   c. the things you did and said while you were there

4. How would you rather study for a test?
   a. read notes, read headings in a book, look at diagrams and illustrations
   b. have someone ask you questions, or repeat facts silently to yourself
   c. write notes out on index cards and make models or diagrams

5. What do you find most distracting when you are trying to concentrate?
   a. visual distractions
   b. noises
   c. other sensations like hunger, tight shoes, or worry

6. How do you prefer to solve a problem?
   a. make a list, organize the steps, and check them off as they are done
   b. make a few phone calls and talk to friends or experts
   c. make a model of the problem or walk through the steps in your mind

7. Which are you most likely to do while standing in a long line at the movies?
   a. look at the posters advertising other movies
   b. talk to the person next to you
   c. tap your foot or move around in some other way

8. You have just entered a science museum. What will you do first?
   a. find a map showing the locations of the various exhibits
   b. talk to a museum guide and ask about exhibits
   c. go into the first exhibit that looks interesting and read directions later

9. When you are happy, what are you most likely to do?
   a. grin
   b. shout with joy
   c. jump for joy

10. Which would you rather go to?
    a. an art class
    b. a music class
    c. an exercise class

11. Which of these do you do when you listen to music?
    a. daydream (see images that go with the music)
    b. hum along
    c. move with the music, tap your foot, etc.

12. How would you rather tell a story?
    a. write it
    b. tell it out loud
    c. act it out

13. Which kind of restaurant would you rather not go to?
    a. one with the lights too bright
    b. one with the music too loud
    c. one with uncomfortable chairs

Total your a's, b's, and c's.
- *If you scored mostly a's,* you have a visual learning style. You learn by seeing and looking.
- *If you scored mostly b's,* you have an auditory learning style. You learn by hearing and listening.
- *If you had mostly c's,* you have a kinaesthetic learning style. You learn by touching and doing.
- *If you picked two letters about the same number of times,* you depend on both of those learning styles.

 File the results of this questionnaire in your portfolio.

Activity 13

Working in Groups and Independently

Your teacher will time you for three minutes. During this time, create a list of musicians— solo artists or groups. Repeat the exercise, but this time do it with two or more of your classmates. Assign one of you to be the recorder. When you are finished, answer these questions on a sheet of paper:

1. Which activity did you prefer? Why?

2. In which situation were you most confident and comfortable?

3. In which situation were you most productive?

4. Think about other situations in which you have worked in a group and on your own. Apply questions 1 to 3 to these situations. You should be able to determine whether you prefer to work independently or in a group.

Write a summary about how you like to learn, and file it in your portfolio.

Your learning style is also influenced by whether you are **right-brained** or **left-brained**. Yes, you read that correctly. Studies have shown that each half of our brain serves a different function. The left half is logical, analytical, and used for language. The right half is used for creative thinking. This does not mean you use only half your brain, but most people have one side that is dominant.

A c t i v i t y 14

Are You Right-Brained or Left-Brained?

Read each question. On a sheet of paper, write down the question number and an "a" or a "b" for the answer that you would most likely choose.

1. Which is more true of you?
   a. I am tense about getting things right
   b. I am relaxed and let things happen

2. Which do you enjoy more about music?
   a. the beat
   b. the melody

3. Which way of learning do you like best?
   a. books and lectures
   b. workshops and field trips

4. Which of these two subjects do you like more?
   a. math
   b. art

5. When you buy something, do you make sure you have received the correct change?
   a. yes, I count it
   b. no

6. How do you figure things out?
   a. a piece at a time, then put it all together
   b. the answer comes to me all at once, like a light going on

7. Which would you rather do?
   a. read
   b. watch TV

8. How are you at putting your feelings into words?
   a. very good
   b. it is hard for me

9. If you practise an instrument or a sport, how do you do it?
   a. the same time each day, for a certain amount of time
   b. when I feel like it and have the time

10. You are riding your bike to a friend's house. You have never been there before. Which method do you use to find your way?
    a. I ask for directions, then write down street names and landmarks
    b. I ask for directions, then look at a map

11. Which of these types of fabrics do you prefer?
    a. fabrics without much texture (cotton, denim)
    b. fabrics with lots of texture (corduroy, suede, velvet)

12. Are you good at remembering faces?
    a. no
    b. yes

13. Are you good at remembering names?
    a. yes
    b. no

14. How do you feel about psychic claims—that there is such a thing as ESP (extrasensory perception), for example?
    a. they are foolish and non-scientific
    b. science cannot explain everything; they are worth looking into

Total your a's and b's. Left-brained responses are a's; right-brained responses are b's.
- *Twelve or more a's or b's* means you strongly prefer that side of your brain.
- *Nine a's or b's* means you somewhat prefer that side of your brain.
- *Seven of each* means you use both sides of your brain equally.

Identify which side of your brain you use most.

 File the results of this questionnaire in your portfolio.

"Your Honor, he was driving his car using the left side of his brain, while his license indicated he was only to drive with the right side!"

If you are right-brained, does that mean you are never logical? If you are left-brained, does that mean you are never creative? Of course not. All it means is that you tend to favour one side over the other. It is just part of your personal style.

Activity 15

Which Side Is in Control?

Which side of your brain controls most of your activities? Find out with this simple exercise. Remember that the left side of your brain controls the right side of your body, and the right side of your brain controls the left side of your body. Write down your responses (R or L) on a separate sheet of paper numbered 1 to 5.

1. Clasp your hands together. Which thumb is on top?

2. Fold your arms. Which arm is on top?

3. Cross your legs. Which leg is on top?

4. Look through a paper tube. Which eye do you use?

5. Kick a ball. Which foot do you use?

   Which side of your brain is in control?

There are many interesting approaches to figuring out who you are. By completing these activities you will become more self-knowledgeable, more self-confident, and more aware of your strengths and weaknesses.

Activity 16

Taking a Personality Quiz

This quiz will assess your preferences at this particular moment in your life. Your preferences will continue to change, so you may want to take this quiz again at a later date.

Read each question, and on a sheet of paper write a Yes or No beside each question number. There are no right or wrong answers. Answer each question honestly, and take as much time as you need. If some questions are hard to answer, discuss them with a partner.

Personality Quiz

1. Do you like to have a lot of freedom when you do an assignment or a job?

2. Do you like to be a leader?

3. Do you like to finish one job before you start the next?

4. Are you generally co-operative?

5. Do you like to work on projects by yourself?

6. Do you keep your things neat and tidy?

7. Do you enjoy writing poetry or stories?

8. Would you enjoy selling things, from apartment rentals to newspaper advertisements?

9. Do you plan carefully before you start to do something?

10. Are social activities very important to you?

11. Would you like to work on research projects?

12. Do you like to follow directions carefully?

13. Are you sensitive to your own feelings?

14. Do you usually look on the bright side of things?

15. Do you like to build things and/or repair them?

16. Are you able to explain things clearly to other people?

17. When you learn something new, do you often try to find out more about it?

18. Do you have clerical ability?

19. Do you like to create things, for example, inventing gadgets or designing posters?

20. Would you describe yourself as being ambitious?

21. Are you uncomfortable when a lot of people pay attention to you?

22. Can you discuss difficult subjects with people without hurting their feelings?

23. Would you want to work in a science laboratory?

24. When you do a project or another job, do you do it carefully, one step at a time?

25. Do you have musical, artistic, or dramatic ability?

26. Do you like speaking in front of a group of people?

27. Do you enjoy working with tools and machinery?

28. Are you able to help people who are upset or worried?

29. Do you read scientific books or magazines?

30. Would you like to prepare letters and written reports?

31. When you have been assigned a project or task, do you like to do it differently from most other people?

32. Are you a person who likes to try new things or experiences?

33. Do you see yourself as a practical person?

34. Are you a good listener?

35. Do you like solving mathematical or chess puzzles?

36. Do you arrange your papers, files, or books in an organized way?

37. Do you express your emotions easily?

38. Do you think you can sell an idea or a product?

39. Do you often take part in sports or athletics?

40. Can you meet new people easily?

41. Do you dig deeply into topics to satisfy your curiosity or to solve problems?

42. Do you see yourself as being calm rather than emotional?

43. Are you basically independent?

44. Are you good at arguing your point of view?

45. Do you think you have mechanical ability?

46. Do you enjoy giving information to other people?

47. Would you rather find out something for yourself than take another person's word for it?

48. Would you like to work at a job where you would operate a computer or other machine?

49. Do you have a good imagination?

50. Would you be interested in organizing a club or another group?

51. Would you rather work at a task than socialize with people?

52. Would you describe yourself as generous?

53. Are you more of a thinking than an emotional person?

54. Do you enjoy working with numbers?

55. Are you able to design, invent, or create things?

56. Have you considered starting your own business?

57. Do you like working with your hands, doing things such as plumbing repairs, fixing cars, sewing, or wallpapering?

58. Are you interested in looking after people when they are sick?

59. Do you have mathematical abilities?

60. When you are given an assignment, do you like to show how well you can do it?

Scoring the Quiz

The chart below contains 60 numbers, one for each of the questions you have just answered. On a sheet of paper, write down the personality types in the order they appear in the chart. For every question you answered Yes, mark an X beside the appropriate personality type. For example, if you answered Yes for question 1, you should put an X beside Artistic. Then count the number of Xs on each line. Write that number at the right. The lines with the most Xs are your strongest personality types.

For a description of each type, refer to "The Six Personality Types" chart on page 43.

Artistic	1	7	13	19	25	31	37	43	49	55
Enterprising	2	8	14	20	26	32	38	44	50	56
Realistic	3	9	15	21	27	33	39	45	51	57
Social	4	10	16	22	28	34	40	46	52	58
Investigative	5	11	17	23	29	35	41	47	53	59
Conventional	6	12	18	24	30	36	42	48	54	60

Developed by the Toronto District School Board.

 You may wish to file your Personality Quiz summary and a copy of your personality type in your portfolio.

The Six Personality Types

Realistic
Technically and athletically inclined people prefer to work with their hands and tools to build, repair, or grow things, often outdoors. **Dislike:** educational or therapeutic activities, self-expression, working with people, and new ideas. **Traits:** stable, materialistic, frank, practical, self-reliant.

Conventional
Data and detail people prefer to work with words and numbers, carrying out detailed instructions. **Dislike:** ambiguity, unstructured, unsystematized activities. **Traits:** conscientious, orderly, self-controlled.

Investigative
Abstract problem solvers prefer to work on their own, observing, learning, investigating, and solving problems, frequently in a scientifically related area. **Dislike:** repetitive activities and working with people. **Traits:** analytical, independent, curious, precise.

Enterprising
People influencers like to work with people—influencing, leading, or managing them. **Dislike:** precise work, concentrated intellectual work, and systematic activities. **Traits:** persuasive, domineering, energetic, ambitious, flirtatious.

Artistic
Idea creators prefer to work with their minds—innovating, imagining, and creating. **Dislike:** structured situations, rules, and physical work. **Traits:** imaginative, idealistic, original, intuitive, expressive.

Social
People helpers like to work with people—informing, enlightening, helping, training, developing, or curing them. **Dislike:** machinery and physical exertion. **Traits:** co-operative, understanding, helpful, tactful, sociable, ethical.

Activity 17

Connecting Your Personality Type to Jobs

Connect your personality type to the possible jobs on the following chart. Select your strongest category across the top of the chart, and then select your second-strongest category along the side of the chart. Find the intersection of these categories. These jobs should relate to your interests and personality type(s).

Career Chart

	ARTISTIC	ENTERPRISING	REALISTIC	SOCIAL	INVESTIGATIVE	CONVENTIONAL
Artistic		Choreographer, Interior decorator, Advertising manager, Film producer/ director	Graphics, Photographer, Sculptor, Sign writer, TV camera operator, Drafter	Model, Teacher, Economist, Musician, Actor, Production manager	Composer, Architect, Sculptor, Sign writer	Props person, Costumes person, TV and film technician, Camera person, Set dresser
Enterprising	Film producer, Disc jockey, Announcer, Baker, Lawyer, Craftsperson, Chef, Interior designer		Pharmacist, Dietary assistant, Sales clerk, Tradesperson	Curator, Systems analyst, Buyer, Auctioneer, Realtor, Sales manager	Insurance investigator, Private investigator, Security, Quality control	Auctioneer, Market research analyst, Sales agent, Insurance inspector
Realistic	Cook, Painter, Cabinetmaker, Mould maker, Photo engineer, Printer, Baker	Plumber, Roofer, Animal breeder, Mechanic		Taxi driver, Meat cutter, Kitchen helper, Server, Chef, Baker, Police officer	Welder, Groundskeeper, Iron worker, Mechanic, Jeweller, Service person	Dental hygienist, Driller, Lather, Truck driver, Letter carrier, Maintenance person, Assembler
Social	Flying instructor, Minister, Priest, Rabbi, Speech therapist, Teacher	Counsellor, Dietitian, Home economist, Restaurant host, Driving instructor	Childcare worker, Employment counsellor, Orderly, Nurses' aid, Waiter		Community organization worker, Social worker, Sociologist, Probation officer, Police officer	Orderly, Cashier, Server, Nurses' aid, Waiter, Host, Probation officer, Police officer
Investigative	Doctor, Law clerk, Mathematician, Scientist, Researcher	Pharmacist, Optometrist, Lawyer, Lab technician, Inventor	Electronics technician, Computer operator, Geological technician	Psychologist, Social worker, Librarian, Veterinarian, Order processor/ picker		Word processor, Camera repairperson, Law clerk, Librarian, Instrument repairer
Conventional	Administrative assistant, Drafter, Computer programmer, Designer	Hotel clerk, Stock clerk, Travel agent, Sewing machine operator	Coding clerk, Order filler, Bank teller, Business machine operator	Travel agent, Receptionist, Library technician, Credit clerk, Bookkeeper	Clerk typist, Methods analyst, Travel agent, Bookkeeper, Stock clerk	

CASE STUDY

Animals of the Workplace

by Diane Stafford

When the lion is away, the otters will play. The beavers will keep on working. And the golden retrievers will sit and smile benignly. That is either a bunch of poppycock or a pretty good picture of the animals in the workplace jungle—if you accept the theory that people can be categorized according to psychological type. Many educators, psychologists, and employment experts believe they can.

Ever since the Myers-Briggs Type Indicator was introduced more than half a century ago, efforts have grown to build teamwork by understanding what makes people tick differently. Several different personality "tests" are in use. One, which uses animal names to label psychological types, was introduced by counsellors Gary Smalley and John Trent. They first applied the lion, otter, beaver, and golden retriever appelations to four personalities they defined in their family counselling work. They and others say personality types can be identified by the way people answer questions about their preferences. By extension, understanding these types can provide keys to workplace harmony.

"Everyone on our staff know what they are," said Dennis Schemmel, a psychologist and director of the Counselling and Testing Centre at the University of Missouri-Kansas City (UMKC). "And by knowing each other's type, we are more attuned to knowing why each of us reacts the way we do." UMKC counselling centre employees do not use animal names to describe their psychological types. But they can reel off four-letter labels familiar to users of the Myers-Briggs assessment. Schemmel, for example, is an ISTJ. He describes himself as a logical, detail-oriented person who is well-organized and takes deadlines seriously. He said he is most comfortable thinking through an issue carefully before he draws conclusions or speaks.

The ISTJ label is Myers-Briggs shorthand for one of 16 personality types obtained by combining four of eight possible preference indicators. An ISTJ personality, for example, tends to answer Myers-Briggs test questions in such a way as to indicate a preference for:

- Introversion (I) rather than extroversion (E);
- Gathering information by sensing (S) rather than intuition (I);
- Making decisions by thinking (T) rather than feeling (F);
- Preferring to deal with the world with schedules and established judgements (J) rather than spontaneity and looser perceptions (P).

An ISTJ boss, Schemmel said, could clash mightily with an ENFP second-in-command who is comfortable with improvisation instead of structured plans and with group brainstorming instead of private thoughts. Could clash but will not, if the ISTJ boss understands why the ENFP acts and reacts the way he or she does. "You cannot change the other person," Schemmel emphasized. "But understanding his type helps enormously to understand what he is about and to understand there is a way to approach him, given his personality."

Psychological type is an explanation of personality developed by the Swiss psychiatrist Carl Jung, who observed that human behaviour is not random. Instead, Jung said, it follows identifiable patterns of inborn preference. People administer the Myers-Briggs or similar tests to persons aged 14 and older to help discover and define those preferences.

Another assessment, the Keirsey Temperament Sorter, explained in *Please Understand Me* by David Keirsey and Marilyn Bates, compacts the four-letter Myers-Briggs types into two-letter labels to identify just four types:

- SJ (sensing/judging);
- SP (sensing/perceiving);
- NF (intuitive/feeling);
- NT (intuitive/thinking).

According to Keirsey, but not yet validated by the extensive follow-up research of the Myers-Briggs test, about 45 percent of people are SJs. SJs are the types Smalley calls beavers, the ones most likely to be detailed, deliberate workers, comfortable with following instructions. Smalley said beavers are most likely to react to a new situation by asking, "How was it done in the past?" Keirsey said about 38 percent of the population are SPs. Smalley calls them the otters. Friendly, fun-loving, verbal, and flexible, otters might offer or respond to new proposals with, "Trust me! It will work out!" Keirsey's NFs are Smalley's golden retrievers. Keirsey said they represent 10 percent of the population. They are, Smalley asserts, loyal, non-demanding, and enjoy routine. They are the most apt to say, "Let us keep things the way they are." That would leave about seven per-

cent as members of Keirsey's NT type. They are Smalley's lions, the goal driven, action-oriented people who are comfortable taking charge. The lion might say, "Let us do it now!"

Psychological typing is not universally accepted, and even its advocates warn against misuse or too-rigid acceptance of the test results. All of the assessments are self-selection, which means that people choose the response, generally to a two-choice question, which they believe fits them best.

1. What are the characteristics of the four animal types—the lion, the otter, the beaver, and the golden retriever?

2. Describe the main characteristics of the Myers-Briggs personality test outlined in this case study.

3. What is the recommended use of personality tests?

4. How does knowing different personality types help develop good working teams?

Creating a Personal Summary

Create a personal summary of each section of this chapter—your intelligences, true colour or personality type, whether you are left- or right-brained, a group or independent learner, and what your learning style and personality type are. Give an example that demonstrates each category.

Expanding on Your Personal Profile

Reflect on how the information you have learned in this chapter has added to your picture of who you are. Has this information changed your outlook about people you know? If so, how? Write a few paragraphs describing your observations in your journal.

Looking Back

1. How will knowing the types of intelligence you have help you choose options at school and career possibilities for the future?

2. Why is your emotional quotient an important part of your personal make-up?

3. How will knowing your personality type help you select activities inside and outside school?

4. Will knowing what type of learner you are change the way you prepare for a test or a presentation? How?

5. How will being a group learner or an independent learner influence your choice of careers and specific jobs?

EXPLORATIONS

Reflections

Write a letter to a teacher from your past, outlining what you now know about your learning style.

Action!

Form groups and determine which types of intelligences are represented in it. Volunteers can assume different intelligences if all the intelligences are not represented in the group. Each student will role-play a cartoon-like superhero that exaggerates one aspect of that type of intelligence.

Featuring. . .

Advice Column: Give advice on how teens of different "true colours" can be friends.

Editorial: Write an editorial on the importance of self-knowledge.

Personal Story/Interview: Does your community give awards to people who are outstanding citizens? Does your school give awards for active involvement in your school, for achievement in academics, music, or athletics? Write the story of someone who has an exceptional talent. You might want to focus on what it is like to be that way and what were the first signs that he or she had this special quality.

Research: Look into other formal methods that can be used to assist a person in answering the question "Who am I?" such as handwriting analysis, numerology, horoscopes, or palm reading. Or investigate one of the following: what emotions are associated with certain colours, what certain colours symbolize (for example, purple is linked to royalty), what effects certain colours have on people.

Advertisement: Create an advertisement for one of the psychological inventories you have explored in this chapter, such as intelligence types, personality types, or learning styles.

Setting Personal Goals

· ·

What You Will Learn

· ·

- The reasons for setting goals.
- What goals are.
- How to set goals.
- How to evaluate your progress in achieving your goals.

Terms to Remember

· ·

goals   short-term goal
action plans   long-term goal
self-esteem   meaningful goals
reachable goals   creative visualization

N ow that you have a clearer idea of who you are, it is important that you continue to grow, and develop your strengths and abilities. As well as asking yourself the question "Who am I?" ask yourself these questions: "Where am I now? Where am I going? How am I going to get there?" **Goals**, or where you want to get to, help you realize that there are things you can do yourself, and that you can make things happen. Translating dreams into specific goals, and goals into **action plans**, is essential for personal growth. Setting goals and striving to achieve them is taking action. Action raises your **self-esteem**, or your opinion of yourself. Set a goal and start doing everything you can to achieve it. Goals give order and direction to your energy.

DREAM

ACTION PLAN
• take drama classes
• job shadow at the local TV station
• figure out how to interview a TV personality
• study television shows—why I like/do not like them
• join a theatre group or school play

GOAL

What Is a Goal?

A goal is something you want to accomplish. For this reason, a goal should be **reachable** or doable. Do not set a goal that is close to impossible to achieve. There are both short-term and long-term goals. A **short-term goal** could be to take better care of your pet, starting today. A **long-term goal** could be to finish high school. Short-term goals, such as getting an A on your next test, often lead to long-term goals, such as graduating to the next grade. Be realistic about who you are and what your strengths and abilities are. A goal should also be **meaningful**. It should move you toward improving yourself. It should agree with your values. Goals are set to help you on your journey to success.

How to Set Short-Term Goals

1. Decide on your goals and list them. Set only three to six at a time so you can reach them. List only those goals you want, not those you think others expect of you. Make sure your goals are achievable and meaningful. Will they help you manage your life in a positive way?

2. Develop a workable action plan to achieve your goals. Create small, manageable steps that build toward reaching your goal.

3. Evaluate your progress—are you completing the action steps? Have you accomplished your goals? After analyzing how you are doing, you might need to revise your goals and action steps. Do not be afraid to make mistakes. Learning from mistakes can help you keep growing.

Setting Goals

4. Revise your goals and plans.

1. Decide on goals and list them.

3. Evaluate your achievement.

2. Develop an action plan to achieve goals.

Setting goals can be depicted by a circle, as shown at right.

Amin's Short-Term Goals

CATEGORIES	GOALS	ACTION STEPS
Friends	• support my friends during personal troubles	• listen without judging • help them to develop solutions
Family/Culture	• take more responsibility as a family member	• respond to others' needs • initiate a family activity
Health/Fitness	• improve my level of fitness • improve my eating habits	• get more sleep • have junk food only once a week • join a fitness class • ride my bike as much as possible • read and follow The Canada Food Guide
Attitudes	• be more positive • use my time more productively	• take time to review my day • remind myself what I do well when I start to criticize myself • keep and follow a daily planner
Helping Others	• help seniors	• volunteer at a seniors centre • shovel snow for an elderly neighbour
School	• meet assignment time lines	• begin research when assignment is given • discuss progress with teacher on a regular basis

Activity (1)

Creating Goal Categories

Study the short-term goals that Amin created. He selected the same categories that you worked with in Chapter 1 with the addition of "school." Working in groups of three, brainstorm other categories that could be added.

Activity (2)

Evaluating Amin's goals

A goal must be *reachable* and *meaningful*. Study the goals Amin has selected. For each goal, indicate whether it meets these two rules.

Developing an Action Plan

Sometimes goals might seem very general. They sound great, but can they be achieved? Developing a workable, manageable action plan is important to your success. Action plans must be very specific and detailed. Following many small steps is the easiest way to accomplish your goals.

Activity (3)

Analyzing Amin's Action Steps

Working with your group, examine the action steps that Amin created for each of his goals. Determine if some should be more detailed, and then record what the additional action steps should be. For example, Amin's goal to improve his health by getting more sleep might require that he add "go to bed at 9:30 p.m. instead of l0:30 p.m." to his action step.

Setting Your Short-Term Goals

To help you determine what you would like to accomplish, do some daydreaming. **Creative visualization** is a method of focussed daydreaming. It can help you with everything from your tennis game, to how well you relate to other people, to planning your future.

Activity 4

Take Time to Dream

1. Visualize what you think a perfect day would be. Start from when you wake up to when you go to bed. Include what you would like to do, not just what you do well. Let your mind create an image for each of the categories in Amin's goal organizer.

2. Next, outline in words or create a storyboard of what you think an ideal week would look like. It is easy to daydream and to make up a new life for yourself. To make it come true, you have to choose one small part of it and decide that is what you are going to try for first.

Identifying a Goal

Write about something at which you would like to succeed. Why is it important? What happened when you tried before? What were the obstacles? What strengths do you need to succeed?

Activity 5

Testing Your Goal

In groups of three, one person states his or her goal. The second person assumes the role of the pessimist, or the negative person, and gives all the reasons the goal cannot be attained. The third person is the optimist, or the positive person, and encourages the goal-setter by offering solutions to problems created by the pessimist. Do this activity three times, each time changing the role you play.

Activity 6

Developing Your Personal Goal Organizer

1. Create a personal goal organizer similar to the one Amin designed. Are there categories from your brainstorming session in the first activity that you want to add to your organizer? Are there some categories Amin selected that you are not interested in?

2. In your organizer, record at least one short-term goal for each category.

3. Setting goals does not do much good if they are not put into action. Design an action plan with steps for each of your goals. Ask yourself "What do I need to do to get from here to there?" Make the steps as small and manageable as possible.

4. Keep your organizer in a place where you can see it several times a day; for example, on the mirror in your room, or in your binder. You might want to create a slogan, such as "Take Action!" or "One Step at a Time!" and put it on your locker door.

Evaluating Your Progress

Self-esteem comes when you know you have accomplished what you set out to do. If you do not meet your goals or follow your action plan for a day, a week, or even longer, do not give up. Pick up where you left off and try again. The following poem offers words of encouragement for when you are in a slump.

Never Give Up

My goals are set. My reach is far and strong

I aim for the highest star in my own sky.

Confidence is overflowing.

The key to success I hold tightly in my hand.

I start my journey.

But the star seems too high, the journey too tough.

Can I attain my dream?

My reach weakens but my arms are still outstretched.

I wipe my tears and flex my heart. I am stronger.

I won't give up.

Firmly in my grasp is the key—the key called perseverance.

—Erin Misener, Mount Albert, Ontario

If you are close to achieving your goal but cannot seem to reach it, you might need to figure out what else to try. Evaluate your action steps to determine if you are following them and decide if they are helping you to achieve your goal. One way to evaluate your progress is to maintain a Goals Journal.

JOURNAL

● ● ● ● ● ● ● ● ● ● ● ●

Recording Your Goals

Create a journal with one page for each of your goals. Choose one or two goals to focus on. A sample journal page is pictured here, but you might wish to create your own style of journal. You could include mementos from your day with your journal entries, illustrate your day instead of writing about it, or use a cassette tape on which you could record your daily activities. Each night for the next week, record in your journal anything you did to help you accomplish your goals. Also record how you felt each day.

My GOALS JOURNAL
GOAL: Meet assignment deadline
DATE: January 13
ACTION STEPS: Made arrangements to meet with Mr. Smith after school.
HOW I FEEL: Feel confident about doing well.

At the end of the first week, analyze how you are doing. Asking the opinion of others can help you to evaluate your progress. For example, Amin could ask his parents if they have noticed an improvement in his eating habits. Look at your goals. Is there someone—a family member, a friend, a teacher—who can give you feedback on how you are doing? Depending on the information you receive, you might want to make adjustments to your goals and your action steps. Or, you might find out that you have been successful!

For each goal, answer these questions:

1. Is there a goal for which you have no action steps?
2. Do you have a goal that has fewer entries than the others?
3. Are there some goals you have already achieved?
4. Are you taking the action steps you outlined but feel they are not helping you accomplish your goal?
5. Are there other resources you can use to help you analyze your action plan?
6. Is there more information you need about what you would like to do? Perhaps there is information in your school or public library, or you could search the Internet. With new information, you might have to adjust your action plan to make your goal achievable.

Evaluation might lead you to making some changes in your organizer. Depending on what your analysis of your Goals Journal tells you, you might have to add some action steps to achieve a goal, or you might have to revise a goal to make it reachable and meaningful. Do not get discouraged. Simply revise the plan to make it work for you!

Creating Action Deadlines

Have you ever postponed doing your homework until Sunday night even though you had all weekend to do it? Sometimes people approach their action plans the same way. One of Amin's action steps was to initiate a family activity. His journal showed that he did not do this during the first week. Amin decided to add "once a month" to his action step. To avoid putting things off, put a specific time on your action steps. Do you need to add some deadlines to your action steps?

Continue with your Goals Journal for two more weeks. At the end of each week, analyze your situation and continue to make changes, if needed.

Because goal setting and action taking is critical to personal growth and self-esteem, continue setting new goals, developing action steps, and keeping a Goals Journal.

JOURNAL

Reviewing Goals

What were the positive rewards you received from keeping your Goals Journal? What did you learn about yourself? What was the hardest action step to accomplish? What was the easiest goal to achieve? Will you continue to keep this journal? Why or why not?

Looking at Long-Term Goals

Achieving short-term goals builds confidence and self-esteem. Short-term goals can also serve as action steps to achieving long-term goals. It is not too early to start thinking about your long-term goals. Just going to school each day can be an action step toward a future goal. It might be an educational, career, personal, or social goal.

 **7**

Creating Long-Term Goals

Choose one of Amin's short-term goals and turn it into an action step for a long-term goal or goals. Amin's short-term goal to improve his eating habits could become an action step toward a long-term goal, such as becoming a nutritionist. Create long-term goals for Amin for each category.

Activity **8**

Expressing a Long-Term Goal

Now it is your turn! Create a bumper sticker, a licence plate number, or a book title to express a long-term goal that you might have. Be creative! But remember, like short-term goals, long-term goals must be reachable and meaningful.

PROFILE

Kwantum Leap

Jenny Wai Ching Kwan is one of British Columbia's first Chinese-Canadian women elected to the B.C. Legislative Assembly. At 21, she had no idea what she wanted to do with her life. At 30, she is a successful politician. Kwan credits her success, in part, to a period of soul-searching that led her to discovering her purpose in life. After graduating from high school, she went on to study business administration at university, but found she really didn't have the interest. Still uncertain as to her direction, Kwan took a trip to Hong Kong and China "to find her roots." When she saw the overwhelming inequalities between the rich and the poor, it made Jenny realize what democracy means and how important it is. She also discovered a new-found pride in her ancestry.

Jenny returned to school, intending to become a lawyer. But a co-op placement in her last term introduced her to a variety of community groups. Realizing she could make changes outside the legal system, Jenny became a community advocate. "What became clear to me is that I wanted to ensure that the community had access . . . to the Charter of Rights and Freedoms." In 1993 Jenny was elected to City Council for Vancouver. In 1996 she ran and won in the provincial election.

In setting and achieving goals, Jenny advises that the basis must be passion and commitment. "You've got to be interested in what you're doing. If you don't know what it is you want to do, then take your time to search for that." In the process, advises Jenny, you must listen to your own instincts.

People tried to discourage her from making the trip to Hong Kong and China. "When you know what it is that you need to do, the amount of self-confidence and esteem you build into what you're doing is enormous. . . . The next step is to find out how to translate your ideas into action."

Jenny believes that "there's still a lot of change that I'd like to see. . . . Equality and justice are the essence of what I live for."

Reprinted with permission from *Career Paths* 1996, published by YES Canada–BC and funded by Human Resources Development Canada and the BC Ministry of Education, Skills, and Training.

1. **How often did Jenny change her direction before finding her number-one goal?**

2. **What is Jenny's attitude toward making changes?**

3. **What personal characteristics does Jenny have that help her to achieve her goals?**

JENNY KWAN'S SIX STEPS TO GOAL SETTING

✓ 1. LISTEN TO YOUR INSTINCTS.

✓ 2. TURN IDEAS INTO ACTION.

✓ 3. BUILD A SUPPORT NETWORK.

✓ 4. SET A TIME FRAME

✓ 5. BE FLEXIBLE.

✓ 6. TRY, TRY AGAIN.

Representing Yourself in the Future

P O R T F O L I O

Find a video clip, a photograph in a magazine or newspaper, or create your own drawing that represents what you will be doing for a career and what you will be like as a person in the future. You determine when the future is. It could be one year or ten years from now. With the image, write a description of your career and personal goals and list the action steps that you will need to follow to achieve your long-term goal.

Before you begin, read the following excerpt for inspiration!

You're Allowed

• To believe there are no limits to your own potential.

• To expect great things for yourself.

• To think and feel that you have the power to go for your own dreams and goals.

• To discover the unlimited potential within you.

• To think and feel you have the power within to change your life circumstances if you are not satisfied.

• To enjoy life.

— Barry Davis

Looking Back

1. Why must goals be reachable and meaningful?

2. Give an example of a short-term goal and a long-term goal.

3. List three action steps you would take to achieve the short-term goal of taking better care of your things.

4. What is self-esteem? Give an example of something that gave you positive self-esteem.

EXPLORATIONS

Reflections

Write a poem or song, or draw a picture, using the theme "Pursuing Your Dreams."

Action!

Review your Goals Journal. Decide if there is an entry in your Goals Journal you would like to share with the group. Select a meaningful entry that you could act out. Feel free to add to it, if necessary!

Or

In pairs, present the following scenario. One of you plays the role of a student without goals. The other acts as a peer tutor who wants to help the student decide on a goal and an action plan for it. Select a goal from one of the categories in your Personal Goal Organizer.

Featuring . . .

Advice Column: Write advice to parents/guardians of students who are without goals.

Research Article: Conduct a survey of your classmates. Ask them if they would be willing to tell you their number-one goal. Report on the survey findings and any conclusions you have reached.

Advertisement: Create an advertisement on the importance of setting goals.

Editorial: Write about the importance of goal setting for teens.

Personal Story/Interview: Interview a teacher in your school. Ask what goals he or she has set and accomplished.

Skills for Success in School

What You Will Learn

- To take personal responsibility for your success at school.
- To develop skills for the workplace.
- To manage your time effectively.
- To prepare for tests and examinations.
- To recognize how peer pressure affects your success at school.

Terms to Remember

responsibility   time management
self-evaluation   peer pressure
personal work area
initiative

The skills you use to succeed at school can often be applied at the workplace and in your personal life as well. It is up to you to become an active learner and to improve areas in your school life that are less than satisfactory. How you see yourself plays an important role in achieving these goals. If you see yourself in a positive way, you can face challenges with more confidence. Evaluating yourself and identifying your problem areas are good starting points. In this chapter, you will evaluate your study habits, your time management, and how you deal with peer pressure. You will also be given suggestions for what to do if you are having difficulty in any of these areas.

Success in School

By the time you graduate from high school, you will have spent approximately ten thousand hours in the classroom. During these hours, your identity, self-esteem, values, career direction, and academic abilities are shaped. As you progress through the grades, you gradually take more **responsibility** for what happens to you at school. You currently play a number of roles: son or daughter, friend, sister or brother, basketball player, reading mentor. Your role as a student will have a major impact on your future.

Activity 1

Reflecting on Yourself as a Learner

What is your picture of yourself as a learner in the classroom? Reflect on this question by completing the following chart.

On a sheet of paper, write the numbers from one to ten. Beside each number, write the number from the scale from one to five that best represents how you see yourself.

How I Feel About Myself as a Learner

1. successful	1	2	3	4	5	unsuccessful
2. satisfied	1	2	3	4	5	unsatisfied
3. confident	1	2	3	4	5	hesitant
4. better than others	1	2	3	4	5	worse than others
5. stimulated	1	2	3	4	5	bored
6. do my best	1	2	3	4	5	do not do my best
7. good study skills	1	2	3	4	5	poor study skills
8. strong test-taker	1	2	3	4	5	weak test-taker
9. use time well	1	2	3	4	5	waste time
10. good relationships	1	2	3	4	5	weak relationships

When you have finished, pair up. Discuss the following questions.

- How do you see yourself as a learner?
- How do you think you got this picture of yourself?
- How would you like to change? (optional)
- How much does the approval of others (parents/guardians, friends, teachers) affect you?

JOURNAL

Reflecting on Your Sharing

In your journal, record the observations made about you during the discussion with your partner. Then write about how you felt when you shared your questionnaire. Were there any surprising differences between your questionnaires? Complete the following sentence starters in your journal.

When I shared the information with my partner, I felt . . .

It surprised me that my partner's questionnaire . . .

The one major difference in results that my partner and I noticed was . . .

Skill Areas for Classroom Success

If you are going to take responsibility for your learning in the classroom, there are important things you can do to ensure that you are making the best use of your time there.

1. Go to every class and get there on time.
2. Take a notebook, textbooks, planner or organizer, and other required materials to class and be sure to copy down important notes and assignments. Record any homework assignments before you leave the classroom.
3. Take careful notes. Details matter. You might not remember later. Underline or highlight important points.
4. Listen carefully. Respond to questions. Sit near the front if you are easily distracted.
5. Ask questions if you need information or clarification on an issue. Ask for extra help after school if you need it.
6. Participate actively in class. Share your views. Be positive.
7. Find someone (a study buddy) in each class who will agree to share information with you and pass on homework assignments if you are absent. Get your study buddy's phone number.
8. Complete your homework each day.

Note-Taking Strategies

The notes that you record in class will enhance your learning and recall. The following strategies will help you to look at the structure and format of your notes as well as the practices of note taking.

Summarize and use key words: The essential element in taking effective notes is to jot down only the main points. Listen for and highlight the main points. If there is information to be read in preparation for the class, make sure that you read it and are familiar with the language, ideas, and content of the subject. Select key words that link concepts and focus on key words that highlight the main ideas, facts, theories, and comparisons.

Organize your notes: Organize and structure your note taking in a way that suits your learning style. Perhaps you want to record all the main points and reorganize them in sequence later. You might be a person who prefers underlined headings with points listed underneath or you might prefer a key word with points written around it. Some people use different coloured pens or highlighters. File folders work best for some, while binders are preferred by others. Should you carry around all your notes for the subject or only the ones for that day? Whatever you do, the structure you use should be one that works for you.

Visualize: Form a mental picture of what the instructor is saying. This visual style of learning will enhance the primarily auditory and verbal style of most lessons.

Use symbols: Devise symbols to speed up and simplify your note taking. Since it is time consuming to spell out every word, abbreviations and symbols can be effective shortcuts. Some examples are shown at right.

Check the chalkboard: Write down everything that is on the chalkboard or is shown on overhead transparencies. Copy down all graphs, diagrams, formulas, and dates that the teacher writes on the board. If definitions, sentences, phrases, or key words are repeated, indicate in your notes that they are important.

SYMBOL	EXPLANATION
Q	question
w/o	without
+	more
bf	boyfriend
^	higher
@	at
>	greater than
*	important idea

Date items and note cross references: Date any handouts or additional materials that are handed out. Do this as soon as you receive them. If the written work in your notes has additional material in a text or is based on textbook information, write the cross reference in the margin of your notes for the day.

Review and revise: Set aside a few minutes at the end of each day to organize your notes. Read them over quickly and highlight information that will be important to study. Copy over or clarify sections that were done in a hurry and might be difficult to understand in the future.

Read and link: Read over your notes and think about how thy tie in with the information previously gained in the class. Ask yourself, How does all this new information relate to what I already know? When you link new knowledge to what you already know, especially within 24 hours of receiving it, you create a lasting impression that is better for recall and higher retention.

Make these guidelines into habits for your note taking to improve your success at school.

Activity ②

Using a Self-Evaluation Checklist

Now that you know how to use class time more effectively, complete the following **self-evaluation** checklist at the end of the week. Try to make it a Friday habit. Do it every week and act on the results.

Classroom Success Checklist

These are the elements that are important for doing well in class, and a rating scale for your self-evaluation. Read each sentence in the checklist. On a sheet of paper, write down the number from the rating scale that is most like you for each sentence.

1 = did very well
2 = did well
3 = did OK
4 = some improvement needed
5 = a great deal of improvement needed

1. I have gone to every class on time.
2. I have taken a notebook to every class.
3. I have taken complete notes.
4. I have listened carefully.
5. I have asked questions as needed.
6. I have participated actively.
7. I have a study buddy in each class.
8. I have done my homework.

Evaluating Your Checklist

Study the results of your checklist. Complete the following sentence starters on a sheet of paper.

When I respond to the questions I feel . . .
After three weeks, my score on the checklist is improving because . . .
The one thing that I still need to work on is . . .
I am most proud of the fact that I now . . .

FOR BETTER OR FOR WORSE © Lynn Johnston Prod., Inc. Reprinted with permission of UNIVERSAL PRESS SYNDICATE. All rights reserved.

Ideas for Study Success at Home

Another key to success at school is creating a **personal work area** at home. It might be a desk, a table, a comfortable chair, or your bed. Whatever and wherever it is, it should be the type of environment that works best for you. If possible, and with permission, make the space your own by having a calendar or your planner (for due dates and to check things off when completed), dictionary, calculator, paper, pens, and pencils. Go to your work area on a regular basis to do your homework. Then follow the guidelines in the Homework Game to develop good study habits.

The Homework Game

START	SCHOOL	I write down homework in my planner as soon as it is assigned.	I make sure I understand the homework before I leave school.
I reflect on my work. How could I do better? How will I use this learning?			
I hand in my assignments on time.			I ask my teacher for help when I do not understand.
My homework is packed by the door, ready for me to take to school.			I have a study buddy I can phone if I am away from school or if I do not fully understand an assignment.
I keep my notebooks, folders, and portfolios well organized.			HOME
I look after myself and take breaks when I need them.	I do my homework early in the evening before I am too tired.	I avoid distractions like phone calls, television, or the stereo.	I have a quiet place to work.

Developed by the Toronto District School Board.

JOURNAL

Planning Your Private Space

Draw a plan for the ideal personal work area and any special features you want it to have. Include the perfect conditions that should exist for you to do your homework. Be as creative as you like. Money, space, and time are no object!

Study Stretches

Have you been studying so long that you are falling asleep in your chair? Do you feel glued to your chair? How can your brain work when it is starved for oxygen? It is time to stretch! Try the Shoulder Shrug.

- Push your chair away from your work area.
- Put your arms by your sides and rotate your shoulders one at a time, then together.
- Try to move your right shoulder up to your ear and then drop it as low as you can. Do the same with your left shoulder.

Now, back to work. Taking a study stretch will help you to study better and longer. Try a stretch every 15 minutes to keep mentally fit.

Activity 3

Writing Exercise Instructions

Write instructions for these study stretches.
- Push-Ups for Toes!
- Awakening All Arms!
- Lift Those Legs!

Developing Skills for Work

Since your future career is probably not yet decided, it is a good idea to take the major subjects at school so that you can change your mind later if you wish. The following chart demonstrates the skills you learn at school in courses and activities and how the same skills can be used in the workplace.

Building Your Work Skills in School

SCHOOL SKILLS	COURSES AND ACTIVITIES THAT BUILD THESE SKILLS	HOW THESE SKILLS WILL HELP YOU IN THE WORKPLACE
Communication Skills • Giving class presentations • Reading articles and books • Writing essays, short stories, and poetry	Language Arts Languages Social Studies Art Student Council School Newspaper	• Prepare presentations • Write clear and concise memos, letters, and reports • Speak well on issues • Explain your ideas effectively • Ask for help when required

Teamwork Skills
- Getting along with your classmates
- Working with others on projects

Social Studies
Science
Physical Education
Trades and Technology
Music
Student Council Clubs
Sports Teams
School Band/Orchestra

- Be a productive team worker
- Accept supervision
- View co-workers as equals
- Know how to be co-operative and share knowledge

Time Management Skills
- Doing homework
- Meeting project deadlines
- Scheduling your day
- Getting to class on time

All courses and activities

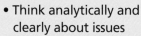

- Get work done efficiently
- Be prepared for meetings
- Meet deadlines
- Plan schedules and set goals

Problem-Solving Skills
- Analyzing information
- Understanding the problem
- Defining the problem
- Solving the problem
- Applying the results

Science
Math
Business
Social Studies
Trades and Technology
Student Council

- Think analytically and clearly about issues
- Pinpoint problems
- Evaluate situations
- Identify risks
- Make informed decisions
- Find productive solutions

Organizational Skills
- Taking notes
- Following written and oral instructions
- Keeping binders of information
- Following a schedule
- Setting priorities and goals

All courses and activities

- Keep a neat workplace
- Take care of equipment and tools
- Keep track of impor-tant details
- Handle interruptions well
- Organize activities to meet deadlines

Learning Skills
- Asking questions
- Reading information
- Using the library
- Researching information
- Joining activities and clubs
- Trying new things
- Meeting new people

All courses and activities

- Think critically and act logically
- Learn from on-the-job training
- Upgrade skills as necessary
- Learn from mistakes
- Increase knowledge and productivity

Computer Skills
- Learning storyboard
- Learning word processing
- Learning database programs

Math
Science
Business
Trades and Technology
Computer Studies

- Be computer literate
- Use technology in the workplace
- Adapt to new tech-nologies

Listening Skills
- Attending classes
- Going to lectures
- Taking notes
- Visualizing what you hear
- Comprehending information

All courses and activities

"I get it!"

- Understand what managers and co-workers tell you
- Help others with their concerns
- Participate effectively in meetings

Creativity Skills
- Learning how others have been creative
- Using your imagination
- Trying new ways to do things
- Looking at issues from a different point of view

Language Arts
Art
Music
Science
Drama Club
School Band/Orchestra

- Be an idea person
- Think of new ways to get the job done
- Create a positive work environment
- Increase motivation

Leadership Skills
- Leading projects
- Being on sports teams
- Volunteering as a peer helper

Science
History
Music
Physical Education
School Activities

- Lead projects
- Manage projects
- Coach others
- Help others reach their goals

Activity ❹ ·····················

Applying School Subjects to the Workplace

This activity focusses on the subjects you are taught at school and how they are used by specific workers. Create a chart like the following sample, and give examples for Mathematics, Language Arts, Science, Health/Physical Education, Technology, and History/Geography.

SUBJECT	SAMPLE JOBS	HOW SUBJECT IS USED
Mathematics	Plumber	• Computes measurements. • Reads plans. • Understands scaled drawings.
	Travel Agent	• Computes discounts, taxes. • Compares prices.
	Language Arts Teacher	• Computes students' marks.
Language Arts	Carpenter	• Reads trade journals to follow new product development.

PORTFOLIO

Reflecting on the School-Work Connection

Complete the following sentences on a sheet of paper.

After completing the chart, I'm beginning to wonder . . .

I think I have changed my opinion about . . .

As I work on these subjects at school, I hope that . . .

Initiative at School and in the Workplace

Initiative means doing what should be done without being told to do it. When you initiate something, it means you start it. Someone who comes up with new ideas, who solves small problems without looking for help or direction, and who can be trusted to work on his or her own is showing initiative. This person will probably do better work and enjoy the job more than someone who must be directed all the time. The chart below illustrates the similarities.

Initiative at School and in the Workplace

AT SCHOOL	IN THE WORKPLACE
• Participates in class.	• Shows a willingness to work.
• Does work as assigned.	• Is busy with assigned tasks.
• Welcomes extra work.	• Does extra work as required.
• Meets after school for projects.	• Works overtime if required.
• Is a mentor for a reading buddy.	• Helps others with work if required.
• Suggests alternatives in group work.	• Presents better ways to get a job done.
• Takes certification courses.	• Takes extra courses to improve performance.
• Understands time management.	• Meets time lines and is prompt.

PROFILE

Two Honoured for Building Racial Harmony

by Debra Black

Abhi Ahluwalia and Trudy-Ann (Debbie) Young believe they can change the world. In their own way, they have already begun to make a difference and help build racial harmony and eliminate discrimination in Ontario.

The pair, recipients of the 1997 Lincoln M. Alexander Awards, were honoured yesterday at a ceremony at Queen's Park in Toronto with both Lieutenant-Governor Hilary Weston and former lieutenant-governor Alexander attending.

"In their determination to promote equality and awareness, these two young people have demonstrated exemplary leadership and commitment," said Alexander, who presented the awards. The ceremony was one of many activities marking the United Nation's International Day for the Elimination of Racial Discrimination.

"This is just the beginning," 23-year-old Ahluwalia said in an interview. "There's lots of work to be done . . . . They say youth are the leaders of tomorrow. I think youth are the leaders of today."

Ahluwalia was nominated for his efforts as a volunteer with the Race Relations Committee of Kitchener-Waterloo. He also has organized three major youth conferences on anti-discrimination, founded a clothing company that features products with anti-discrimination messages, and done work in conflict resolution training.

Trudy-Ann Young is a 19-year-old student at Jarvis Collegiate Institute in Toronto. She believes a lot of work remains to be done if true equality is going to be achieved. But she believes her generation has the tools to make that happen.

"There is a stereotype that this generation, my generation, is apathetic," said Young, who plans to study sociology and English at McGill University. "But we're not. We're very politicized. I think it's important to point out there are a lot

Trudy-Ann (Debbie) Young and Abhi Ahluwalia with Lieutenant-Governor Hilary Weston and Lincoln Alexander.

of young people out there doing what we're doing. I work with all kinds of exemplary youth. I see their drive and passion."

Young won her award for her efforts to deal with racism and discrimination. She is the editor of *The Jarvis Jargon*, which was selected as the best school newspaper by *The Toronto Star*. She also co-ordinated a school-wide Black History Month, hosts and produces a talk show for young people on CKLN radio, is president of the African History Club, and has led anti-racism youth training groups.

Reprinted with permission—The Toronto Star Syndicate.

1. List the projects that Young and Ahluwalia initiated. Beside each activity, indicate who would be influenced by it.

2. Ahluwalia says, "They say youth are the leaders of tomorrow. I think youth are the leaders of today." Look around your school community. In what ways do you see youth living up to this statement?

3. Young says that "there are a lot of young people out there doing what we're doing." What evidence do you see?

4. If you could recommend someone in your school for this award, who would it be? Why?

Activity 5

Taking the Initiative at School

One of the ways that you and your classmates can show initiative is to plan an event or activity to help another class or group in your school community.

1. Brainstorm some ideas.

2. Ask these questions about each idea:
   - Is it practical?
   - Is it fun?
   - Will it help?
   - Do we have enough time to do it?
   - What help do we need?

3. Make a chart to compare the ideas.

Decision-Making	Is it practical?	Is it fun?	Will it help?	Do we have time?	Who can help?
Idea 1					

4. Make a decision based on the criteria.

5. Begin the planning of the group's choice. Use an organizer to help you.

Things We Will Need	Steps to Success	Possible Problems	Solutions

JOURNAL

Reflecting on Opportunities to Show Initiative

Complete the following sentences in your journal.

When I am in situations in which I have opportunities to show initiative, I must remember . . .

It is important for me to . . .

When I am part of a project planning team, I . . .

Where Is Your Time Going?

Using a chart similar to this one, keep track of your time for a week. Your total might not add up to 24 hours exactly, but try to be as accurate as you can.

ACTIVITY	SUN.	MON.	TUES.	WED.	THURS.	FRI.	SAT.
Sleep	8	8	8	8	8	8	8
Travel to/from school	0	1	1	1	1	1	0
School classes	0	6	6	6	6	6	0
School clubs, teams	1	0	0	1	0	1	0
Homework	0	1	1	1	1	0	1
Volunteer work, jobs	$\frac{1}{2}$	0	1	0	1	0	1
Household chores	0	$\frac{1}{2}$	$\frac{1}{2}$	$\frac{1}{2}$	$\frac{1}{2}$	$\frac{1}{2}$	$\frac{1}{2}$
Eating	$1\frac{1}{4}$	$1\frac{1}{4}$	$1\frac{1}{4}$	$1\frac{1}{4}$	$1\frac{1}{4}$	$1\frac{1}{4}$	$1\frac{1}{4}$
Dressing	$\frac{1}{2}$	$\frac{1}{4}$	$\frac{1}{2}$	$\frac{1}{4}$	$\frac{1}{2}$	$\frac{1}{4}$	$\frac{1}{2}$
Hobbies/interests	3	1	1	1	1	1	3
Sports	1	$\frac{1}{2}$	0	$\frac{1}{2}$	$\frac{1}{2}$	0	1
Telephone calls	$\frac{1}{4}$	0	0	$\frac{1}{4}$	$\frac{1}{4}$	$\frac{1}{4}$	$\frac{1}{2}$
Watching TV/videos	3	1	1	2	1	1	3
Listening to radio/music	1	$\frac{1}{2}$	$\frac{1}{2}$	$\frac{1}{2}$	$\frac{1}{2}$	1	1
Other (specify)	2						
Total hours	$21\frac{1}{2}$/24	21/24	21/24	$23\frac{1}{4}$/24	$22\frac{1}{2}$/24	$21\frac{1}{4}$/24	$20\frac{3}{4}$/24

1. Look over your chart and write a summary of how you spend your time. Some of the questions to consider while you are writing are:
   • Where is most of your time spent?
   • How is most of your time spent?
   • In which areas can you save time?

2. Choose one category; for example, sleeping or eating. Compare your results in that area with five other people. What did you learn about yourself by making the comparison? Are you planning to try to make any changes in any of the categories?

Activity  6

Managing Your Time

If you think you need help with the way you spend your time, or **time management**, here are some questions to guide your reflections and your decisions for change:

- Do you spend too much time doing certain things?
- In what ways do you waste time?
- What is a problem area for you in managing your time?

- Do you postpone doing important things? Why?
- Do you have difficulty fitting everything into your day? Why?

Identify the areas where you could trim some time and where you need more time. Set a goal to change at least one area at a time. Keep track of your goal and your results.

Preparing for Tests and Examinations

Prepare early: Prepare for tests and examinations from the first day of the course, when the teacher outlines the course and the course expectations. Keep complete notes and review them as the course goes along. Your focus from the first day of the course is a major factor in how well you will do on tests.

Clarify expectations: Make sure that you know the details about the test or exam. What subject matter is it based on? How many questions will there be? What format will be used? How much time will be given? Arrive early and listen to the test instructions carefully.

Observe and question: Observe your teacher during class to see what he or she considers to be important. Notice which points and key words are stressed. If the teacher writes formulas on the board, repeats dates, or illustrates concepts on overhead transparencies, you can be sure that these are important. Ask questions in class as you read, take notes, and review chapter material. Save questions, quizzes, and activity sheets. Use them for review.

Review: Start the review process by previewing chapters and notes before class. Becoming familiar with a new topic opens your mind to receive new information and to link the familiar with the new. Review notes after class consistently as the course progresses and your notes increase. A week or so before the test or exam, commit time to a major review of notes, texts, and supplementary materials. Summarize what you have learned in preparation for your final study time.

Use a study team: Use your time with a study team to exchange notes, make up sample questions, and summarize chapters.

Get organized: As soon as you get the test, organize yourself. Scan the test quickly, preview the questions to see which ones you can answer quickly and which will take more time. Pace yourself according to the time allowed and make the time count by looking at the points for each question and determining the importance of each section.

Move quickly: Move through the test. Don't panic if you do not know an answer. Leave it and answer the questions you do know. Rephrase questions that you are having difficulty with, write down what you do know, and come back to it.

Reread, recheck, and rethink: Once you have finished, read the test over again and check for careless mistakes and spelling errors. If you have extra time, add points to essay questions or fill in other details.

Strategies for Taking Tests and Examinations

The thought of taking a test causes some people to feel anxious and others to feel physically ill. The strategies listed below will help you to accept the challenge of tests and examinations

Reflect on the purpose: Tests provide feedback on what you have mastered during the course. They do not measure your self-worth, your intelligence, or your ability to contribute to society.

Distance yourself: Distance yourself and do not exaggerate the pressure of test taking. Look for solutions, not problems.

Be prepared: The best way to control test anxiety is to go to every class, review your notes, and study in advance. Work smarter, not harder.

Join a study team: Join a study team and draw strength, ideas, support, and commitment from each other. Develop a team spirit and study together to reduce anxiety.

Practice: Make up questions and test yourself and your classmates, if they are willing. When you rehearse a stressful event, your mind does not see it as a fearful unknown.

Exercise: The day before the test, go for a long walk or jog. Exercise is a good way to reduce stress.

Pace yourself: Last minute cramming creates a hectic climate and increases anxiety. Make your test day peaceful by having everything ready, getting up in time for breakfast, and getting to class early.

Breathe and relax: Deep breathing is calming and increases the oxygen supply. Take a deep breathe, hold it for two or three seconds, and then breathe out slowly through your mouth. Relax your muscles by systematically progressing down your body, tensing and releasing each group, until you have curled and released your toes.

Imagine success: From the time you wake up until right before the test, it is important to create a positive state of mind. See yourself as relaxed, calm, confident, and recalling information easily.

Use self-talk: Tell yourself that the text or exam is an opportunity to indicate what you know. Make sure that you use positive self-talk!

Focus: Focus on the subject. Get involved with answering the questions and do not think about other things.

Be objective: After the test, look objectively at how you did. Evaluate your grade, preparation, anxiety level, and answers. Look at the results and prepare for the next time.

Writing Self-Talk Sentences

When you look over the list of strategies for preparing for a test or exam, you will realize that some of these suggestions will be easier for you than others. Which three ideas will help you and why? In your journal record three positive self-talk sentences that will work for you in a stressful test situation.

Analyze and Assess

When you get the test or examination back, analyze and assess it. Ask yourself the following questions:

- Did I anticipate the style, format, and questions?
- What didn't I expect?
- What did I do right?
- What should I have studied more?

- How was my recall?
- Did I prepare enough?
- Did I handle test anxiety well?
- Did being part of a study group help or hinder me?

Activity 7

Improving a Younger Student's Classroom and Study Habits

Imagine that you have been asked to help a younger student to prepare for a test in a subject in which he or she usually does not do well. Review the note taking and test strategies outlined previously and decide how you can help the student to use the information that you have just learned. List the steps that you will employ to help him or her.

Peer Pressure

Peer pressure is a term that we hear quite often these days, especially in reference to preteen and teenage students. It has to do with feeling obligated to follow the wishes of your peers in spite of your own wishes.

IN THE NEWS

Growing Pains

by Louise Brown

Children are shaped as much by their peers and their genes as they are by the home, so society should get off parents' backs. This bold claim by sociologist Anne-Marie Ambert, a professor at York University, flies in the face of popular pro-nurture theory, which places the burden of raising happy kids squarely on parents' shoulders.

Yet when Ambert asked 1400 undergraduates between 1974 and 1989 to write about what had made them most happy and unhappy as they grew up, parents were mentioned in not even one-third of these memories. Instead, peers played the leading role, especially in negative memories.

"By far the most common unhappy recollections were of abuse inflicted by their peers, yet parents are the ones who always get blamed (when kids are unhappy)," said Ambert at a parenting conference.

More than half of Ambert's students wrote about how incidents of "peer abuse" had made an impact on their lives. They traced ailments such as ulcers or personality traits such as shyness and self-consciousness to being abused by a peer, verbally, emotionally, or even physically. Surprisingly, very few pinned such problems on parents.

"Don't get me wrong. Parents are a key influence, usually for the good, but these essays suggest it's not parents who play a role in the most pronounced happy or painful memories of childhood. It's peers. I believe society definitely puts too much blame on parents (for problems with children). Kids can get abused by peers and suffer a lot of stress, but they won't tell their parents. Then the kids end up with ulcers, the parents don't know why, and in the end the parents get blamed!"

Even when kids beat each other up, as seems a growing problem in some schools, people ask what the parent did to create the bully or create the victim, says Ambert, "rather than asking the better question: 'What is it about our society that fosters this climate of violence in the first place?'"

Ambert believes a "good home atmosphere is very important. I'm not arguing that but I'm saying it suddenly can be changed by peers. The peer group itself has an effect that may be more powerful than parents. A great proportion of minor delinquents come from average families. I'm suggesting that maybe parents don't have the power to make or break a child. They are made or broken by other children."

I'm not sure I'm convinced parents play this minor a role. Surely one reason Ambert's students rated parents so low in importance is simply a function of their age. University is a time when young people make their first big break from their parents and they almost need to downplay their parents' importance as part of growing up. It's an age when many of us can recall dismissing our parents' importance as minor—a view we later revise.

Still, Ambert makes an important point: that the whole focus of science has been "How do parents affect their kids?"

which neglects other important factors in child development, such as the role of peers and the child's own temperament.

"We have inherited an entire psychological culture, starting with Freud, that sees the child as moulded by the parent, as a clean slate to which the parent adds. How the child turns out is supposed to be entirely the responsibility of the parent. Yet new research suggests the child is co-producer of his or her own development, that children are born with personalities in the making."

Some parents have told Ambert they find the thought of peer influence frightening, but she argues it should be comforting to realize we parents aren't as responsible for our kids' happiness as we had thought. It takes the load off, in a way. We may not be able to guarantee them happiness, but nor can we singlehandedly spoil things for them, either.

Reprinted by permission of Louise Brown.

1. Discuss whether or not you agree that children are shaped as much by their peers and their own temperament as they are by their parents.

2. Write about an incident when you were strongly influenced by peers. Why were you influenced? Was it a positive or a negative influence? What would you do the next time? How can you be sure?

Activity 8

Role-Playing Difficult Situations

With a partner, create conversations using two of these situations as the starting point. Then create two of your own, based on your experiences.

- A few minutes before math class, a friend asks you to give her your homework to copy.
- As you are leaving school, some friends from another class invite you to play basketball. You have a science test and a book report due; they do not.
- Your older brother offers you one of his English essays in exchange for cleaning up the kitchen for him.
- Your best friend wants to be your partner on a project. The last time you worked together, you did a second-rate job.
- Just as you start reviewing for a math quiz, your best friend from camp makes a surprise visit.

JOURNAL

Responding to the Role-Play

Even though you were only role-playing difficult peer situations, real feelings might have been aroused. Respond to the following:

- When I think about responding to a friend in a negative way, I . . .
- Even though I was only role-playing in an activity, I felt . . .

Describing Expectations

In a chart like the following, write on the arrows at least five expectations you feel people have of you. Consider those that can be met and those that will take a long time (or can never be met), and decide on their priority by numbering your statements in the circles provided. Then make a personal comment about each expectation. For each item, consider a plan of specific actions you could take to meet or deal with these expectations.

Expectations

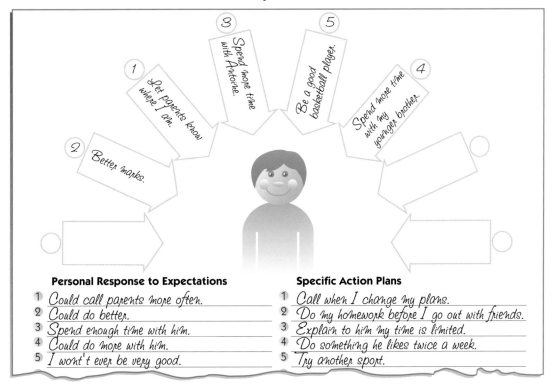

Personal Response to Expectations
1 Could call parents more often.
2 Could do better.
3 Spend enough time with him.
4 Could do more with him.
5 I won't ever be very good.

Specific Action Plans
1 Call when I change my plans.
2 Do my homework before I go out with friends.
3 Explain to him my time is limited.
4 Do something he likes twice a week.
5 Try another sport.

 You might wish to file the completed chart in your portfolio.

Looking Back

1. Which of the chapter activities will help you to take responsibility for your own success in the classroom? In what ways will they help you?

2. What are two benefits of managing your time?

3. Peer pressure often interferes with school success. Discuss this idea in terms of your own experience.

EXPLORATIONS

Reflections

Saying no to your peers is difficult. For each of the following statements, outline a situation when you might say:
- No, thanks.
- That's not for me.
- I'd rather not.
- You've got to be kidding.
- Sorry, not now.

You might wish to draw the scenario or create a cartoon strip or a storyboard.

Goals

Think of a short-term goal that you have achieved recently. How many steps did you have to take? Which was the most difficult? How did you feel when you achieved your goal?

Action!

Use one of the statements from the Reflections activity in a skit in which a friend is trying to influence you in a negative way.

Featuring. . .

Editorial: You are the editor of your school newspaper. You are graduating to another school and leaving your readership of three years. Write an inspirational editorial about the value of the effort you have spent in the position of editor.

Advice Column: Write a letter advising a peer to try to improve his or her school attendance. Include suggestions on how to get up and get to school, as well as the benefits of regular attendance.

Advertisement: Prepare an advertisement to attract students from another province to attend your school as a part of an exchange program. Your advertisement should contain a variety of features, available at your school and in your community, which will appeal to a wide audience.

Research: Survey fellow students to find out their homework habits. Include the categories of time, duration, location, and rewards. Graph the results.

Personal Story/Interview: Ask several students to share their journal entry about their ideal private space, on page 66. Write an article reporting on the one that is both practical and creative.

Discovering Pathways

Making decisions about your future involves exploring different pathways. Now that you have a good understanding about yourself and know how to set goals, you can begin to determine where you are heading.

Some decisions will need to be made sooner than others. Choosing which high school courses to take is more important at the moment than making choices about education after graduation. Choosing volunteer activities or part-time work needs to be explored before making decisions about careers and full-time employment. Yet, what you do now affects decisions you will make later. For example, volunteering to assist in the primary grades could help you decide to work with children as a future career. If you work in a clothing store, you might decide that retail is not what you want to do in the future! Knowing all your options is essential as you start down the path to your future.

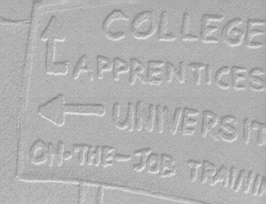

Educational Opportunities

What You Will Learn

- What to expect when in high school.
- Types of high school programs and subjects that are offered.
- What options you have if you cannot attend school full-time.
- About apprenticeships and youth apprenticeships.
- The differences among college, university, and other educational institutions.
- What post-secondary institutions are located in your local community, your province, and in other provinces.

Terms to Remember

credits
compulsory
community involvement
optional
full disclosure
semester
alternative education programs
term
co-operative education
work experience

youth apprenticeship
correspondence courses
independent learning courses
distance education
secondary
post secondary
apprentice
trade
diploma
degree

Education constantly increases in importance as the workplace continues to change. You need more education to give you more job choices and flexibility in the job market. There is a direct relationship between education and work in terms of job availability and job satisfaction. A lack of education limits a person's job choices and often leads to job dissatisfaction.

For year 2000+:

- The minimum requirement for 80 percent of jobs will be a high school diploma. This means that only 20 percent of jobs will be available for workers without a high school diploma.
- Without high school, you will be unemployed for 35 percent of your life. Entry into the better-paying jobs will continue to be severely limited for such workers.
- Of the 80 percent of jobs requiring a high school diploma, 50 percent will require five years of education beyond high school. This means 17 years of education, training, or on-the-job experience with training.
- In the growth areas, 90 percent of jobs will require college, university, or other educational training.

Education and the Job Market

35% of time will be spent unemployed

No high school diploma: 20%

High school plus five years or more education and training: 40%

High school only: 40%

Growth Areas

High School

We know that high school is mandatory until you are 16. We also know that it is important for employment. To discover what your high school education could be like, you need to ask a lot of questions and get solid answers from those who know. You can talk to you guidance counsellor, your teacher-advisor, or any of your teachers. Older students and peer helpers are also a good source of information. Remember, you must make decisions based on what is best for you and your future goals.

Diploma Requirements

Compulsory credits (total of 18): All students in Ontario must complete the following credits to graduate with a diploma.

4	credits in English (1 credit per grade)
1	credit in French as a second language
3	credits in mathematics (at least 1 credit in Grade 11 or 12)
2	credits in science
1	credit in Canadian history
1	credit in Canadian geography
1	credit in the arts
1	credit in health and physical education
$1/2$	credit in civics
$1/2$	credit in career studies

Plus:

1	additional credit in English, or a third language, or a social science, or Canadian and world studies
1	additional credit in health and physical education, or business studies, or the arts (music, art, drama, or dance)
1	additional credit in science (Grade 11 or 12), or technological education (Grades 9-12)

___
18

Community involvement: Every student must complete 40 hours of community involvement as a compulsory graduation requirement.

Optional credits (total of 12): In addition to the 18 compulsory credits, you have to earn 12 optional credits in courses of your choice, selected from the full list of courses available in the school. Optional credits allow you to build an educational program that suits your individual interest and meets university, college, apprenticeship, or work requirements.

Full disclosure: In Grades 11 and 12 (and OAC until 2004) in Ontario, your achievement for all courses taken or attempted is recorded. This is shown as percentage grades earned, credits granted (if successful), or "w" (if you withdraw from the course before completing it). If you repeat a course for which you have already received a credit, you will have all marks recorded but will receive only one credit.

Course Types

In Grades 9 and 10, you can choose from Academic, Applied, and Open courses. Transfer courses may be taken if you wish to change the type of course you have been taking.

Academic courses: In an academic course, the essential concepts of a subject are learned and related materials are explored as well. Although knowledge and skills in the subject will be developed through both theory and practical applications, the emphasis will be on theory and abstract thinking as a basis for future learning and problem solving.

Applied courses: An applied course also covers the essential concepts of a subject. Knowledge and skill will be developed through both theory and practical applications, but the focus will be on practical applications. In applied courses, familiar, real-life situations will be used to illustrate ideas, and more opportunities will be given to experience hands-on applications of the concepts studied.

Open courses: These courses are not specific to destination and are appropriate for all students.

In Grades 11 and 12 you may choose from four types of courses—Workplace, College, University/College, University, and Open. The type, or stream, of courses is geared to the destinations following high school.

Streaming Model of Courses for Grades 11 and 12

WORKPLACE	COLLEGE	UNIVERSITY/ COLLEGE	UNIVERSITY	OPEN
Courses designed for students planning to enter the workplace directly following high school.	Courses designed to prepare students for entrance to most college programs following high school.	Courses designed to prepare students for entrance to specific college and university programs following high school.	Courses designed to prepare students for entrance to university programs following high school.	Courses that are not specific to any particular post-secondary destination, are appropriate for all students, and that students may take to meet compulsory or optional requirements and/or for personal interest and growth.

Annual education plan: Appropriate selection of courses is essential for two reasons:
• success in high school
• career requirements

Completion of your Annual Education Plan will ensure that you are getting the most out of your course offerings. It is also important to choose wisely because of the policy of full disclosure.

What is the best advice a new high school student could receive?

- Use every opportunity to learn in the classroom and participate in extra-curricular activities.
- Ask questions and listen carefully to the answers.
- Look for a challenge and always try to do more than the minimum required.
- Take advantage of facilities such as the gymnasium and the resource centre or library.
- Make friends. High school friendships might last the rest of your life.

There are other factors to consider when planning your high school program.

Location: Do you have a choice of schools? Some communities are large and have several high schools that you could attend. You need to know what is available. For example, one school might specialize in the arts, while another might feature technology and science. Choosing a school because that is where your friends are going is very appealing, but you must look at your interests, skills, and abilities. Choose the school that has the best opportunities for you.

Alternative programs and schools: Are there **alternative education programs** available? Some communities offer schools that vary from the traditional structure. For example, an alternative school might be designed for independent learners who require a less formal structure. Also, traditional schools might offer alternative programs, such as enrichment programs for students who excel in science and technology.

Program focus: You have already discovered your areas of strength and ability and might have an idea of the career area you would like to pursue. The optional subjects should be examined with this in mind to help you follow your career pathway. For example, if you are musically intelligent, what courses are available? What is the physical education program like if you are bodily intelligent? If you are language intelligent, how many language courses are available beyond what is required?

Career education: You have started on your career path. There is more to learn before you make some final decisions. Other than career studies at Grade 10, what career preparation courses and career guidance counselling are available?

Extra-curricular activities: There are many activities that take place before and after school; for example, sports, music and drama productions, travel opportunities, clubs (language, chess, computers, photography), student council, athletic council, dances, concerts, school newspaper, and school yearbook. Which ones that interest you are available?

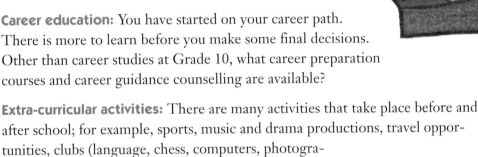

Schedule: There is a variety of schedules on which a school might choose to operate. A two-semestered system divides the year into two equal parts, or **semesters**. Your school might be on a four-**term** schedule. Another schedule is a full school-year. If you have a choice of schools you can attend, and they are each on a different schedule, what are the advantages or disadvantages of each one?

Community-based learning: Many high schools now have a broad connection with the community. Are there opportunities for you to gain credits for learning that occurs outside the classroom? Are there **co-operative education** or **work experience** opportunities? Is there mandatory community involvement as a requirement for graduation? Are **youth apprenticeship** programs offered?

Activity 1

Gathering Data

There are many sources for finding the information you need to help you choose the right courses and to enable you to take full advantage of all that your school offers.

1. With your teacher and classmates, decide who you want to come and speak to your class.
   - Invite a student from a co-operative education program and a student from a youth apprenticeship program to speak about their experiences.
   - Ask some of last year's high school graduates to participate in a panel discussion about their high school experiences and how their choices have affected them.

   - Ask a guidance counsellor to come and speak to your class.
   - Ask your student activity council president to speak about extra-curricular opportunities.

2. Thoroughly read your school's and/or school board's course description booklet to ensure that you are aware of all that is being offered. Make note of the courses you wish to take. Check your annual education plan and update it if necessary.

3. Many boards of education have information on a web site on the Internet. Use the Internet to gather data.

Activity 2

Analyzing Data

With all the information gathered in Activity 1, make a list of the key information you will use to determine what the remaining two years of your high school education will be like. You may wish to use the headings on pages 84-87 to assist you.

JOURNAL

Reflecting on Your High School Experience

Reflect on your Grade 9 and your Grade 10 years so far. Outline the positive and the negative aspects. What can you do to make your high school experience positive and memorable?

Alternative Ways to Complete Your Education

Not everyone can attend high school full-time due to a variety of reasons—the need to work, poor health, or family responsibilities. For others, the traditional route just might not appeal to them. There are numerous options available:

- Alternative education programs (described earlier) might enable you to attend school on a flexible time schedule.
- You can attend school by taking night school and summer school courses.
- In **correspondence courses** or **independent learning courses**, study materials are mailed to you to complete at home. You then return your work by mail to be marked. Once you have completed all the course requirements, you receive a diploma.
- **Distance education** involves using computer connections and telephone conference calls. You communicate with an instructor and classmates to complete course requirements. Some courses are also available over the radio.
- Youth apprenticeships combine in-school learning and on-the-job training. See the following section for more information.

Youth Apprenticeships

Would you like to be a plumber, a hairstylist, or a motorcycle mechanic? Many schools across Canada offer youth apprenticeship programs starting in Grade 11. You can train for a career while still in high school, with work-site learning and a paycheque from the employer. When you graduate, you continue working toward your goal.

Some of the more common careers available through youth apprenticeships are:

- glazier
- electrician
- tool and die maker
- small-engine mechanic
- auto body repairer
- automotive painter
- fuel and electrical systems mechanic
- heavy duty equipment mechanic
- plumber
- general machinist
- industrial woodworker
- pattern maker
- steam fitter
- painter and decorator
- mould maker

- cook
- automotive machinist
- farm equipment mechanic
- motor vehicle mechanic
- sheet metal worker
- general carpenter
- ironworker
- hairstylist
- fitter (structural steel/plate work)

Alternative Ways of Learning

Suppose that in the future you are unable to attend school full-time. In your journal, write what the advantages and disadvantages are of each of the alternative ways to get an education. Which type would best suit your learning style? Why?

After High School

High school is often called **secondary** education. *Post* means *after*. Therefore, **post secondary** means after high school. As you learned from the statistics at the beginning of this chapter, post-secondary education is very important for pursuing future career opportunities. Post-secondary education might seem like a long time away for you, but it is never too early to start thinking about the choices that are available. Post-secondary education can be achieved in a variety of ways—apprenticeships, on-the-job training, college, technical school, university, and private institutions.

To increase your options, you can gain more skills and further your education while working through apprenticeships and workplace training programs.

IN THE NEWS

When Normal High School Is a Bad Fit

by Todd Mercer

Julie Lee became a self-described skipaholic when she was in Grade 10. Her A marks fell and she dropped out. "I took a year off, worked, got laid off. I didn't want to go back to school because my friends would be graduating and I'd still be in Grade 10." Instead, Lee enrolled in an alternative school. She admits to goofing off her first year, but "eventually you realize you're not getting any younger."

Like mainstream high schools, the alternative schools offer core subjects from Grade 10 through to graduation. However, they deliver these courses without formal classes or daily attendance requirements. This flexible scheduling particularly serves the needs of mature students who have other demands on their time, such as a job or children. Students must see each subject teacher at least ten hours during the course, usually in half-hour appointments once a week. The one-to-one tutorial meetings are key to learning. The learning is self-paced. Students can work intensely to complete a course over four or five months or, if their schedule demands it, over a longer period of time. Without the alternatives offered by such schools, many students claim they would simply drop out.

Reprinted by permission of Todd Mercer.

Students Gain a Better Understanding of the RCMP

In October 1995, G.P. Vanier Work Experience Co-ordinators Isabelle Pacholuk and Fiona Tayless and Constable Derek Kryzanowski of the Courtenay, B.C., Royal Canadian Mounted Police (RCMP) detachment launched the idea of a Mountie training camp (the first of its kind in Canada).

For six days 65 students lived in barracks and dressed in regulation RCMP uniforms, shirts pressed, shoes shined, and hats on. The day started at 5 a.m. and a few students managed to last until lights out at 11.

Based on the model of the Regina, Saskatchewan, RCMP training academy, drill, Cooper's Run, physical training, PARE testing, law classes, Deadly Decisions, traffic control, crisis intervention, firearms training, emergency response, underwater recovery, drug control, tracking with police dog, helicopter (rides for some!), and more drill (one student complained his brand new pair of shoes had no soles left after camp) were all part of the experience.

Twenty-five RCMP officers and 13 auxiliary members volunteered their time—240 volunteer hours. And what did they hope to get out of it? Constable Kryzanowski stated their objectives: give the students the opportunity to experience the training and working conditions of police officers, develop a better understanding and appreciation of the police, provide a

setting that enables officers and students to work together in a positive fashion, enhance students' self-esteem and leadership skills, and educate the public about positive youth/police contacts. Judging by the student evaluations, all of these goals and more were achieved. Their major complaint was that one week wasn't long enough!

On Sunday March 17th, 65 "green recruits" walked through the main gate, many of them looking like they doubted the wisdom of their choice. On Monday in parade square they looked like the misfits from *Hogan's Heroes*. However, on Graduation Day, Saturday March 24th, goose bumps ran down our arms, and tears of pride filled our eyes as our 65 young officers marched in unison and stood at attention before an emotional Constable Kryzanowski. This is what made one of the largest projects our work experience program ever tackled so worthwhile!

As we told our students on Graduation Day: "What you obtain by reaching your destination isn't nearly as important as what you become by reaching that destination!"

Due to the overwhelming success of this camp, both the RCMP and School District #62 ran a second training camp during spring break, March 1997.

Article written by Isabelle Pacholuk, Work Experience Co-ordinator at G.P. Vanier Secondary School in Courtenay, B.C.

Getting an Education Using the Internet

by Peter Giffen

When high school student Kerry Shipton discovered she could not take an English course because of a timetable conflict, she decided to use the Internet. The 16-year-old phoned the government and arranged to do the course via e-mail.

"The whole thing was done over the computer," recalls her father, John Shipton, a French teacher. "She would receive an assignment one day, do it the next, and have it returned and marked on the following days. The whole process was fast and efficient. She polished off the course in ten weeks. She wouldn't even let me help her."

From "The Virtual Classroom" by Peter Giffen, *Sympatico Netlife*, Sept./Oct. '96

What Is an Apprenticeship?

If you do not enter a youth apprenticeship program while you are in high school, you can enter into an apprenticeship after graduation. While you are working, you are trained as an **apprentice**. This involves on-the-job training done by a qualified person, and it involves some time spent taking courses—usually at a college. The training is in a **trade** (a job or business involving manual or mechanical ability or buying and selling). This leads to jobs for men and women as skilled tradespersons. Apprenticeships are regulated by the government and, therefore, are well-recognized in industry.

Some of the advantages of becoming a skilled tradesperson are that, on average, wages for full-time positions are higher than in many other businesses or industries. There is a growing demand in Canada for tradespeople. Switching jobs when you are ready for a change is therefore easier. Depending on the career you choose, the hours you work, where you work, and the technology you use might vary a great deal. If you are looking for job flexibility, learning a trade might be one answer. The combination of learning in the classroom and hands-on learning in the workplace can be very appealing.

Colleges, Technical Schools, and Universities

The careers you are interested in might demand a college or technical school **diploma** or university **degree**. Colleges and technical schools offer one-, two-, or three-year diploma courses. Universities offer three- or four-year degrees and offer post-graduate degrees called Masters and Doctorates.

All have registration costs of several thousand dollars. You might not have a college, technical school, or university in your community. If this is the case, then the additional costs of either living away from home or driving a long distance add to the expense of post-secondary education. To help with these costs, student loans and bursaries, or grants, are available. Also, you might be able to win a scholarship.

One way to get information is to use the Internet and the World Wide Web. SchoolNet is a source of information about all colleges, technical schools, and universities in Canada. Also, every college and university offers information on all their courses, fees, admission requirements, and so on. Most post-secondary institutions hold special "open houses" and information nights.

Information is also available from bookstores, guidance offices, career centres, or university, college, and technical school admissions offices. Former students have also written books giving their opinions about what is good and bad about their college, technical school, or university. *Maclean's* magazine does a yearly analysis and rates the major universities.

Activity 3

Researching Colleges, Technical Schools, and Universities

Using a variety of sources of information, find:
- The location of the nearest college, technical school, and university to you
- The names of colleges, technical schools, and universities in your province

Choose one college, technical school, or university, and gather as much information as you can about:
- Courses offered
- Tuition fees
- Admission requirements
- On-campus residences and housing

Other Educational Institutions

Post-secondary education is not limited to government-run colleges, technical schools, and universities. There is a vast number of privately run institutions that provide training for a variety of careers. These include computer training, business courses (accounting, word processing, desktop publishing, management), child care, health care (dental assisting, laboratory assisting), travel, dance, dramatic arts, hairdressing, cooking, languages, modelling, photography, theatre make-up, music, electronics, and even truck driving.

There is a fee to attend these schools. Course lengths vary from one month to several years. As with colleges and universities, you can apply for student loans and bursaries.

What Is Out There?
Here are some choices you have:
- Colleges of Applied Arts and Technology
- Private Vocational Schools
- Hospital-Based Programs (technicians, assistants)
- Universities
- Agricultural Colleges
- Colleges of Art and Design

PORTFOLIO

Researching Educational Requirements for Your Career

Choose a career that interests you. What education will you need for that career? What high school courses prepare you for post-secondary education for that career? What courses must you take in college, technical school, or university? Which college, technical school, or university in your province offers these courses?

Use the information sources discussed in this chapter to answer these questions. File your findings in your portfolio.

PROFILE

Building Skills

By Catherine Patch

Put on your hard hat and construction boots, grab a coffee, and head for class. But don't bother to log on, sit down, or get out your books – this class is being held in a field. Well, it's not exactly a field and it's not exactly a class, either. Some Ontario high school students have been reporting for work on real-life construction sites, where they work alongside building tradespeople, guided by on-site consultants and supervisors from the building industry.

Al Schmidt, left, of the Waterloo District Board of Education, is joined by high school students Jacinta Avery, Tim Casson, and Chris Pyle at a house they built.

One of the most recent triumphs of co-operation between the private sector and the school system took place in January, when senior officials from Monarch Construction Ltd. and the Waterloo Region School Board joined students from Jacob Hespeler Secondary School for a ribbon-cutting ceremony at their recently completed house in Doon Mills, Kitchener. The co-operative project was launched in 1997, and so far, students from Jacob Hespeler, Galt Collegiate Institute, and Elmira District Secondary School have built seven homes that have been sold and now are occupied. Students work in as many as 30 building trades during the year, which gives them a chance to find out which trades they are interested in for apprenticeship training even before high school graduation.

Mattamy Homes founded a classroom in a field in Cambridge about three years ago. "We got into this by chance," says Bernie Torchia, vice-president of construction operations at Mattamy. "Al Schmidt, a teacher in Cambridge, had an idea and approached me on one of our sites." The idea was that Mattamy would allow a team of students to build a house. Torchia was interested in Schmidt's idea and took it to the company's senior management team, who decided to go for it. Three years later, Mattamy is in four school board regions and deals with six different school boards.

"It's an ongoing thing," says Torchia. "Right now we've got classes in Oakville, Markham, and Mississauga. And I'm talking to another school board next week." At the time of the Kitchener project, Mattamy wasn't building in Cambridge, so it handed the project over to another large builder, Monarch Homes. Mattamy expects to be active in Cambridge again by next year.

"The main benefit to this program is that we're introducing our industry to the high-school-age student and we're introducing it when that student is still a mainstream student," says Torchia. "Our industry has always been one where you sort of fall into it by default or failing at everything else. What we have to do in this country is to introduce skills – construction trades, automotive trades – whatever the skills are, we have to introduce them at almost a grade school level. If we keep attaching this stigma to kids who are interested in trades, that if you can't recite Shakespeare, then you might as well go become an auto mechanic. . . we're not going to have the skilled tradespeople in the future."

"The beauty of this program is the kid is still a Grade 11 or Grade 12 mainstream student at the local high school. If he's on the volleyball team, he gets back to the school in time for the practice. In the past, trade-related programs have always been treated as somewhat less than what you would want for your children." Hespeler teacher and co-op project leader, Schmidt, who got the ball rolling, has been sending students out on co-op framing jobs for years. "But it doesn't give them a realistic view of the industry," he says. "If we do the whole house, we can appeal to a broad range of interests. The kids fill out an option sheet and then do an interview – we very rarely get dropouts."

For 19-year-old Jacinta Avery, the Doon Mills house was her third time out. She's already worked on two houses for Mattamy Homes in Cambridge. Avery has always done woodworking with her father and has studied it since Grade 7 and with Schmidt since Grade 9. "I've been learning all aspects of building," she says. "Every day, my skills just get greater." Renovation is the area where Avery will build her career. "But I really wasn't sure until last semester," she says.

Chris Pyle is a Grade 12 construction technology student at Jacob Hespeler, another of the 12 who helped build the Monarch home in Doon Mills, Kitchener – his second house. "When I started the program, I already had a general idea of what I wanted to be – a framer," Pyle says. "But I wanted some insight into what my career would be like. It also offered good experience – to go through school at the same time as learning about my job. I also got to look at other trades. The

first house I built, I really got into plumbing. But this year, I'm back into framing." This semester, Pyle will be working on his third house and already has a job waiting. "I've got a job offer with one of the other guys on the crew this summer and it's with a past member of the co-op."

Pyle and his peers, like Avery, are arriving on the construction trades scene at an ideal time, says John Latimer, head of Monarch Development Corp., who has worked on the Mayor's Homeless Action Task Force in Toronto and is active in home builders' associations. "From a builder's point of view, everyone is aware that the trades in this province are getting older. The average age of bricklayers, carpenters, and others is in the 50s, and we just don't seem to be producing the kinds of skilled labour, particularly building labour, that we are going to need for the future," says Latimer. "I think these kids have a great opportunity to learn, hands-on. There's nothing like experience to gain knowldege," notes Latimer.

1. If you were a parent, why would you want your son or daughter to participate in this program?

2. Why would a builder take the trouble to have teenagers at the building site?

3. Write a letter that a Grade 12 student who had participated in the program might write to a Grade 11 student who was thinking about it.

4. If you were a student participating in the program and the group decided to put a time capsule in the cement of the house's basement, what items would you want to include?

Activity  4

Listing Other Educational Institutions

Look in the Yellow Pages of your telephone book under the heading Schools. Make a list of other educational institutions in your community. Select two or three that relate to a career or careers that interest you and contact these places for information. Find out the length of the courses, the fees involved, and whether you need particular high school credits to enroll.

PORTFOLIO

Reviewing Your Research

Review the research you have completed on the post-secondary opportunities that are available in your community. Select three you researched that appeal to you the most. On a sheet of paper, list the reasons why you selected them.

Activity 5

Researching Educational Institutions

Choose one of the following activities to research information relevant to your educational and career plans.

• Check with your guidance office or school library to see what material is available on apprenticeships, or contact your provincial Ministry of Labour and ask them to send you information.

• Choose one college, technical school, or university and, using a variety of resources, gather as much information as you can about courses offered, tuition fees, admission requirements, and on-campus residences or housing.

• Using a variety of resources, make a list of other educational institutions in your community. Select two or three that relate to a career or careers that interest you and contact these places for information. Find out the length of the courses, the fees involved, and whether you need particular high school credits to enroll.

Activity 6

Reviewing Your Education Options

1. Review the courses you have been taking in high school. What are the education options available to you when you graduate? Have you been taking courses that enable you to enter college or technical school? Are you able to meet the requirements for university?

2. From the research done in Activity 5, make a list of the options that are available to you.

3. When you have completed high school, do you want to stay in your town or city to continue your education? What options are available to you?

Identifying Your Career Options

In Chapter 1, you completed a quiz in which you assessed your personallity type and compared it to a chart of possible jobs (see page 44). Are there other jobs you are interested in now? If so, write them down.

Looking Back

1. Why is choosing the right high school so important?

2. Identify a career that interests you. List the extra-curricular activities you could join that relate to that career. Describe what skills you might gain from them.

3. What are the differences among college, technical school, university, and other educational institutions?

4. Would you continue your education if you could not attend a secondary school full-time? Why or why not?

5. List the advantages of an apprenticeship.

EXPLORATIONS

Reflections

Create a cartoon for the caption "Don't Drop Out."

Goals

What do you think your post-secondary education will be? Give reasons for your answer.

Action!

In pairs, act out one of the following situations:
- Education is important.
- Choosing a non-traditional school or program is a challenge.
- I got ahead and I did not have any education!
- Marks are not everything!

Portray different viewpoints, such as those of a parent, a teenager, or an employer.

Featuring. . .

Advice Column: Write letters of advice from the perspective of three people who graduated from your school ten years ago. These three people are writing to your magazine to give advice to students who are currently in school.

Research: Complete a cost comparison among a college, a technical school, a university, and a private institution (admission fees, books, other fees).

Advertisement: Create an ad for an alternative school.

Editorial: Write about future trends in education.

Personal Story/Interview: Interview an adult about his or her opinion of education today. Then write an article that summarizes the interview.

Career Choices in a Changing World

What You Will Learn

- The four career clusters.
- The characteristics of each cluster and how to match the best one to you.
- How education affects career choice.
- Where to find information on careers.
- A job that interests you in your community.
- Future career trends.
- New ways of working.
- The impact of technology on the workplace.
- Jobs that are growing or declining.

Terms to Remember

futurist	career goals
demographer	career plan
career	trends
cluster	downsize
occupational research interview	globalization
	outsourcing

There will be many exciting opportunities for you when you are ready to enter the work force. The challenge is to keep up with the many changes that are occurring at an ever-increasing rate. Changes are occurring for several reasons:

- Computers and other technologies. Current jobs are replaced with new ones. Robotics and the Internet are two examples of how the way in which work is done is constantly changing. Business is no longer limited to one's own country; the world is available to all.
- Data, knowledge, and information are the new products of the workplace.
- The changing needs of people. The aging population of Canada affects what people buy, do, and use.

Some people wish there were a crystal ball that could tell exactly what the future will hold. In its place, however, there are ways that predictions are made about the future. For example, **futurists** specialize in watching what is currently happening, observing what changes are starting to occur, and predicting what will happen in the future. **Demographers** study the population of a country and determine what the future needs and actions of the population will be. It is important to study the predictions of futurists and demographers. You need to direct your talents, abilities, and energies down the right path.

In this chapter, you will study career clusters and some of the occupations that are available in each cluster. Future trends in careers and ways of working will also be examined.

You might know exactly what you want to be, or maybe you cannot decide. Either way, you have to find a good match between yourself and the constantly changing world of work. In this chapter, you will begin the process of career planning.

Career Clusters

All **careers** in our society can be categorized under four main headings. The **jobs** in each group, or **cluster**, require the same interests and abilities. The four clusters are:

- Communication and the Arts
- Engineering, Industrial, and Scientific Technology
- Health, Human, and Public Services
- Business and Marketing

You have learned a great deal about your abilities, personality, skills, intelligences, and goals. As you consider future career possibilities, you need to think about those that fit well with all your characteristics. Now you can start to focus on careers that will best suit you.

Activity 1 ••••••••••••••••••••••••••••••••••

Describing Unfamiliar Jobs

The following Career Clusters chart lists the types of jobs that can be found in
each cluster. For each career cluster, read the jobs that are listed. Write down
any jobs that you have never heard of or that are unfamiliar to you. As a class,
help one another describe these unfamiliar jobs. Make a list on the board and
then, together, describe the jobs.

•••

Career Clusters

COMMUNICATION AND THE ARTS	ENGINEERING, INDUSTRIAL, AND SCIENTIFIC TECHNOLOGY	HEALTH, HUMAN, AND PUBLIC SERVICES	BUSINESS AND MARKETING
• musician • artist • actor • dancer • choreographer • interior designer • fashion designer • costume designer • set designer • writer • publisher • multimedia expert • reporter • curator • photographer • make-up artist • editor • producer • director • agent • TV and radio announcer	• environmental planner • surveyor • software engineer • computer programmer • plumber • contractor • builder • miner • logger • landscape architect • aerospace engineer • inspector • machinist • mechanic • auto body technician • mason • electrician • electrical engineer • diagnostic technician • researcher • robotics expert	• home health-care worker • physician • educator • religious leader • child-care provider • psychologist • dentist • dental assistant • police officer • speech therapist • nurse • dietitian • veterinarian • emergency medical technician • physical therapist • biomedical technician • caterer • restaurant worker • cosmetologist • hotel manager	• purchasing agent • travel agent • store owner • advertiser • sales associate • market researcher • office manager • loan officer • stockbroker • accountant • economist • personnel manager • systems analyst • meeting planner • buyer • image consultant • comptroller

Activity ②

Listing "Smarts" and Career Clusters

1. With a partner, list the types of smarts that would be needed for success in each of the career clusters listed in the chart. (See pages 27-33 to review the types of smarts.) For example, jobs in Communication and the Arts would require word and picture smarts. What other smarts would be useful for this category? Add them to your list.

2. Which career cluster includes the greatest number of smarts that you possess?

3. Are there other similarities within each cluster, such as working for others or for yourself or working in large institutions or outside? List any similarities you find.

In addition to being categorized in career clusters, jobs can be classified under three main types. There are jobs that involve: working with people, working with information, and working with things. Each career cluster contains all three of these classifications.

Activity ③ ···

Playing the Job Trek Game

On a sheet of paper, write down the number of each statement that describes you well. When you have finished, match up the numbers you picked with the number groups following the statements.

1. I would rather make something than read a book.

2. I enjoy problem-solving games and working at puzzles.

3. I like helping people when they need it.

4. I enjoy learning about new topics by reading about them.

5. I like working with my hands.

6. I like being the leader in a group of people.

7. I prefer to know all the facts before I tackle a problem.

8. I like to take care of other people.

9. I enjoy designing, inventing, and creating things.

10. I enjoy expressing myself through art, music, and writing.

11. I would like a job that lets me deal with people all day.

12. I like working with materials and equipment.

13. I enjoy learning new facts and ideas.

14. I find that co-operating with others comes naturally to me.

15. I like finding out how things work by taking them apart.

16. I would choose working with machines rather than working with people.

17. I can usually persuade people to do things my way.

18. I enjoy building and repairing things.

19. I enjoy the research part of my projects.

20. I like interacting with people.

21. I enjoy thinking up different ideas and ways to do things.

22. I like hearing other people's opinions.

23. I enjoy learning how to use different tools.

24. I find it easy to follow written instructions.

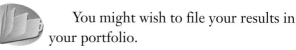 You might wish to file your results in your portfolio.

1, 5, 9, 12, 15, 16, 18, 23

Things are your thing.
You enjoy:
• Using tools and machines.
• Making objects with your hands.
• Maintaining or fixing equipment.
• Finding out how things work.

Jobs related to things are found in:
• Engineering
• Product manufacturing
• Construction
• Repair and servicing
• Transportation
• Trades and technology

3, 6, 8, 11, 14, 17, 20, 22

People are your pastime.
You enjoy:
• Caring for or helping others.
• Persuading people or negotiating.
• Working as part of a team.
• Leading or supervising others.

Jobs related to people are found in:
• Health care
• Education and training
• Social work and counselling
• Religion

2, 4, 7, 10, 13, 19, 21, 24

Information is your passion. You enjoy:
• Expressing yourself through writing, music, art.
• Doing experiments or researching a topic.
• Solving puzzles or problems.
• Studying or reading.

Jobs related to information are found in:
• Arts and entertainment
• Business and finance
• Scientific research
• Sales and services
• Tourism
• Law

Developing Your Interests into a Career

Through hobbies, interests, and extra-curricular activities you may discover a career field that you had not considered and that you are already knowledgeable about and have experience in. To decide on a career that you would enjoy, begin by considering your interests. Looking at your interests and assessing what skills and knowledge you have already developed may guide you in deciding on an education path; volunteer, co-op placement, or job-shadowing experiences; and activities that will further develop your ability in that area.

While pursuing your career goals, you may have to accept a job in an area of work that seems unrelated. However, you could choose a temporary or part-time job that will at least build skills that will contribute to your future career. You may also have to start in a position that is in your area of interest, but is at a lower level of responsibility than you hope to attain one day. If this is the case, keep your goal in mind, learn the most you can in that position, perform to the best of your ability, and find out as much as you can about other positions within the company or business. In this way, you can advance closer to your desired job over a period of time. Develop a professional network and draw upon your people resources for information in the meantime. You could also take specific job-related courses that would upgrade your skills and give you more of an advantage.

Perhaps when you initially chose a career field to become involved in, your aims were too high for you to attain a specific job or your knowledge was too limited to know how you would really feel performing this job. If this is your experience, you could choose a job in the same field, but something more in line with what you have learned about yourself or the business.

Attitude is an important aspect of finding a job that you will enjoy doing and of advancing in a job that you already have. Keep a positive frame of mind and be open to as many options as possible. These two characteristics will allow you to be open to change and to have more control over your career.

Activity 4

Mind-Mapping Your Interests

Think of your favourite subjects at school. For each one, mind-map all the careers you can think of that relate to that subject. Share your list with friends, teachers, and counsellors, and ask them to help you think of jobs that would incorporate these subjects. For example:

Education and Job Choices

In Chapter 5, you set educational goals. Your level of education influences the types of job you can pursue. The following graph shows a variety of jobs or occupations organized by career cluster and levels of education and/or training. Note that you might have several jobs in your lifetime, but all in the same career, or field of interest. There are many more opportunities if you have a university degree, a college or technical school diploma, or apprenticeship training.

Education and Job Choices

Arts
Human Services
Technical
Business

- Graphic Artists
- Photographers' Assistants
- Special Effects Technicians
- Announcers
- Medical Technicians
- Dental Technicians
- Health Care Technicians
- Paralegals
- Social Services Workers
- Ministers

- Creative and Performing Artists
- Writers
- Librarians
- Probation Officers
- Psychologists
- Teachers
- Lawyers
- Pharmacists
- Veterinarians
- Dentists
- Doctors
- Computer Programmers
- Land Surveyors
- Architects
- Engineers
- Investors
- Counsellors
- Accountants
- Auditors

- Assembly Supervisors
- Process Operators
- Processing Supervisors
- Fishing Vessel Skippers
- Logging Machine Operators
- Underground Miners
- Forestry Supervisors
- Mapping Technicians
- Industrial Engineers
- Technical Inspectors
- Administrative Assistants
- Clerical Supervisors

- Health Services Assistants
- Assemblers
- Machine Operators
- Agriculture and Horticulture Workers
- Oil and Gas Drillers
- Logging and Forestry Workers
- Mine Service Workers
- Clerks
- Office Equipment Operators
- Distributors

- Food Counter Attendants
- Medical Assistants
- Labourers
- Primary Production Labourers
- Plant Labourers
- Cashiers

| Education and/or Training Required | University | College, technical or apprenticeship, or two-years' training beyond high school | High school diploma, or some high school and on-the-job training | Some secondary school and some on-the-job training |

Activity 5

Creating a Personal Venn Diagram

A Venn diagram is used to demonstrate at least two different subject areas to see what they have in common and what is different about the two. On a piece of paper, draw two overlapping circles. Label one circle "Interests" and the other circle "Skills." Using information you have gathered about yourself from activities in previous chapters, list your interests and skills in the appropriate circles. Write anything that is both an interest and a skill in the section where the circles overlap. See the sample Venn diagram at right.

Review the Career Clusters chart on page 103. Identify the jobs that would require the majority of characteristics listed in the central part of your Venn diagram. List these jobs underneath your diagram. You might wish to file your Venn diagram in your portfolio.

INTERESTS

- bicycling
- tv, movies, computer games
- reading magazines
- playing chess with friends
- friends and family

- good with hands
- good with people
- like animals
- like science
- good memory
- have good marks in math
- have logical-mathematical intelligence and inter-personal intelligence
- my "true color" is gold

SKILLS

- am good at planning ahead
- can save money

PORTFOLIO

Creating a Family Tree of Careers

Talk to as many family members as you can about the career paths they have chosen. Ask each person to describe his or her employment history while you take notes. Ask your relatives about past generations. When you have gathered all the information, create a "Family Tree of Careers." A sample is included to get you started.

Do you notice any patterns in the jobs your family chose? Are the career choices you are interested in similar to those of your family? You might wish to share your family tree with the class and then file it in your portfolio.

Grandfather	Grandmother		Grandfather	Grandmother
investor	teacher		architect	homemaker
Uncle	Aunt		Aunt	Aunt
banker	fund raiser		accountant	dean's assistant
Sister	Brother		Brother	Sister	Sister
caterer	missionary		real estate broker	artist	bookkeeper

nurse–Mother   Father–carpenter

Researching Career Options

Once you have identified possible occupations, the next step in forming a career plan is to research these options. It is important to have an accurate understanding of any occupation in order to determine how appropriate it is for you. Career information can be obtained from the following sources:

- **Career centres.** Your community, your board of education, and/or your school may have a career centre that has information on careers as well as tests to help you determine appropriate occupations.

- **Guidance offices.** Your school guidance counsellor can provide you with detailed career information.

- **Career counsellors.** These people are specially trained in helping others to select the most appropriate occupation. They may work independently or be part of a career centre, and their services may require paying a high fee.

- **Libraries.** Use the library to research occupations that interest you. You can also use libraries to find out what services are available in your community to assist you.

- **Career Fairs.** These fairs provide information on different career areas. They are usually held in the community or in schools with individuals, educational institutions, companies, agencies, and trade associations participating.

- **Canada Employment Centres.** At these offices you can obtain brochures, job postings of jobs available in your area, speak with employment officers, and gain information on job-training programs sponsored by the government. Provincial government employment offices will also have valuable information.

- **Armed Forces.** The Canadian Armed Forces offer valuable work experience and will assist with education, such as a university program, in exchange for work for a specified period of time.

- **Human resource departments.** Contact these departments in large companies to request information on the opportunities and the range of occupations in a company.

- **Newspapers, magazines, and trade journals.** Publications that focus on a particular occupation can supply information as well as job advertisements.

- **Parents, relatives, friends, neighbours, and other contacts.** Ask people you know what they do for a living and what qualifications are needed in their fields.

- **Volunteer work, job shadowing, co-operative education, and part-time jobs.** Experience an occupation in order to determine whether it is right for you and to learn valuable skills. For more information on these activities, refer to Chapter 9.

- **Computer databases.** Databases are available to assist people in making career decisions. Many are available, including *Choices*, an interactive computerized career information system, and *Horizons*, a program that provides information about post-secondary education. These types of programs are available in some schools and Canada Employment Centres.

- **Unions and professional associations.** Some have education departments that will provide information on occupations.

- **Occupational research interviews.** One way to find out first hand about an occupation is to talk to people who are in it. You can interview people in various jobs to better understand the demands and rewards of these occupations.

Activity 6

Exploring Career Information Sources

1. Work in groups to explore what career information resources are available in your community. For example, one group could visit your school's guidance department and make a list of all the services and resources that are available to students. Some options on the list may not be available in your community; for example, a group exploring the career centre option may need to write or phone for information if the closest centre is too far away to visit. Another group could access the Internet to find numerous sites that can give career information. Another group may wish to read texts on career planning and give a book report on the content.

2. Compile the information from your research and give everyone in the class a copy. Include a brief description of the resources and services offered by each source.

Activity 7

Conducting an Occupational Research Interview

1. Return to the mind map you created in Activity 4. Draw a circle around your ideas. From that circle, generate names of stores, companies, agencies, and people in your community that you could approach for more information. As part of your research, conduct an **occupational research interview** for one of your two occupations. With a partner, create a list of questions you have about the occupation. Some questions you may wish to ask are:
   - What education and experience do you need as background for this career?
   - What specific training do you need for this career?
   - What is a major temperament, physical skill, or mental ability necessary for this career?

- How did you become interested in this career?
- What aspects of your job bring a smile to your face?
- What are the positive and negative aspects of this career? What do you like and dislike?
- What does it mean to be successful in this workplace?
- How do you balance your career with your family and personal life?
- How is the world different because of what you do?

2. Ask your teacher to review your questions and approve the person you have selected to interview. Then telephone a person in that occupation to request an occupational research interview. Explain who you are and why you want the interview. During your conversation, write down the company name, the person's name, the interview time, and the address. Be sure to bring a pen and paper to the interview. Write a thank-you letter to the person after your interview.

PORTFOLIO

Summarizing Occupational Research

Complete a summary similar to the one that follows, for each occupation you researched in Activity 7. Create a file for each occupation, and put it in your portfolio. Continue to collect and file information about the occupations that interest you.

Occupational Summary

Occupation: *High School Teacher*

Entry-level position: *The positions of educational assistant and supply teacher are often used to get experience as a teacher.*

Responsibilities: *To teach a full load of classes—prepare lessons, teach, evaluate, organize excursions, etc.*

Education required: *University degree, Bachelor of Arts (B.A.) plus a Bachelor of Education (B. Ed.)*

Supervisory position: *Department Head*

Responsibilities: *Regular teaching duties plus administration of a department of teachers.*

Education required: *Additional courses needed to become a subject specialist.*

Management position: *Vice-Principal/Principal*

Responsibilities: *Supervise all teachers, set time tables, enforce policies, set the tone of the school, hire staff, evaluate teachers.*

Education required: *Usually a Masters degree in education (M.Ed.) plus two additional courses (Principal I and II).*

Top-level position: *Director of Education*

Responsibilities: *Oversee all schools, teachers, students, and support staff for a district or board of education.*

Education required: *Usually serve as a principal then as a superintendent. Selected and interviewed by the trustees.*

Working environment: *A school setting—large, small, urban, or rural.*

How the working environment could change: *Dramatic cuts in money available, reduced extra-curricular activities.*

Salary or wages and benefits: *Starting salary is approximately $27 000. Director earns $100 000+. Benefits include medical, dental, life insurance, workers' compensation coverage, and employment insurance.*

Future trends in this occupation: *Undergoing major change in administrative structure and funding procedures. Have to do more with less—fewer teachers, administrators, programs. Increased technology must be available for students.*

The impact of technology on this occupation: *The teacher will become a facilitator.*

Skills I will need for this occupation: *Excellent communication, organizational, and people skills, love of young people, sense of humour!*

My interests that relate to this occupation: *Teach little league, peer tutor. Top computer skills. Like people.*

What I like about this occupation: *Working with young people, variety in the day and what happens in the classroom. Opportunity to coach sports, take trips.*

What I might not like about this occupation: *Demands of difficult students, being "up" for every class, giving the students what interests them.*

Other comments:

PORTFOLIO

Evaluating Your Career Choices

A good tool to evaluate your choices is the Personal Career Profile Form shown on the following page. This is a chart in which you can arrange side by side what you have learned about yourself and what you have learned about a career option. In the third column, use a 1-to-10 rating scale system to express how suitable the match is between you and your career option, with 10 being the best match. Complete a Personal Career Profile for your top three career options. How do you rate?

Personal Career Profile Form

Name: *Samantha N. Robin*   Date: *December 14*   Career: *Nutritionist*

Personal Information	Career Information	Match (1-10)
Your Values *I believe that people should take good care of themselves through good eating and physical exercise.*	**Career Values** *I would be able to help others achieve a healthy lifestyle.*	9
Your Interests *I love to cook and have a collection of cookbooks. I also work out a lot.*	**Career Duties and Responsibilities** *I would meet a lot of people. I would have to experiment with different foods and combinations of foods.*	8
Your Personality *I am quiet and have a few special friends.*	**Personality Type Needed** *A nutritionist can work in a lab or with clients. I would prefer to work with people. I can work on my interpersonal skills.*	7
Information-People-Things Preferences *I like experimenting and researching and I also like people, but in small numbers.*	**Information-People-Things Relationships** *Nutritionists have a choice of the type of environment they want to work in.*	8
Skills and Aptitudes *My best subject is science. I also like English. I prefer facts over fantasy. I do get creative when I cook.*	**Skills and Aptitudes Required** *Thorough research skills, accuracy, and good communication skills.*	9
Education/Training Acceptable *I would like to go to university with a co-op component to combine theory with practice.*	**Education/Training Required** *A university degree is best.*	9

Forming Career Goals and a Career Plan

Once you have researched educational and career options, you will need to make a decision about what occupation you wish to pursue and how to pursue it. Analyze the educational and career information you gathered to determine your **career goals**. To set effective goals, use these guidelines:

• Set one goal at a time.
• Make sure that your goals leave as many opportunities as possible open to you. For example, continuing your education after high school will allow you more job opportunities.

- Conceptualize a goal and clearly identify the first few steps that need to be taken toward this goal.
- Believe you can reach your goals.
- Be sure that your goals are attainable in terms of your strengths and abilities.
- Identify the factors affecting your goals that you can control as well as those you cannot control. For example, you may not be able to control the availability of a job opportunity at a company that interests you, but you can actively seek out an opportunity at that company.
- Set goals that can be measured in some way, such as in time or in quantity. For example, your goal may be to achieve a certain grade level in school or to attain a diploma or degree.
- Be sure that your goals are what you really want, rather than what you think you should want.

Once you have set your career goals, develop a **career plan** on how to attain them. To do this, set short-term goals or smaller achievements that lead to your long-term goals. Identify the challenges that face you and how you can cope with these challenges. A sample career plan follows for a 17-year-old co-op student in his last year of high school.

Career Plan for Jeremy Lang

Career Goal: Hazardous Waste Management Technician

Goals	Challenges
Short-Term Goals • Complete my work experience • Take a senior math and physics course • Apply for part-time work at my placement (Smithers Waste Management Co.) • Volunteer to work for Ecology House	• Maintain a positive relationship with the people at my placement • Return to studying • A job may not be available • Manage volunteer work and studying
One-Year Goals • Graduate from high school with a focus on math and science • Apply for community college courses in waste management	• Graduate with good marks in order to get into college • Save enough money for college by working part-time and during the summer • Move to an unfamiliar place to attend college
Three-Year Goals • Graduate from college • Obtain a part-time job while at college • Continue to take courses relating to waste management • Take courses on becoming an entrepreneur	• Maintain good marks • Balance college and work • Budget my finances effectively
Long-Term Goals • Contribute to waste management in a unique way • Own my own company	• Keep aware of future trends by reading trade magazines and attending seminars • Develop the skills and abilities required to become a successful entrepreneur

Activity 8

Forming Your Career Plan

1. Create a career plan using the sample on page 114 as a model.

2. Discuss your career goals and plan with a partner. Try to give your partner helpful, friendly advice about his or her career plan.

 You may wish to file your career plan in your portfolio.

Evaluating a Career Plan

Once you have formed career goals and a career plan, remember to continue to evaluate and modify your goals. As you progress in your career, there may be many reasons to modify your career plan. In order to manage change, you need to seek out opportunities for yourself. People change their career plans for many reasons; for example:

- A person might review his or her personal goals and determine that they are not currently being met.
- A unique and unexpected opportunity may present itself.
- A spouse may have to relocate.
- A person may need to adapt to a new situation, such as moving to a city with more opportunities or a town with a different occupational focus.
- A person may change occupations due to limited opportunities for advancement.
- A company may close or merge with another company, causing a person to lose his or her job.
- New technology may make a job obsolete.

JOURNAL

Assessing Present and Future Career Plans

In your journal, respond to the questions below.

- How will my career plan affect my high school behaviour?
- How will my high school course selections and activities affect my career options?

PROFILE

Calgary Stampeder, Roger Reinson, Talks About What He Does

"You guys are paying me to play football? That's crazy!" This is still Roger Reinson's reaction when he contemplates his good fortune. Six years a line-backer with the Calgary Stampeders, at age 30 Roger feels blessed that he's been able to translate his lifelong passion into a career. "You have to be happy to go to work in the morning," the well-known long-snapper says, reminding job-seekers thinking about long-term employment: "You want a job to be more than a source of income. It might as well be doing something you enjoy!"

"Sports has created who I am," Roger confides. "The skills learned are so transferable to life. You develop a work ethic and commitment, you see end results, and get out of it what you put in." In sports and business, he points out, you're focussed on the goals.

Roger always manages to apply something from football to his other jobs. "I pull something positive out of every single experience. Even the horrendous situations teach you, benefit you. They tell you 'Don't do it!' When you hate a job, let it go, don't get locked in. Fear doesn't help. That's when you have to dig deep and think positive, know it's time to move on."

1. Why does Roger feel fortunate and blessed?

2. Why isn't income the most important component of Roger's job? Do you agree? Why or why not?

3. List Roger's transferable skills.

4. What is Roger's advice if you find yourself in a job you do not like? Do you agree with this advice?

Activity 9

Inviting Career Speakers or Planning a Career Day

As a class, decide on people who would be interesting to hear speak about their careers. Decide on who and invite them to speak to your class. Or, as a class, decide to plan a career day for your school.

A c t i v i t y ⑩

Problem-Solving Situations

1. Raymond learned from his research on careers that the one he would like to pursue required a senior secondary mathematics course. Raymond struggles with mathematics. What strategies can Raymond use to continue to take and be successful in mathematics courses?

2. Andrew has just graduated from high school. He plans to build a career in the communications industry. He has just been offered an excellent job as publicity co-ordinator for a local radio station. The problem is that it is a full-time job with irregular hours and Andrew has been planning to attend college full-time. How can Andrew reach a decision? What do you think a good decision might be?

In the Future

It is impossible to predict the future accurately. For example, futurists of the 1960s and 1970s foretold that there would be a greater use of computers. However, they did not foresee how computers would become an essential part of our lives and work. Still, it is possible to look at the facts today and imagine what could happen in the future. The following chart shows **trends**, or general directions, in Canadian society that are changing the workplace today and are creating new possibilities for tomorrow's workers.

TODAY'S FACTS	TOMORROW'S POSSIBILITIES
An aging population: The baby boomers are getting older. As a result, there will be more people in the 50-60 age group after the year 2000.	**More jobs for young people:** As the baby boomers age, many will retire. Since there aren't as many young people entering the work force as there are older people leaving, there will be more career opportunities for young people. **More job opportunities in services for older people:** An aging population will increase demand in areas such as health care, leisure activities, and educational services for older people.

More women in the work force: Women's participation in the work force is growing: many are mothers with children under 18 years of age.

More family-friendly workplaces: To ease the stress on working parents, more companies will allow flexibility in work schedules and family leave.

More jobs for people who provide services to working women: Child-care workers, homemakers, house-cleaning services—there will be increasing demand for people who provide support services for families.

More education = better opportunities: Workers with good education and skills are getting jobs with good wages and career prospects. Workers with less education and skills are moving down the employment ladder in terms of wages, benefits, and prospects.

A more divided population: Canadian society could be divided into those who have wealth and those who don't. If unemployment remains high and the economy fails to generate a significant number of well-paying jobs, social problems may increase.

Growth of service jobs: Most new jobs today are in retail and wholesale business, financial and real estate services, entertainment, personal services, health, education, and social services, and transportation, communication, and utilities.

Continued demand for services: Increasingly, Canadians will turn to the service sector for employment. Business managers will seek out markets where they can supply products and services that are in demand.

One Hundred Best Careers for the Twenty-First Century

MEDICAL TECHNOLOGY AND HEALTH CARE CAREERS
Physician • Podiatrist • Chiropractor • Audiologist • Registered Nurse (RN) • Licensed Practical Nurse (LPN) • Nurse's Aide • Home Health Aide • Dental Hygienist • Dental Assistant • Alcohol and Drug Abuse Counsellor • Dietitian • EEG Technologist/Technician • Cardiology Technologist • Emergency Medical Technician • Medical Records Technician • Surgical Technologist • Physician Assistant • Clinical Laboratory Technologist • Respiratory Therapist • Physical Therapy Assistant • Occupational Therapist • Music Therapist • Dance Therapist • Veterinarian • Veterinary Technician

GERIATRICS CAREERS
Geriatric Social Worker • Geriatric Assessment Co-ordinator • Nursing Home Activities Director • Geriatric Care Manager • Recreational Therapist • Retirement Planner

SCIENCE AND ENGINEERING CAREERS
Meteorologist • Biochemist • Civil Engineer • Mechanical Engineer

CONSERVATION AND ENVIRONMENTAL CAREERS
Environmental Engineer • Environmentalist • Environmental Technician (water and wastewater) • Hazardous Waste Management Technician

COMPUTER CAREERS
Word Processor Operator • Systems Analyst • Technical Documentation Specialist • Computer Programmer • CAD Specialist • Computer Salesperson – Retail • Computer Service Technician • Computer Trainer

ADVERTISING, COMMUNICATIONS, AND PUBLIC RELATIONS CAREERS
Copywriter • Graphic Artist • Radio/Television Advertising Salesperson • Reporter (print) • Print Advertising Salesperson • Public Relations Counsellor • Marketing Manager

SALES AND SERVICE CAREERS
Accountant • Actuary • Insurance Sales Agent • Lawyer • Paralegal • Salesperson • Personal Shopper • Hairstylist • Child-Care Worker • Secretary • Private Investigator • Property Manager

HOSPITALITY AND TRAVEL CAREERS
Hotel/Motel Manager • Restaurant Manager • Travel Agent • Pilot • Flight Attendant

EDUCATION CAREERS
Teacher (elementary and secondary) • School Counsellor • Adult Education Teacher

FITNESS AND NUTRITION CAREERS
Aerobics Exercise Instructor • Sports Fitness Nutritionist • Personal Trainer

HOME-BASED BUSINESS CENTRES
Catering Service • Bed-and-Breakfast Inn Owner • Word Processing Service • Desktop Publishing Service • Gift Basket Service • Image Consulting Service • Child-Care Service • Publicity Consulting Service • Home Instruction Service • Cleaning Service • Event Planning Service • Pet-Sitting Service • Bookkeeping and Accounting Service

New Ways to Work

Not only are new jobs being created all the time, but new ways of working are being created too. The 8-hour workday and 40-hour work week is becoming a thing of the past. For many reasons—personal lifestyle choices, availability, advancement of technology, and the cost of how work is done—flexibility concerning where and when people work is becoming more and more important for both employers and employees. Here are some new ways they are choosing to schedule their work time.

Telecommuting: Employees work at home, linked to the workplace by computers and fax machines.

Flex Time: Workers start and end their days on flexible schedules—for example, 7 a.m. to 3 p.m. instead of 9 to 5—within limits set by management.

Work Sharing: To avoid layoffs, an organization's work force might share the available work.

Job Sharing: Two people share the responsibilities, salary, and benefits of one full-time job.

Permanent Part-Time: The employee works fewer hours, but enjoys the same job security and benefits as a full-time employee.

Compressed Work Week: Employees work longer hours for fewer days.

Phased Retirement: This allows people to retire gradually by reducing their hours of work.

Leave Time: The employee may be absent from work without loss of employment rights for such options as family leave, maternity leave, educational leave, sabbatical leave, and personal leave.

CASE STUDY

Why Normal Workers Are in the Minority

by Bruce Little

What is a normal job? If that question evokes a person who trundles off to work each morning to nine-to-five, Monday-to-Friday, full-time work with a company or government agency, you might want to think again. Only one in every three Canadian workers has such a "typical" job. The rest are caught up in a dizzying variety of flexible work arrangements that are far more normal than most people realize. The list seems endless: self-employment, temporary jobs, part-time jobs, jobs requiring more than 49 hours a week, job sharing, home-based or telework, flextime, weekend work, shift work, compressed work weeks.

Brenda Lipsett and Mark Reesor, analysts with the federal Human Resources Development department, have written an extensive paper on flexible work based on the 1995 survey of work arrangements sponsored by their department and carried out by Statistics Canada. To find the proportion of typical workers in the work force, they

use what might be called a process of reductive reasoning.

First, the whole work force is split into those with paid jobs (84 percent) and the self-employed (16 percent). (All the figures refer to different groups as a percent of all workers.) The latter either work on their own, as consultants or freelancers, for example, or they run a small business that employs other people. In theory, they can set their own working hours, but in fact, their work week will be dictated by the demands of their clients or the hours needed to keep their business running.

Next, the 84 percent with paid jobs are divided into those with permanent jobs (74 percent) or temporary ones (10 percent). Temporary workers have jobs that will end on a specific date. They may be filling in for someone on vacation or maternity leave, working on a specific project (like introducing a new computer system), or hired to handle a short-lived surge in demand (like retail clerks around Christmas).

The remaining 74 percent of workers are now split into those with full-time jobs (62 percent) and part-time jobs (12 percent). Some work part-time as a matter of choice; often, they are women with small children at home and students whose jobs finance their way through school. The rest are part-timers only because they cannot find full-time work.

Now we are down to the 62 percent with full-time jobs, and they can be divided into the 56 percent who work at their employer's office or factory and the 6 percent who work out of their homes. This group can include the growing new breed of workers in the information industry who keep in touch with the office by computer, but it would also take in the low-paid worker doing piece-work sewing for a clothing manufacturer.

The 56 percent who leave home to work each day can now be split into those who work normal hours (51 percent) and those who work long hours (5 percent). Long hours in this case means anything over 48 hours a week. Other surveys have shown that those working long hours tend to be managers, teachers, and those in the construction business. Among the 51 percent who work normal hours, almost all (50 percent) are content to work only in that job. But the other 1 percent hold a second, or perhaps third, job as well. These are probably people who run a small business on the side even though they have a full-time job.

We are down to half of all workers now, but we still have to split them into those who work Monday-to-Friday (37 percent) and those who work other days (13 percent). You need only look to people like police, firefighters, store clerks, and restaurant workers for examples of those who are not working an "ordinary" week. Even the 37 percent who get their weekends off are not all working daytime hours. That privilege is reserved for only 33 percent, while the other 4 percent work shifts, almost always because that is what the job requires.

Finally, we have reached the 33 percent of Canadian workers holding one of those so-called normal jobs. Of that group, 26 percent work for a business and the other 7 percent work in the public sector. The only thing that makes them close to typical is that there are more of them than any

Canadian Work Patterns

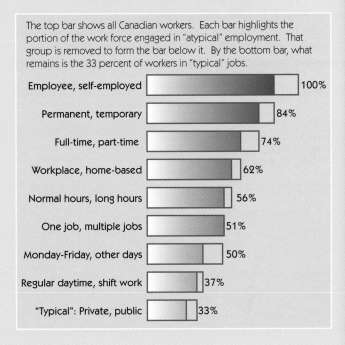

The top bar shows all Canadian workers. Each bar highlights the portion of the work force engaged in "atypical" employment. That group is removed to form the bar below it. By the bottom bar, what remains is the 33 percent of workers in "typical" jobs.

Employee, self-employed	100%
Permanent, temporary	84%
Full-time, part-time	74%
Workplace, home-based	62%
Normal hours, long hours	56%
One job, multiple jobs	51%
Monday-Friday, other days	50%
Regular daytime, shift work	37%
"Typical": Private, public	33%

other single group of workers. But, in the end, you have to wonder why their jobs came to be thought of as normal. Every day, we encounter hundreds of people who are hard at work outside those hours. Every time we turn on a radio or television, fill up the car with gas, take a bus or train or plane, eat in a restaurant, shop in a store, or listen to the siren from a police car, fire truck, or ambulance, we are dealing with some of the two-thirds of Canadian workers whose jobs are anything but "normal."

1. **Give a definition for the following terms.**
   - **temporary worker**
   - **self-employed**
   - **part-time**
   - **shift work**
   - **piece work**

2. **Add to the list of occupations mentioned in the Case Study that require working outside the "normal" Monday to Friday, nine-to-five jobs.**

3. **Predict how the percentages of work patterns will change in the year 2010.**

P O R T F O L I O

Identifying Your Career Options

Based on your study of who you are, predicted future trends, your lifestyle needs, career values, and the level of education for which you are striving, brainstorm a list of three occupations that are appropriate for you. Rank your occupations in order of preference.

Technology

Change is happening all around you. But nowhere is change occurring faster than in the area of technology. People have come a long way since the television was introduced a mere fifty years ago. At home people have TVs, VCRs, cable, satellite dishes, personal computers, CD-ROMs, and microwaves. They can program the functioning of their homes—for example, set the thermostat or turn on the oven before getting home—using the Smart computer. Although the home has been revolutionized, the most dramatic impact has been in the workplace. A *Times Mirror* survey found that among the countries of North America and Europe, Canada has the highest level of home PC use. An international survey in 1996 found that Canadians and Americans lead the pack in the rate of Internet access at home. In many instances, Canadians equal or surpass Americans in the popular adoption of technology. How did people work before the invention of faxes, e-mail, voice mail, laptop computers, cell phones, pagers, teleconferencing, modems, and most importantly, the Internet? People are *wired* wherever they go!

Technology has had an impact on the workplace in other ways as well. Robotics has caused many traditional factory workers to be replaced by machines. Traditional office workers, such as receptionists and secretaries, have also been replaced. Companies have **downsized**, or reduced the number of employees, as a result. The challenge for young people today is to choose growth careers in the field of technology and to use technology to their advantage.

Globalization

Technology has introduced **globalization** by making the world one large community—boundaries and borders are becoming even more artificial. The Internet has connected the world. No longer is the market for a product limited to a local region or home country. Technology has also had an impact on the ease with which goods can be sent to all parts of the world. On the downside, for many North American workers, this has enabled the growth of **outsourcing,** or having goods produced in Third World countries where labour costs are a fraction of North American costs, to occur.

Activity 11

Stating Your Opinion

In his book *Sex in the Snow: Canadian Social Values at the End of the Millennium*, Michael Adams makes the following statements. For each statement, explain why you agree or disagree. Give examples to support your opinions.

1. "The adoption of technology in Canada is slanted toward younger rather than older users, urban rather than rural users, and toward the better educated and more affluent."

2. "Canadian youth, although disadvantaged at the ballot box, might reasonably expect a greater degree of fairness and success on-line than in many other arenas of life."

3. "Younger Canadians are more attracted to the experience-seeking, exploring and communi-cating with friends and strangers, whereas older Canadians (mainly boomers) are more attracted by the time-saving convenience and the informational content of the Net."

4. "Despite the misgivings of some critics that the new technology is dissolving attach-ments to traditional forms of community, such as the family, church, and state, there has actually been a *broadening* of the defini-tion of community to include new relation-ships and new possibilities for contact that were formerly impossible, or prohibitively difficult, to establish. In the past, you had it made in Canada if they let you join the club. Today, you have it made if you can network in cyberspace."

Activity 12

Presenting Arguments on Globalization

Form into small groups. Half the groups will research and present arguments on the benefits of globalization; the other half will take the opposite viewpoint.

You may wish to file points from the arguments in your portfolio.

© Tribune Media Services, Inc. All Rights Reserved. Reprinted with permission.

IN THE NEWS

Lessons from the Future

by Frank Ogden

Imagine yourself back to the year 1905. You work for a company that manufactures buggy whips.

You learned leatherworking from your father, and your skills have guaranteed you steady employment since you were 14 years old. You don't worry about the future, because people will always need horses, buggies, and buggy whips.

Those new-fangled automobiles? They're expensive, unreliable, and dangerous—just a passing fad!

Technological Change Is Nothing New

Canadian workers today are in a situation similar to that faced by workers a hundred years ago. Technology has created hundreds of new products, making old ones obsolete.

Our economy is no longer fuelled by selling natural resources or mass manufactured products. More and more Canadians are working for industries that market ideas, information, and technology, including software developers, telecommunications companies, and businesses that develop and manufacture instruments such as robotics and computer controls.

The incredible advances in knowledge and technology are

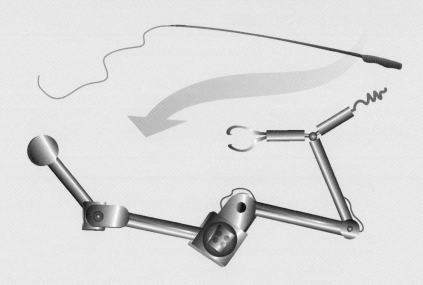

changing our work and lifestyles so completely that many people were calling the 1990s the dawn of the Information Age—a time when ideas and knowledge are the main forces in the development of new goods and services.

Jobs in the Future Will Be Constantly Changing

The leatherworker only knew one skill—how to work leather into buggy whips. If you're looking for a job in today's economy, you may have to add a few skills to those you already have.

Whatever kind of job you're looking for, chances are it now requires some computer skills. For example, if you want a secretarial job, you'll have to learn word-processing and electronic filing systems. If you're interested in shipping and warehousing, you're going to need to be familiar with computerized dispatch and inventory controls.

Acquiring these skills may mean some computer training and learning some basic math skills. It may mean sharpening your communications skills in reading and writing.

The most important skill, however, is one you probably already possess—the ability to be flexible and adaptable. Change in the Information Age is happening so quickly that no job will remain the same.

From Dr. Tomorrow's "Lessons from the Future." Reprinted by permission of Frank Ogden.

1. How might computer inventions, such as multimedia development and country-wide networks, affect our lives?

2. What do you think of an increasingly technological environment? Do you look forward to it or do you wish it would slow down? Do you look forward to the jobs it will result in?

Job Trends

The following lists forecast jobs that will be growing and declining in the future.

JOB GROWTH	JOB REDUCTION
• Technicians—computer, environmental, medical, automation, quality control	• Court reporters
• All aspects of film and television production	• Legal secretaries
• Food preparation—take-out, delis, home delivery	• Print journalists
• Private school teachers	• Doctors (except for those working with the elderly)
• Hospitality—adventure tours, luxury hotels	• Traditional farmers
• Retailers—large discount stores, home office products	• Bank tellers
• Home renovators	• Inventory takers
• Farmers specializing in local markets	• Printers (other than desktop)
• Private security firms	• Department store and supermarket jobs
• Massage and relaxation therapists	• Public school teachers
• Funeral directors	
• Drivers for mail order or home shopping items	
• Information technologists	
• Paralegals	
• Financial planners	
• Marketing specialists	
• Activation co-ordinators	
• Registered nursing assistants/health care aids	
• Software developers	
• Engineers—electrical and mechanical	

In the future, robots will replace workers in performing many routine functions, particularly where danger, accessibility, or great strength are factors.

Looking Back

1. Name three places where you can gather information about careers.

2. List two changes in today's society that will affect jobs in the future. Explain the effect they will have.

3. Do you agree with the lists on job growth and job decline? Are there some that you question? Make a list of the occupations that fall into these categories and the reasons why you picked them.

EXPLORATIONS

Reflections

What are your dreams for the future? Do you also have some worries or concerns about what is ahead? Reflect on what you think the future might hold for you.

Goals

Based on the information you now have about future career possibilities and what your interests and abilities are, select the career that interests you the most. Make that your career goal. In order to achieve that goal, you will have to also set educational goals. Include educational goals for high school. Revisit the goals you chose for post-secondary education in Chapter 5. Do they need to be changed to meet your career goal? Create three action steps that will start you on the path to your future career.

Featuring. . .

Editorial: Write an editorial on the topic "The Changing Workplace."

Advertisement: Create an advertisement for an interesting job for today and for the future.

Advice Column: Respond to two readers who have written to the magazine asking for advice on how to choose a career that they will like.

Research: Conduct research on Canadian futurists and summarize what their predictions are for future workplace trends and job opportunities.

Personal Story/Interview: Interview someone you or your parents/guardians know whose job includes at least one of the "new ways to work" mentioned in this chapter. Find out how the change has affected his or her life. Prepare your interview for publication.

Action!

Imagine that there is a psychic who is able to see the future by looking into a crystal ball. Several clients come to visit, asking questions about the future—careers, workplace trends, job opportunities, working in outer space, and so on. Role-play this scenario.

Role Models, Mentors, and Networks

What You Will Learn

- To identify characteristics of positive role models.
- To reflect on the importance of mentors and role models.
- To identify people in your life who are mentors to you and to others.
- To discover your network possibilities.

Terms to Remember

role model
characteristics
mentor
network

A **role model** is a person whose part played in life is especially worth copying or imitating. Role models can have a big influence on the lives of many people, in many different ways. What characteristics make a worthy role model? What choices have they made and what actions have they taken that make them outstanding individuals? This chapter offers profiles of people who are role models for others. As you read about them, you can think about your own role models. You can determine what you can do to become the person you want to be.

What Is a Role Model?

Think of a person you admire. It could be someone famous in his or her field of work, someone in the community, or someone in your family. What special **characteristics** or qualities does that person have that make him or her admirable? What do you like about how that person acts and what he or she does? The following chart lists some characteristics and resulting actions that most people would find worthy.

CHARACTERISTIC	ACTION
Aware of the needs of others	Works as a volunteer
Resourceful	Creates new clothes from old ones
Reliable	Never breaks promises
Optimistic	Can find something positive in every situation
Brave	Stands up for people's rights

Activity 1

Identifying Characteristics

Think of other admirable characteristics to add to the chart and give examples of actions that illustrate them. Record the results so they can be shared with the class and referred to in future activities.

C A S E   S T U D Y

Inspired Connections

by Sharon Doyle Driedger

Dr. Arlette Lefebvre and some of the young people she's helped with Ability OnLine.

Dr. Arlette Lefebvre's voice falters, remembering her first encounter with a young patient named Laura. The Grade 3 student had contracted meningitis and—to save her life—doctors had to amputate her legs. "She was a figure skater," says Lefebvre, a psychiatrist at Toronto's Hospital for Sick Children where Laura was treated. "She woke up without legs—she was depressed, she didn't want to live, she didn't want to eat. I thought, 'How can I give this kid hope that there is life without legs?'" To help Laura deal with her loss, Lefebvre hooked her up to Ability OnLine, an innovative electronic support group she had established a year earlier. "One good role model is worth a thousand psychiatrists," Lefebvre contends. "I put her in touch by computer with Carlos Costa, a wonderful swimmer without legs. Now, she is Rollerblading with her prosthetic legs."

Ability OnLine—the first service of its kind in Canada—handles about 1200 calls a day across Canada, the United States, Europe, and Australia. The free e-mail link allows chronically ill, disfigured, or young people [with disabilities] to communicate from their homes or hospital beds with others who have a disability, as well as with friends, family, classmates, and volunteer mentors. "We've just had our millionth call," says Lefebvre, who started the program six years ago with a single computer.

In 1992, she realized her plan for a "friendly on-line environment" with the help of Brian Hillis, a retired firefighter and computer wizard, volunteers, and donations from private sources. Ability OnLine now has more than 5000 current users, but Lefebvre is determined to expand. "My dream is to have a laptop in every [hospital] room," she says.

Lefebvre spends five hours every evening answering young people's e-mail messages. "Putting people in touch with each other," she says, "is my main goal." With Ability OnLine, Dr. Lefebvre found a way to do just that.

Maclean's, July 1, 1996. Reprinted with permission.

1. Make a list of words that you think best describe Arlette Lefebvre. Which of these characteristics do you admire the most? Add them to your chart, if you have not already included them.

2. How do Lefebvre's characteristics suit the career she has chosen? What other jobs do you think she would do well, and why?

JOURNAL

• •

Identifying Your Positive Qualities

What you do shows people who you are. Think about yourself in a variety of situations with people from different age groups. Some sample situations are:

• Visiting your grandmother in a seniors' residence.
• Attending a large family celebration or reunion.
• Going to a younger brother's or sister's baseball game.
• Going to a sporting event.
• Participating in a school play production.

Which of your character traits come to mind when you picture yourself in these situations or others that you think of? Record the situation and the character traits in your journal.

Activity ② •

Identifying Role Models

1. With your classmates, make a list of people who are positive role models. They can be people in your family, people in the community, or famous people in any professional field.

2. Work independently to list the qualities each of these role models has that make him or her admirable and the actions that demonstrate these qualities.

3. Share your findings as a class.
   • Which role models are most popular with your peers?
   • What characteristics do many of the role models have in common?

• •

FOR BETTER OR FOR WORSE © Lynn Johnston Prod., Inc. Reprinted with permission of UNIVERSAL PRESS SYNDICATE. All rights reserved.

IN THE NEWS

Turning Tragedy into Triumph

By Heather Finley

In June, 1996, Jeremy D'Souza was running for the bus at a Scarborough, Ontario, intersection when a pickup truck going through a yellow light hit him. After a week in a coma, he awoke at Sunnybrook Hospital, unable to recognize his own family.

D'Souza—a high achiever who had spent four years at Royal Military College and had just completed his first year in information systems at St. Lawrence College—had damage in a crucial area of his brain. He spent two weeks in intensive care, then two-and-a-half months in rehabilitation, undergoing speech pathology and occupational therapy, and had to learn to walk again. He also found that his memory and some thinking abilities were impaired

Then he tried to start working. But because he could no longer multi-task, keep track of time, or remember things the way he once did, he was fired from three jobs. The physical and professional struggles left him frustrated and angry, too, making rehabilitation even more painful.

Then D'Souza signed up for Goodwill Toronto's Webmaster/ Developer program for youth with disabilities, a 32-week intensive course that includes

Jeremy D'Souza fixes a computer problem at Scotia bank.

counselling and life-skills courses, internships, and training in specific programming languages. Scotiabank, a Goodwill corporate partner, agreed to hire him as a condition of his being accepted into the Goodwill program. And last June, at the end of this training, Soctiabank gave him a permanent job.

Happily, D'Souza, 29, is now a technical trainee working toward a position as data security officer with the bank's data centre in Scarborough. He loves his work, and says the company understands and supports his disabilities—even going as far as moving him into an internal computer support position after he found his original Web development position was too difficult for him. Now he's helping other bank employees and programmers with computer-related

problems. Goodwill even sent in a job coach to help him cope with the time-mangement problems the brain injury had left him with.

Like any new employee, D'Souza worried about fitting in. But when he had his first performance appraisal, he came out feeling very positive about his future. "They're very happy. In no way am I being held back, in no way am I being babysat."

1. **How do you know that Jeremy D'Souza was a young man with long-term goals before June 1996?**

2. **What admirable characteristics does D'Souza have?**

3. **List the ways D'Souza is a role model for a wide variety of people.**

Setting a Fine Example for Native Youth

by Janice Turner

Strong family support and an Olympic champion for inspiration gave Sara Beaudry enough confidence and determination to "stay on the right path." She took up cross-country running, completed high school, and is proudly raising a son on her own. In 1990, she earned a gold, silver, and two bronze medals in track and field at the North American Indigenous Games. Three years later, the team she coached at the games brought home 14 medals. And just last year, she won herself another silver.

Today, the 24-year-old Ojibway volunteers with the National Native Role Model Program in hopes of making a difference in the lives of Native youngsters. The program dates back to the 1984 summer Olympics in Los Angeles when Beaudry's hero, Quebec Mohawk Alwyn Morris, won gold and bronze medals for Canada in kayaking. After winning the gold, he held up an eagle feather—the symbol of honour, friendship, and life—as a gesture to all North American Native people. A year later, he received the Order of Canada.

The program focusses on education, motivation, and positive reinforcement, and encourages Native American youth to realize their potential by taking control of their lives.

Sara Beaudry (left) and friend.

It is federally funded, Native designed and operated, and rooted in the tradition of the seven sacred gifts: wisdom, love, respect, bravery, honesty, humility, and truth.

Beaudry and Morris have met five times during the past ten years. "I've been in total awe of him," says Beaudry, who named her son after her personal role model. "I know first-hand the impact that a role model can have on one's life," she says. "He inspired me to be the best I could be. He challenged me to make a difference and to believe in myself and my dreams. The circle is complete as I am now the role model."

Beaudry was appointed to the two-year position with the role model program in February [1996] and has already visited with more than 15 Native American youth groups, most of them on reserves. She continues to run several times a week. "I think the strongest message I can send out is that my running has helped me stay on the right path," she says. "It's given me something to focus on and helped me to lead a healthy lifestyle."

The youngest of ten children, Beaudry spent most of her youth in Sudbury. In May, she moved to the Wikwemikong reserve on Manitoulin Island with her five-year-old son Alwyn to join the rest of her extended family. Beaudry is currently recreation co-ordinator for the reserve's youth centre.

"I try to get my message across by talking about my life and I haven't had an easy life raising a son by myself," she says. She separated from his father before their child was born. It also wasn't easy being the only Native American student at her Sudbury school. "I was teased," she recalls.

When speaking to kids, Beaudry then turns to the positive things in her life—her family and her commitment to physical health and her determination to stay in school. "I try to make them (Native American youths) understand that there's more out there than drugs and alcohol. There's their education and their culture. I know sometimes I'm getting through to them." She encourages young people to be active in their communities and to organize local youth councils.

"I want them to take responsibility for who they are and to try to build a future for themselves," she says. "I just try to encourage them to not listen to what other people have to say about who we are and where we come from. If you listen to that and believe it, it's just going to bring you down."

Reprinted with permission—The Toronto Star Syndicate.

1. How did having a role model help Sara Beaudry decide to become a role model?

2. What are the positive suggestions that Sara has for other Native youth?

Describing a Role Model

PORTFOLIO

Write a description of a role model who interests you. Include such details as personal traits and life events that shaped the person's character, education, and job history. You might need to research the information or, if your role model is someone who lives in the community, you might be able to interview him or her.

Or

Mount a picture of a role model on a background that represents something about that person's job; for example, an artist on a painter's palette, a musician on a lyric page, a computer programmer on a printout. Include a few important facts about the person on your display.

File your description in your portfolio.

PROFILES

Mary Simon

by Brian Bergman

For a brief moment, Mary Simon is savouring the comforts of home—in her case, a two-storey wood-frame house in central Ottawa. The bookshelves are filled with volumes on northern Canada, and soapstone carvings, prints, and paintings by northern artists adorn nearly every centimetre of display space. Just back from a five-day trip to Norway, Simon has only a few days to unwind before embarking on a ten-day journey to Greenland and Russia. It is all part of her job as Canada's ambassador for circumpolar affairs and chairperson of the Arctic Council, an eight-nation organization that is designed to foster co-operation in the northernmost regions of the planet. It also means spending more than half of each year on the road—a wanderer's existence that is nothing new to the Inuit leader. "I seem to have been travelling all my life," she says with a hearty laugh.

Born in Kangirsualujuak (George River) in northern Québec, Simon spent much of her first 15 years moving with her family from camp to camp by dog team or canoe. Her Manitoba-born father, Bob May, who is white, went north as a Hudson Bay manager. He stayed on to found a fly-in fishing and hunting business and to marry Simon's mother, Nancy, who is Inuk. The second eldest of eight children, Simon says she learned early on about "living close to the land" and how to sew her own parkas, and *kamiks*, or traditional boots made of caribou, walrus, or seal hide. The family spoke Inuktitut and Simon took much of her schooling through correspondence courses. She credits those years with giving her a firm

Mary Simon, Canada's ambassador for circumpolar affairs and chairperson of the Arctic Council.

grounding in two very different cultures. "I can live down here in a house like this," she says with a sweep of her hand, "or I can go north and live in a tent. I'm comfortable either way."

Good thing, too. These days, Simon's life is punctuated by cellular phone calls, faxes, and complicated plane schedules. Since 1994, when she became the first Inuit ambassador in Canada, Simon has worked tirelessly to help found the Arctic Council, which held its first meeting in Ottawa in September [1996]. Her goal, she says, is to show that international co-operation can have results—preserving, for example, the Arctic environment and creating northern jobs through free trade in northern products.

For Simon, the Arctic Council is the culmination of a career that has seen her play a leading role in several Inuit institutions. But it required some sacrifices. For most of her adult years, Simon has had to make her home base far from northern Québec, where her parents and siblings still live. Before pulling out pictures of herself and the fish she caught during a recent visit home, Simon remarks sadly, "The hardest part of my job is being away from my family so much." She has also had to adjust to life in urban Canada, where the casual friendliness of a Northerner is sometimes viewed with suspicion, if not outright alarm. "At first," she recalls with a smile, "I'd say hello to strangers and make eye contact. People would look at me like I was crazy."

To relax, Simon and her husband, former CBC broadcaster Whit Fraser, canoe, camp, and ski at every opportunity. She also cherishes her time with her three grown children, from a previous marriage, and the four grandchildren that they have given her. As her long-distance duties beckon, those moments seem increasingly precious.

Maclean's, December 23, 1996. Reprinted with permission.

• •

Serving as a Surrogate

By Allan Maki

The telephone would ring and it would be her son's school calling, and right away Bernice would cringe. "What now?" she'd ask. Sometimes the teachers would tell her that Ryan, her 13-year-old son, had been caught goofing off and disrupting the class. Sometimes they'd say Ryan was refusing to do his homework and that his grades were falling fast. A few times enough was said and left unsaid that Bernice, a single mother of three, wondered where her son was headed.

Thankfully, Berenice says, things are better. When she talks to her son's teachers now, they tell her what a joy Ryan is and how his whole attitude toward school has changed. He does his homework, plays guard on his junior high basketball team, and has his mind made up that one day he's going to the University of Calgary.

That's where his buddy David Sol goes to school. That's where the two of them have hung out and become fast friends—the 2.3-metre middle blocker on the Calgary Dinos volleyball team and the 1.5-metre live wire from northeast Calgary. They may look like a strange pair, but theirs is a compelling story. "Ryan's pretty quiet," Sol said. "He doesn't talk a lot. But I don't know if I've ever met a more pleasant kid, regardless of the situation." "I like David," Ryan said. "Mostly

University of Calgary student David Sol tackles Ryan Bishop as the two play some hoops in Calgary.

we talk about school, like the differences between university and my school."

Six months ago, Ryan and Sol were paired together in a Calgary mentoring program involving university athletes and boys in need of positive role models. It was the second year of a partnership between the Catholic Family Services and University of Calgary coach Greg Ryan, who figured his players could use a few lessons in life as well as how to spike a volleyball. When Greg Ryan approached Sol and asked whether he was interested in spending time with a teenaged boy whose behaviour was making his mother extremely nervous, Sol surprised him by saying yes. It was the start of an agreeable friendship and a remarkable turnaround in Ryan's life.

"From what I understand, Ryan's one of the better kids involved in social services," Sol said. "His parents split up, but he lives with his mom and two sisters. There was never a custody battle. He was a prime candidate for this program because of his age and personality. He's really interested in sports, and just being athletes at the university level, kids look up to you. What we're doing is cool."

Sol, 21, grew up in Calgary with an older brother and younger sister and a love for sports. He was an all-round athlete in high school but never thought he was good enough to play at the next level. When he did make it with the Dinos, his life became an endless shuffle between classrooms and the university gym.

One day he watched as two of his senior teammates were paired with young boys from social services in need of some male encouragement. Sol had no idea his turn was coming the next October. "Greg Ryan ran [the mentoring program] last year and approached me and asked if I'd be interested," Sol said. "I didn't know much about it. Basically, the approach to this is that I give what I can offer and, quite honestly, after a long day, a long practice, it's something you have

to want to do. I know my mom and dad were a little surprised when I agreed to do it. It's a little out of the ordinary. Usually, it's just volleyball and school for me."

"The best thing about it is helping someone. Plus, it's an affirmation about the good in people. This child is such a good guy. If he's at that pivotal stage in his life, maybe I can make a difference in which way he falls as an adolescent."

Sol was screened by the police and interviewed by social services, and it was during the volleyball season that Ryan and Sol got to know each other. Ryan would go to the university Wednesday after school, watch the practice, and fetch balls. Afterward, Ryan and Sol would hang out, talk, and go to a movie. It was awkward at first, but the two got along so well that Sol began to spend more time with Ryan than the required few hours each week. It wasn't long before Bernice noticed the changes in her son.

"He's definitely more positive because a lot of the male role models in his life have left," Bernice said. "My own dad doesn't have much to do with my kids. My brother is in Texas. The dad is doing his own thing. I wanted Ryan to have a positive role model, and when I was told about the mentoring program with university athletes, I jumped at it. I wanted this for him."

• •

Mag Ruffman's Remarkable Teachers

"I fiercely loved all my public school teachers," Mag Ruffman asserts, "but I managed to select three."

In 1963, Avonel Monkman taught Grade 1 at L.M. McConaghy Public School in Richmond Hill. "She was very stern with us," says Ruffman, "but she clearly loved us and she taught me how to read. For this I am forever indebted to her." Although she wanted to be an astronaut then, not an actor, Ruffman loved to read out loud. She used to flip ahead through the reader, looking for

the passages with the most exclamation points, like when the dog got into the swimming pool. "When we got to that page," Ruffman recounts, "I would carry on, I poured my heart into it, and I would make these really dramatic scenes. Mrs. Monkman must have appreciated it because somehow I got the idea this was fun."

"That's one of the reasons I'm citing these three teachers, because they put up with me, because I had way too much energy," Ruffman says. The energy that made her a rambunctious student continues. Mag Ruffman is an actor (Olivia Dale in "Road to Avonlea"), contractor, and carpenter, and host, creator, and writer. She currently has two shows on WTN, "A Repair to Remember" and "Men on Women," and a third in development.

Ruffman encountered her second remarkable teacher, Marilyn Letcher, in Grade 6. "That was the year everyone was starting to get bras and it was a huge scourge if you didn't have a bra. Mrs. Letcher had this really calming effect on the Grade 6 mentality. For one thing she was a total babe. She had that high beehive hair and was just so hip, and she spoke with the clearest diction I can remember in a teacher. She was strict but had a really even hand in the classroom. She was noble. You wanted to be like her." Ruffman remembers her class as terribly boisterous and that she used to fall down dramatically, just for fun. "You can see what Mrs. Letcher had to put up with," says Ruffman, "but she had this quality of self-possession and grace and yet leadership that was inspiring."

Joyce Insley was Ruffman's Grade 8 teacher. "Mrs. Insley was a true grammarian," says Ruffman. "Consequently my grammar rocks. I can write because she was extremely encouraging. Taking a sentence apart and breaking it down into pieces—I loved doing that. But you had to have someone instructing you who thought it was fun, too, or you were going to hate grammar. I just love it when somebody knows whether to use a colon or a semicolon. It's like knowing how to set

a table and which fork to pick up first." Ruffman also credits Insley with teaching her how to crochet. "I was left-handed and so she had to reverse everything for me. Now I work in a different medium – construction or carpentry or wood. But that was when I learned I could create something."

That year, Ruffman also got her first taste of stage glory. She recalls, "We did the hippie version of *'Twas the Night Before Christmas* and Mrs. Insley gave me the biggest part – the narrator. Not that I was that good or even that people told me I was good. But that was the beginning of a career. It was so fun."

Ruffman concludes: "I was passionately devoted to these teachers. And because I felt that way, I did really well in school. I think that if a teacher can create that bond with their students, where the students truly love them, well then the whole world is a better place. You're fascinated by everything and curious. You think your mind can go on expanding forever because somewhere along the line back in public school, somebody gave you the idea that it could."

1. The role models about whom you have read have made important choices about who they are and where they want to be. Discuss the challenges they faced, and what they might have given up to pursue their dreams.

2. For each of the role models, identify the benefits they have gained from their experiences.

Learning from Role Models

Many people attribute their success to a famous person they admired when they were young. That role model might have been a movie star, an inventor, a surgeon, or an athlete. They probably never spoke to that person, and yet he or she set a worthy example to follow.

People in the media also trigger the popularity of certain occupations. For example, there was an increase in the number of students who chose computer careers after the success of Bill Gates, who developed MS-DOS and founded Microsoft®. Every four years, the Olympics renews people's interest in sports careers. The "overnight successes" of performers like Alanis Morissette might spur individuals on to becoming singers. Because of the exposure, or extensive coverage, that people receive in the media, their actions have a strong impact on young people and the careers they choose for themselves.

Activity 3

Comparing Professionals

With a partner, pick a career that would be highly visible in the media; for example, politician, model, athlete, medical researcher, musician, or lawyer. Review back copies of newspapers and magazines at the library to find as many articles as you can on people in that profession. Identify the individuals who are receiving the most media attention. Record any personal attributes and actions that are mentioned in the articles. Then outline why that person would or would not make a good role model for young people. Report your findings to the class.

JOURNAL

Making Choices

In your journal, write an entry about education and career choices that you might make in the future and how they will affect your life as an adult.

PORTFOLIO

Visualizing What You Would Say

If you could spend ten minutes talking to a person you admire, what would you say? Would you explain why you admire him or her? Would you ask who he or she admired as a young person? Would you get an autograph? Would you ask about something specific he or she did? Write your reflections on a sheet of paper, or create a song about the experience, or draw a storyboard about the incident. File it in your portfolio.

What Is a Mentor?

A **mentor** is a trusted counsellor or guide. Many adults remember a person who played a special role in their personal development. That person, often older, gave support not available from peers or family members. He or she might have provided inspiration, information, career guidance, and exposure to new activities and ideas. You also might have had mentors in your life without even realizing it. In this section, you will identify past mentors in your personal life, find new ones to help you, and learn how to become a mentor yourself.

PORTFOLIO

Identifying Past Mentors

Identify people in your life who have been mentors, or who have guided and encouraged you along the way. They might be people in your family, at school, or in the community. In a web like the one here, write their names and describe what they did to help you (action).

Mentors in My Life

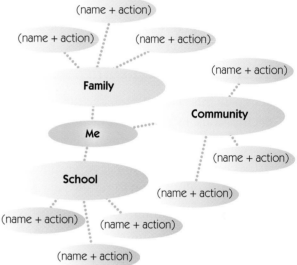

(name + action)
(name + action)   (name + action)
                                   (name + action)
Family
                    Community
Me
                    (name + action)
School
(name + action)   (name + action)
          (name + action)

Being a Mentor

In the past, you may have been a mentor without even realizing it. Have you:
- been a reading buddy to a younger student when you were in elementary school?
- helped a teammate to improve and practise a skill in which he or she was weak?
- acted as a lunch, hall, or bus monitor?
- coached a friend through a difficult personal situation?
- studied for a challenging test with a classmate who needed encouragement?

Reflecting on Your Mentoring Experience

Think back to a time when you have been a mentor to someone.

- In what ways did you help?
- Did you do it more than once?
- How did you feel?
- What did the other person do or say to show he or she enjoyed being with you?

   Describe your experiences in your journal.

Activity 4

Presenting Your Mentoring Abilities

1. Set up an information page like the following, listing your personal traits, talents, skills, interests, past mentoring experiences, and times when you would be available to perform the role of mentor.

2. Ask a classmate who knows you well and with whom you feel comfortable sharing the information to review your list and add anything you missed.

3. Make copies of your information to take to future mentoring opportunities.

Name: _____

Address: _____

_____

Phone Number: _____

Personal Traits: _____

_____

Talents: _____

_____

Skills: _____

_____

Interests: _____

_____

Mentoring Experiences: _____

_____

Times Available: _____

IN THE NEWS

Respite Services in Mentorship Project

Durham Family Respite Services has received a federal grant for young adults, as mentors, to team with special-needs families in four geographical areas of Durham, Ontario.

The participants of the mentorship project will be working with families who have children with developmental disorders. They will work directly with the families to provide support for the children. This could include strengthening social skills, tutoring, positive peer-interaction, community interaction, educational support, and family relief.

The mentorship project promotes an alternative and cost-effective way for communities to support exceptional families in a "dignified" fashion. It fosters a natural exchange of skills between the families and their children's mentors.

While the families mentor the young adults in areas of job skills, they will in turn support their children in specific areas of their development.

Reprinted by permission of the *Whitby Free Press*.

1. **Why would a mentoring opportunity such as this appeal to young people?**

Activity 5

Mentoring a Younger Person

As a class, brainstorm possible opportunities for you to be a mentor at school, in the community, or in your immediate neighbourhood. As a class, research these possibilities and develop guidelines for the types of mentoring you find. Select a mentoring opportunity that appeals to you and in which you have skills and experience. With permission from home, make the necessary arrangements and volunteer to be a mentor.

Finding a Mentor

Before you begin to look for your own mentor, you have to decide what you want to gain from him or her. You have to decide whether you want to get to know someone new or be with a person whom you already know, respect, trust, and can learn from. Do you want to investigate careers? Do you want to learn more about an industry? Do you want to spend time with someone you admire personally and find out more about him or her? Study this chart to help you decide whom your mentor could be.

WHO/WHAT	GOAL	LOCATION
• Teacher	• Improve attendance • Get better marks	• School
• Service clubs • Social service agencies	• Learn skills • Do volunteer work related to future job	• School • Community
• Employee in your area of career interest	• Experience what it is like on the job	• Workplace
• Educator from an area of educational interest	• Become more informed • Become more aware of skills needed to proceed	• College • University

Activity 6

Defining the Qualities of Mentors

Look over the following list that some students created, of desirable qualities for a mentor.
• Cares about others.
• Listens without judging.
• Advises without lecturing.
• Accepts and values differences.
• Is patient.
• Speaks at a level that is easy to understand.
• Is reliable.
• Wants to make a commitment.
• Is an advocate for others.
    Add any other qualities you think are important.

Contacting a Mentor

Imagine that you are contacting a possible mentor. Choose at least four personal qualities from the list in Activity 6 and tell why they are important to you. Then explain why you would like to have a mentor.

PROFILE

Students Give and Get Career Help

by Paul Luke

The last recession did its best to strangle the ancient art of mentoring. However, Melody Lever, 22, insists on keeping the practice alive because it helped make her what she is—and what she's becoming.

Influenced by a mentor she had as a Grade 10 co-op student at the Vancouver aquarium, Lever decided to enrol in Simon Fraser University's co-op studies program.

Now, a fourth-year biochemistry student on a co-op placement at Vancouver's Terry Fox Labs, Lever has become a mentor herself.

Her protégé is Esther Tang, a 15-year-old student from Burnaby South Secondary School. Tang is one of 45 high school students from the Lower Mainland matched with Simon Fraser University co-op student mentors at 35 workplaces. Participants in the program work four days a week and spend one day taking courses at the university.

A researcher in a medical genetics lab, Lever urges Tang to ask questions, although fielding those questions can prolong her own work day. Lever says mentoring is circular. Even as she supervises Tang, she herself is informally mentored by other researchers in the lab.

Paul Luke/*The Province*.

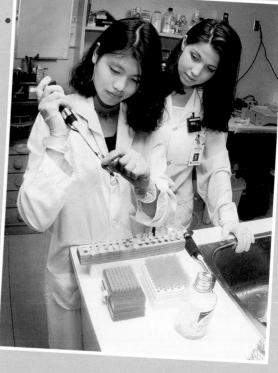

Esther Tang with her mentor, Melody Lever, at Vancouver's Terry Fox Labs.

1. Why would a recession affect a corporate mentoring program?

2. Why does Melody Lever believe in mentoring programs?

Activity 7

Describing Yourself

Write a description of yourself to give to a potential mentor. Include what your interests are, what your likes, dislikes, goals, and dreams are, and anything else that would help a mentor get to know you better.

Organizations That Provide Mentors

There are many organizations that provide mentors for young people. In the following pages, you can read about these groups and meet some mentors.

The YMCA's Black Achievers

The YMCA's Black Achievers program links young people with positive role models in the community, according to Annie Bynoe, who co-ordinates the project in Peel Region, Ontario. More than 400 students between the ages of 14 and 21 participate at the six sites operated by the YMCA in the Greater Toronto Area. The program has run in the area for years. "The program exposes youth to a wide range of educational and career opportunities while raising their academic standards," she said.

"The objective is to inspire youth to realize their career goals by linking them with black mentors who are successful in their professions." Bynoe said participants meet twice a month and focus on life skills, career development, and cultural identity.

Deann Lunan, left, and
Leonard Smith, right,
with their mentor
Juliet Jackson

Deann Lunan, 19, an OAC student at West Hill Collegiate Institute, said she was helped greatly during the three years she's been involved. "I've done a lot of networking with professionals," said Lunan, who is enrolling in a pharmaceutical technology course at Seneca College in Toronto. "It has benefited me a lot. There are a lot of professionals who serve as mentors who I can ask about career decisions."

"It's a really great program," said Juliet Jackson of Brampton, Ontario, a social worker who has volunteered with the project.

Mentors have discussions with between 50 and 60 students during the school year and work to instil feelings of self-respect and the need to achieve.

Leonard Smith, 17, a Grade 12 student at Bramalea Secondary School in Brampton, said he was motivated by the program. "It gives me self-confidence, self-esteem, and makes me work harder to reach my career and goals in life."

Big Sisters

The Big Sisters Associations across Canada assist girls and young women in the development of self-esteem through a voluntary, caring relationship with an adult female volunteer. Little Sisters are referred from a variety of sources: physicians, teachers, public health nurses, social service agencies, parents, and even friends who are Little Sisters themselves. Little Sisters come from a variety of cultural and economic backgrounds. They could live in a

"It's lots of fun having a Big Sister," says Little Sister Jenna. "Nancy helps me with my homework sometimes. I want to be a doctor and I know I have to do well in school to become a doctor. I went to Nancy's company Christmas party and got to see where Nancy works. With my Big Sister I get to do things I wouldn't normally do at home."

single-parent, mother-led family, in a single-parent, father-led family, or in a family in which both parents are present.

Volunteers undergo an extensive application and screening process before being matched with a Little Sister. Matches are based upon mutual interests and personality traits, among other factors. The Big Sister's major role is being a special friend to a girl who will benefit from the attentions she will receive. Part of the Big Sister's role is to participate in activities with her Little Sister, to share time together, and to develop their friendship. Some Big Sister agencies offer special programs and workshops on issues that are important to girls and young women.

What Is a Network?

Involvement in your community and participation as a member of a family and a group of friends leads to a **network** of people who know a variety of things about you. They might know you well enough to describe your personal strengths, or perhaps they know your abilities in the swimming pool. The network of people you know includes four types of connections: personal, professional, organizational, and those that occur by chance.

Successful Networks

CONNECTION	DESCRIPTION	EXAMPLES
Personal Connections	People who know you well enough to be able to describe your personal strengths	Immediate family, other relatives, family friends, friends
Professional Connections	People who know you through work or school and can describe your employability skills	Teachers, co-workers, supervisors, coaches, mentors
Organizational Connections	People who know you through non-job or school-related organizations such as faith communities and/or community clubs	Computer club, hiking club, community choir, faith community
Chance Connections	People you encounter by chance. They may find out your interests from talking to you and be able to give you a job lead, or introduce you to someone who can help.	Store clerk, waiter, person sitting next to you in the dentist's office, a service person at your home

Activity  8

Webbing Your Networks

Using the Successful Networks chart as a guide, create a web like the following and complete it with the names of specific people you know who qualify for your personal and professional network.

Your Network Possibilities

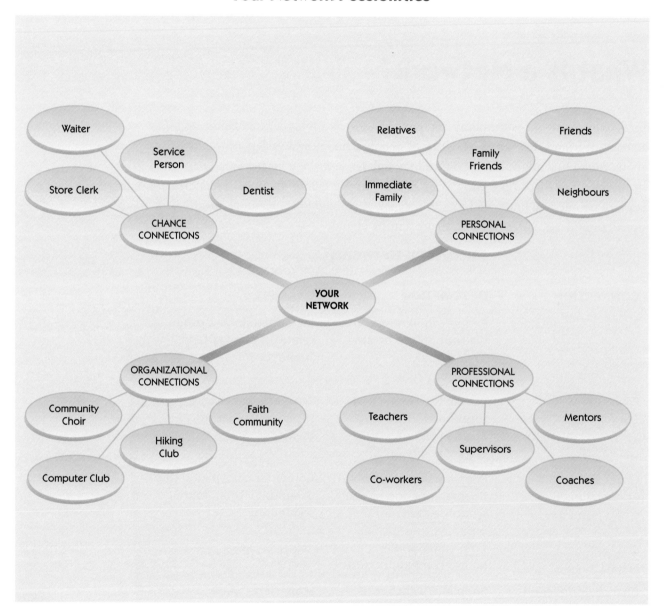

 You may wish to file your web in your portfolio.

Activity 9

Are You Building a Network?

Think about the people that you have identified as being in your network. Do you know their likes and dislikes? Are you aware of their concerns and needs? Successful networkers share in the lives of others by giving and receiving information, advice, and support. Check on your networking skills by answering the following questions on a sheet of paper. Beside each question number, put a Y for Yes, an S for Sometimes, and an N for No to indicate the answer that best applies to you.

1. I check with my friends regularly to see how they are doing.

2. I enjoy the challenge of helping people with problems.

3. I congratulate people on special occasions.

4. I ask others for advice when I need it.

5. I know how to listen to others when we are interacting.

6. I connect with people from my network when I see or hear something that would interest or affect them.

7. I try to meet new people who could become a part of my network.

8. I thank people who help me.

9. I celebrate the accomplishments and successes of others.

10. I share my ideas, interests, and plans with others.

What's your score?

Count the number of times you answered Yes to see how you scored.

Seven or more: You are a terrific networker.

Four to six: You are a good networker.

Under six: Start working on your networking skills!

Looking Back

1. When you think back on the characteristics of the role models and mentors you have read about, met, and/or discussed in this chapter, what are some of the personal characteristics they have that you would like to have?

2. Who are the important people in your network now? Who will become important members of your network in a few years?

EXPLORATIONS

Reflections

Imagine yourself as a role model for the next generation of students at your school. Describe the characteristics about yourself that will make you valued as a role model. What job will you be involved in? What will your work environment be like? With whom will you be interacting? What advice will you offer?

Goals

The role models and mentors profiled in this chapter had, and continue to have, a focus for their future. List three goals that you have for your future that are similar.

Action!

You are a successful vice-president who has worked up from the bottom of a construction company, where you started as a labourer. With three other students in your class, role-play a scene in which you tell your family (partner and children) that you want to give up your office job and return to physical labour.

Featuring. . .

Editorial: Write an editorial about the importance of positive television role models for young people.

Advertisement: Ask classmates for a picture or description of one of his or her role models, mentors, or network members. Create a poster with the headline "Thanks for the Inspiration."

Advice Column: Write a letter of advice to a young girl who is planning to quit school as soon as she turns 16. Write it as if you are her teacher, her younger brother, or her Big Sister.

Research: Go to the biography and autobiography sections of a library. Skim through several books to see who others identify as the person(s) who affected them most.

Personal Story/Interview: Write a personal story about a peer whom you consider to be a good role model in his or her day-to-day life now.

Experiencing the Community

Every community, large or small, is filled with opportunities for you. It is important to find out as much as possible about your community and how it works. Recognizing how you fit into the community is the first step to being a contributing member of it. This part of the book has you meet people from your community and discover more about yourself by interacting with them. After you find out more about your community, who works there, and how you can help to make it an even better place, you will be ready to live in it as a contributing member.

Resources in Your Community

What You Will Learn

- To gather information about your community.
- To discover the strength of community co-operation.
- To reflect on the aspects that make your community unique.
- To identify volunteer opportunities that interest you and will develop your skills for a future career.
- To recognize the ways in which you are a part of your community.

Terms to Remember

community	services
residents	retail
economy	community services
products	

The dictionary defines a **community** as "a body of people living in the same place under the same laws." But is it not much more than that? People create the community, and it is what happens in it that makes it important to them. A community might have ten, a hundred, ten thousand, or a million people or **residents**. It might have a thousand buildings set very close together or fifty buildings set apart. It might have a few businesses or many. It might be built on a lake or it might have a river running through it. The streets might be straight and flat or twisted and hilly. Whatever the characteristics, it is still a community, and what happens in it depends on the people.

Businesses in Your Community

A community's **economy**—the management of material resources—is very important to its well-being. Consider the businesses that are necessary for people's day-to-day lives. What types of **products** are made locally? Visualize the stores on the main streets and throughout the area. What kinds of products are for sale? Think also about the **services** that must be provided to enable community homes and businesses to operate and the people to live comfortably. All of these factors contribute to the well-being of a community.

The Retail Community

The **retail** community consists of stores that sell products such as groceries, hardware, clothing, and electronic equipment directly to the consumer. Most communities have retail stores that provide not only products, but also jobs.

Activity 1

What Stores Are in Your Community?

1. Make a list of products that your family generally needs to purchase in the stores where you live.

2. Create a chart, using the headings from the sample that follows, to show what stores are available in the area where you usually shop.

3. Indicate which of these stores also sell on the World Wide Web.

Stores in My Community

Name of Store	Type of Store	Estimated Number of Employees	Distance from My Home	Frequency of Use by My Family
SNAPS	Convenience	8	.25 km	daily
Bob's	Bakery	3	.25 km	daily
Loblaws	Supermarket	65	1 km	weekly
Your Hardware	Hardware	16	1 km	weekly
Planit	Building Centre	11	3 km	monthly
Greens'	Fruit/Vegtable	6	.25 km	weekly

When you have completed the chart for all the stores in your community, compare your results as a class.

- Which stores do all families use?
- Which ones do most families use?
- Which ones do only some families use?
- Are there products that are not available in your community? If so, how far must you go to get them?
- Do most families walk to the stores or get there by transportation?
- Which stores have the most employees? The least employees?
- Which stores are used the most frequently?

CASE STUDY

Building Stronger Communities—a Success Story

A Community in Trouble

Port au Port, Newfoundland, sprawls across 96 kilometres of rugged coastline and includes 25 small towns with a population of about 8000. At one time, it was a thriving community with a successful local fishing industry and a limestone mine. There were a lot of jobs, including those generated by a nearby U.S. military base.

Then the bad times began. The military base closed, limestone no longer had a market, and the fishing industry hit rock bottom when an important fish-processing plant closed in 1987.

The changes hit Port au Port hard. The adults lived on seasonal work and unemployment benefits. The drop-out rate at the high schools was between 60 and 70 percent.

A vicious cycle had begun. Young people routinely left school at 16 years old. Many girls became single mothers living on social assistance. Their children weren't doing well in school—possibly predicting future school failure and more drop-outs.

And people with potential were leaving. "I questioned the future of our rural community," says Mark Felix, of the Port au Port Economic Development Association. "I wondered where the leadership was going to come from in 30 years' time when most of our population [was] high school drop-outs and dependent on social programs."

Education Is Key

The residents of Port au Port decided they had to do something. And what they chose was to look at their community's education as a whole.

The community's call to action included people not normally involved in education. Members of social agencies and businesses joined school boards and residents to promote social change. "It was a new idea at the time," Felix points out, "but this agency co-operation turned out to be our greatest strength."

Calling themselves the Community Education Initiative, the group put several programs into place:
- Pre-kindergarten day care to provide children with an enriched environment and parents with support programs.
- A variety of reading programs in the schools.
- Family Resource Centres within the schools, offering drop-in play programs, after-school programs, and family recreational events.
- The Pathfinder Learning Centre, providing other ways of learning for people who have dropped out of school and then returned to finish their education.

Port au Port also applied its teamwork approach outside the school system. Discussions with federal and provincial social agencies started other changes.

Developing an Economic Base

"We also want to develop an economic base in the community," says Beverley Kirby, the Co-ordinator of the Community Education Initiative. "And we want to nurture an educated population that can make the most of local opportunities." Port au Port is working to build on several areas of economic activity: tourism, aquaculture, and sheep farming.

The schools have developed careers in entrepreneurship, aquaculture, tourism, and agrifoods. "We're providing a lot of career awareness information," Kirby adds, "and not just to kids. We want to train parents to help their children make good career choices."

The Community Education Initiative has a number of successes under its belt. Teachers are reporting higher reading levels, the drop-out rate is decreasing, and more parents are actively involved with their children's education.

A student hard at work at the Pathfinder Learning Centre in Port au Port West, Newfoundland.

"Now we're working on helping high school students make the change to college or university," Kirby says. And the community has also started a series of televised town-hall meetings to discuss the future of Port au Port.

Interested in Helping Your Community?

What advice would Felix and Kirby give other struggling communities? "The main ingredient is people," Felix says. "You have to develop human resources, not infrastructure (the basic parts of a structure or system). You can always build infrastructure later. Kirby adds, "Focus on everyone working together to get things done."

Port au Port still faces an uphill battle, but its residents have taken action that will help keep young people in the community and create hope for the future.

Adapted from Canada Career Information Partnership, *Canada Prospects*, 1995/1996.

1. The changes in Port au Port must have been a challenge for some people to accept. Write a few paragraphs from the point of view of a teenager, a woman, or an older man living in Port au Port. Include your reflections on how you felt about Port au Port before the changes, after the first meeting about the changes, and, finally, after the changes had begun and the town started to recover.

Service Businesses

Many business opportunities in your community will be in the area of service. Who repairs a flat tire? Who do you call if a pipe bursts? Who provides fuel for heating systems? Who cuts people's hair? Where do people go for entertainment or a meal? Who repairs computers? Who sets up web pages? These businesses are not always easy to see, but they are essential to the community. Service is the fastest growing sector for employment.

What Services Are Available in Your Community?

Refer to the Yellow Pages in your telephone book and the advertisements in your community newspaper to get you started on this activity. Create a chart similar to the sample below.

Services in My Community

Name of Business	Service Offered	Estimated Number of Employees	Distance from My Home	Frequency of Use by My Family
Carpet Delight	Carpet Cleaning	3	2 km	1/year
Hair After	Hair Care	6	.5 km	1/month
Plumber Brothers	Plumbing	3	.5 km	as required
Keen Klean	Cleaners	3	.5 km	1/week

As a class, combine your findings and compare your results.
- What surprised you about the services available in the community?
- Which services are lacking?
- Which services are most numerous?
- Which services are used most?
- Which services employ the most people? The least?
- Which businesses interested you? Why?

Representing Your Community

Create a web site or a brochure that highlights all aspects of your community.

Community Services

Community services are organizations that add to the quality of people's lives by providing services that promote health and well-being. They provide recreation and leisure activities as well as physical and mental health support-systems. Many of the services assist individuals and families; others interact with schools. The employees of community service organizations are people who like working with other people rather than with things. Many of them are volunteers from the community.

Activity 4

Identifying Volunteer Jobs

With your classmates, brainstorm a list of your community service organizations. Then refer to your local newspaper or telephone directory to see if there are any services to add to the list. Find out if the services use volunteers. Which volunteer activities appeal to you? What kind of skills would you develop if you volunteered in each? Which community service would help you develop skills for a future career? Record your findings on a chart like the following.

VOLUNTEER ACTIVITY	SKILLS PRACTISED
Serving in a Breakfast Program.	
Helping drivers deliver Meals on Wheels.	
Shelving books at a library.	
Copying, collating, and stapling.	
Answering the phone.	
Shovelling snow or mowing the lawn.	
Sorting and packing food at a food bank.	
Playing with preschoolers.	
Reading to seniors.	
Visiting seniors.	

Contact the services in your community to discuss the possibility of volunteering there as a component of your community involvement graduation requirement. Add the chart to your portfolio. Include volunteering as one of your short-term goals.

IN THE NEWS

A Little Time Goes a Long Way

by Janice Turner

It's a glorious summer's day and Lisa Mak, 18, a high school graduate who's university bound, is serving a picnic lunch to a group of seniors. And she's smiling. Non-stop.

The night before, she'd spent three hours making assorted sandwiches and designing fruit trays. Before that, she'd picked up groceries for 17 guests—all members of Support Services for the Elderly.

"I've never shopped for so much food in my life!" says Lisa.

Mak and about 15 of her schoolmates raised the $100 for the food and drink by selling posters during the school year. They also received an $85 grant from the Bell United Way program—100 percent of what they asked for.

The program encourages youth aged 14 to 20 to come up with projects that will improve their communities. The funding comes from Bell Canada and is distributed through the United Way. The grant to Mak and her colleagues paid for door-to-door transportation to the park for all the guests.

"It's just marvellous," enthuses Olivia Berry, 74, relaxing after lunch in the bright, midday sun. "Without them, we wouldn't be out here today. We'd be sitting at home, and sitting at home does you no good. It's very nice that they've taken the time to be with us."

The group of teens has brought along a portable stereo for background music—a mix of pop and classical. Before and again after lunch some of the youngsters play bingo, chess, and checkers with their older friends. Others simply pair off and talk.

"When you help the community you feel good about yourself and the seniors don't feel so isolated," says Mak. "It helps them know what's going on through a teenager's perspective."

Eighty-something Ted Nielsen says the teens have demonstrated that they truly care. "They're beautiful, just terrific," he says. "With young people you have interesting things happening. It keeps you up to date."

Michael Follert, 16, notes that everyone will grow older, and no one should be forgotten. Besides, he thoroughly enjoys the company. "They've been young before and they understand what it's like. I do learn from them."

The students keep in touch with the seniors by phone, speaking to them once or twice

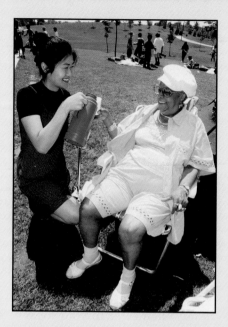

Lisa Mak and Olivia Berry enjoying themselves at a picnic sponsored by Support Services for the Elderly.

a week. The picnic is a chance for them to get together and celebrate.

Reprinted with permission—The Toronto Star Syndicate.

1. Discuss how each group (the volunteers and the Support Services for the Elderly participants) benefits from activities like this picnic.

2. Make a list of other activities that you think these picnic participants would enjoy.

3. These young people received a grant for this project to "improve their community." Discuss what kind of similar project you would like to do in your community.

Activity 5

Visiting the Community

As a class, identify two or three businesses or services in your community that interest you the most. Arrange to visit these sites and speak to a resource person, or have the resource people visit your classroom if you live in a rural area and cannot arrange transportation to the site. Before the meeting, prepare some questions and choose the students to ask them. Here are some categories and sample questions to get you started. Brainstorm to lengthen and strengthen the list.

Purpose of the workplace
- What product/service do you provide?
- Who buys/uses your product/service?
- How do you attract customers?

Scope of the workplace
- How many employees do you have?
- How many people use your product/service?
- How long has the business been in operation?

Employment profile
- What types of jobs are performed?
- What responsibilities do employees have?

Skills needed
- How did the employees learn to do their jobs?
- What skills will be needed in future employees?

Future trends
- How has this workplace changed?
- How will it change?
- How might increased technology affect your workplace?

Ideas for visits:
- Note the location of the site and its convenience for employees.
- Note the atmosphere of the place and the feelings you had there.
- Note the equipment and furnishings. Note the employees' behaviour, their clothing, their interaction.

After you have prepared a question sheet, use the following checklist to plan your visit.

Visiting the Community Checklist

❑ Pick a site to visit.

❑ Make an appointment to visit the site.

❑ Arrange transportation.

❑ Meet the resource person.

❑ Explore the site. (Look. Listen. Ask questions. Get involved.)

❑ Make notes about the visit with the help of your question sheet.

❑ Summarize your question sheet and write a report.

❑ Send a thank-you note.

❑ Discuss your reports with your class.

People Are the Key

While you have been studying your community, you have probably realized the strength of the people. Many of them might be people you know. Some might even be your relatives. As a class, start a list of the people who help to make your community a good place to live. Begin by listing the people who support your school, other than your teachers. Add to the list as you continue your study of communities.

Inviting Guest Speakers

Look through some copies of your local newspaper and clip articles about people in the community who interest you. Identify those you would like to have visit your class. You might need to contact the community's Chamber of Commerce, government offices, or the newspaper itself, or check the Yellow Pages, to find out how to get in touch with them. When you invite a speaker to the classroom, offer some guidelines about what is of interest to the class.

After each visit, fill out a report like the sample that follows, especially if the speaker's career, business, or volunteer activity is one that interests you for the future. File it in your portfolio.

Guest Speaker Report

Speaker's name: **William Keith**

Job: **President and CEO of Printers Inc.**

Overview of business/service: **Supplies all business printing needs to both large and small businesses.**

Previous jobs: **Always in the printing business. Outlined jobs held over 26 years — sweeper to CEO.**

Education/Training required: **High school graduation and on-the-job training with 10-week college courses for specialty areas.**

Skills needed: **quick-thinking, clear reasoning, mathematics**

Future of speaker's workplace/service: **Good. Workplace is always changing, getting more computerized. He plans to keep up with the changes.**

Speaker's advice: **Stay in school, keep up with all subjects, get involved in your community, work hard, play hard.**

How can I find out more about this job? **Visit him, guidance counsellor, library, the Internet, college guide.**

My observations: **He likes his job. He speaks favourably about his employees. He's up-to-date.**

Is the speaker a possible contact for the future? **I'm not really interested in this field.**

PROFILE

· ·

Helping the Homeless

by Scott Steele

From 1989 to 1994 Ken Lyotier, the self-described 49-year-old alcoholic and "full-time dumpster-diver," combed the alleyways and garbage bins of downtown Vancouver—which has no blue-box recycling program in high-density buildings—for bottles and cans he could return to local retailers. The problem was, there were limits on how many each would accept. Lyotier and other street people in the city's downtown Eastside—the neighbourhood with the lowest per capita income in Canada—decided to begin a grassroots recycling initiative. Predicting that they could gather five million bottles and cans a year at a central location, pay cash to the collectors, and then return the containers to manufacturers for a deposit and a small handling fee, they approached VanCity Community Foundation. The foundation agreed to give them an interest-free loan of $12 500—and extended a further $12 500 line of credit, personally guaranteed by an anonymous VanCity member. In 1995, United We Can opened in a storefront on Vancouver's East Cordova Street.

According to the soft-spoken Lyotier, now general manager of the facility, which employs four full-time sorters and four part-timers, up to 400 people a day bring in bottles and cans for cash. Hauling their spoils in shopping carts and green garbage bags, many are homeless, have problems with substance abuse, or suffer from mental illness.

In just 18 months, United We Can has not only met its commitments to VanCity, but has also paid out $600 000 in cash to the collectors—and has provided a much-needed environmental service.

Maclean's, July 1, 1996. Reprinted with permission.

Frank Lyotier turned bottle and can collecting into a recyling business for the homeless.

1. Create a poster that Ken Lyotier can post around Eastside that tells people how they can get involved in the United We Can project as a collector or as a supplier of bottles and cans.

2. What two questions would you like to ask Ken Lyotier about his involvement in United We Can?

3. What two questions would you like to ask one of the people who bring in bottles and cans each day?

4. "People are the key" is a phrase used earlier in this chapter. Frank Lyotier and his supporters are the key to the success of an initiative that helps hundreds of people while improving the environment. Create a plaque to be presented by the City of Vancouver to United We Can.

Activity 7

Creating an Information Kit

Imagine that a furniture refinisher is thinking of moving a small business into the community where you live. He is married and has two children. For his workshop, he will need a location that is close to transportation. He plans to hire four employees.

Work with a small group to plan an information kit for this family. What facts will they need to know about your community before they can make up their minds? What aspects of the community will they find suitable and appealing?

How Will You Fit into the Community?

Now that you are familiar with the characteristics of a community and all the people and services that work together to make communities successful, visualize the part that you will play in a community in the future. What will be your responsibilities as a community member?

With your classmates, paint a mural depicting how you see your roles in a future community.

Or

Create a mock radio or television program, in which you interview classmates about how they see their roles in a future community.

JOURNAL

Reflecting on Choices

Reflect on the mural or interview that you and your classmates created. What surprised you about your classmates' choices? What were the reasons behind your contribution to the mural or interview? Record your observations in your journal.

Looking Back

1. In your opinion, what are the important parts of a community?

2. Define the word *economy* and describe why it is important to a community's well-being.

3. Name three service businesses that have characteristics in common.

4. Describe three different types of community services in your area.

EXPLORATIONS

Reflections

Write a reflection on how the various components of your community have shaped who you are.

Goals

Look back at the educational goals that you have set for yourself. How do they fit with some of the jobs in your community that you found out about in this chapter? Which of these jobs now interest you? Try to find out more about them. Add any information you obtain to your portfolio.

Action!

Prepare a sales presentation for your local city or town council on why your community needs its own web site. Outline the strategies that you will use to attract people to the web site. Explain how the web site will attract people to use the retail, service sector, and community services.

EXPLORATIONS

Featuring. . .

Editorial: Write a letter to the editor either to complain about the lack of community services in your area or to praise the work of one of the community services in your area.

Advice Column: Write a response to the following letter.

> Dear Andy,
> I hope that you can help me. We are getting ready to move to a new town. I am looking forward to it, but feel very nervous about going to a new school where I do not know anyone. Please give me some advice on how to adjust to my new situation.
>
> Thanks in advance,
> Roy, 17 years old

Personal Story/Interview: Interview a person who volunteers in your community. Write a story that outlines the person's previous relevant experience, describes the type of volunteer work done, and expresses the volunteer's reasons for involvement. Add a photo if possible.

Research: Speak to a real estate salesperson in your community about local sales statistics on a yearly basis. Compare yearly sales for a five-year period. What trends can you see? Ask the school secretary for statistics of how many students move away and how many move in by year. What comparisons can you make?

Advertisement: Create a radio script for an advertisement that will attract new families to your community. Include local attractions, businesses, and services that will be of interest to newcomers.

Connecting in Your Community

What You Will Learn

- What job shadowing is and the procedures involved in it.
- What volunteer activities are available in your community and what skills you have as a potential volunteer.
- How to fulfill your community involvement graduation requirement.

Terms to Remember

job shadowing
volunteer training programs
volunteer co-ordinators

There are many ways to make connections in your community. In the last chapter, you found out more about what makes your community function. You might have discovered information that was new to you, especially in the area of the actual jobs that people do. Now you can choose to make a stronger connection and learn even more by spending time volunteering, job shadowing, and working in your community.

Job Shadowing

Does participating in a **job shadowing** experience for a day interest you? Job shadowing means spending a day at work with a person in a particular career, at a particular job that interests you. During the day, you will observe what the job involves, talk to other employees, and, with permission, take pictures at the site. Your school might already do this as a part of Career Week or to encourage students to participate in a co-operative education program. Job shadowing—in places like hospitals, trucking depots, design studios, auto repair shops, banks, news rooms, or offices—is exciting, and an excellent learning opportunity.

You might have had this type of experience in Grade 9 through the Take Our Kids to Work day which is held in November.

Activity 1

Preparing Questions

When you are job shadowing, you could ask some of the same questions you asked your community visitors. (See Activity 5, Chapter 8, page 159.) Or, you could design a Know-Want-Learn (KWL) Chart as your guide.

The Know-Want-Learn Chart   Topic _____

What do I already **Know** about __'s job?	What do I **Want** to know about __'s job?	What did I **Learn** about __'s job?
_____	_____	_____
_____	_____	_____
_____	_____	_____
_____	_____	_____
_____	_____	_____
_____	_____	_____
_____	_____	_____

You could also make up your own questions. Keep in mind that people respond in different ways to different types of questions. There are four types for your purposes. Look at these samples to see which type gives the most information.

1. Yes/No questions
These can be answered simply and give little information. For example, "Do you like your work?"

2. Fact-finding questions
These are specific and give more information. For example, "What four things make your work challenging? What do you like most? What do you like least?"

3. Open-ended questions
These questions are more personal and can lead to more questions. For example, "What are the things you like about your job? How did you get started in this job? What do you need to know to be successful in your job?"

4. Follow-up questions
These questions are used to get more information or to clarify an answer. They keep the conversation going. For example, "That's interesting. Can you tell me more?"

TIPS FOR A GREAT INTERVIEW

✔ Prepare the questions you want to ask the person at work.

✔ Ask the most important question first, in case you run out of time.

✔ Listen carefully. Give the person your full attention.

✔ Ask "Why is that?" or "Please tell me more" when you want to know more.

✔ Tell about your own experience that relates to something he or she tells you.

✔ Jot down specific information.

✔ Write up your notes afterwards.

✔ Thank the person for his or her time.

Recording Your Job-Shadowing Day

A day planner could be used to record an hour-by-hour, task-by-task description of your job-shadowing day. It would also be an excellent keepsake of your experience and a handy reference when answering your classmates' questions about your day.

There are other ways to share your day: a talk show, a photo essay, a newspaper article, a report, or a video or audio tape.

File the material on your job-shadowing day in your portfolio.

Activity 2

Evaluating the Day

Here is a guide to use after your job-shadowing day to share your experiences, in groups, with your classmates.

1. Whom did you "shadow"?

2. What is his or her job?

3. What other jobs did you find out about?

4. What did you like about the day?

5. What did you dislike?

6. In your opinion, how could the day have been improved?

7. What did you learn?

8. What else would you like to say?

Community Involvement

Like job shadowing, community involvement offers you another unique experience. It is not about learning from books. It is learning by being around different people, doing things that you would not normally do, and seeing things from a different point of view. By volunteering, you will have a chance to exercise your independence, assume more responsibility, negotiate with adults on a more equal footing, and gain employability skills. You will have the opportunity to develop your own identity, based on what you can do and what special gifts you have. Volunteering also helps solve the problem of "I need a job to get experience. I need experience to get a job." As a student attending school in Ontario, you are required to complete 40 hours of volunteer community involvement as part of the graduation requirements for a secondary school diploma. The purpose of this requirement is to encourage you to develop awareness and understanding of civic responsibility and the various roles that you can play in strengthening your community. At the same time, you will be meeting possible mentors and role models as well as exploring career areas. These hours may be spent in your community at any time during your secondary school program outside of school hours, for example during lunch break, in the evening, on weekends, during school holidays and summer vacation. It is your choice. It is also your responsibility to decide on the activity and obtain approval on the choice from the principal before you undertake it.

Finding a Place to Volunteer

When you consider volunteering, four questions need to be asked:
• What skills can I offer?
• What skills do I want to gain?
• What group do I want to work with?
• What time do I have available?

Look around your neighbourhood and think of a place where you would like to get involved. Reflect on your strengths and how you can share them with others. Here are some ideas.

Helping your neighbours by
• providing a regular service to a person who cannot get out by shopping, running errands, or visiting with him or her.
• sharing your interest in science with a neighbour's child or taking the child to the library on a regular basis.
• helping to organize local community events such as the annual Terry Fox run, the Santa Claus parade, or a food drive.

Helping your community by
• assisting with the coaching, score keeping, or field maintenance for a local sports league.
• serving breakfast at your local breakfast club.
• becoming a peer buddy to a student with special needs.
• becoming a peer mediator or mentor.
• working with others to organize a welcome event for Grade 9 students.
• helping at school events such as parents' night, graduation, music night, or athletic events.

Many organizations have **volunteer training programs** and **volunteer co-ordinators**. Most have a contact person for you to call to set up an appointment. You can find out how to get in touch with these people in your local Yellow Pages or, in some cases, on the Internet.

Some national organizations you might wish to contact for a list of their local branches are:
Volunteer Canada
Canadian Centre for Philanthropy (charity)
United Way of Canada-*Centraide Canada*
YMCA Canada
Canadian Environmental Network
Canadian Parks and Recreation Association
Canadian Association for Community Care
Community Foundations of Canada
Canadian Conference for the Arts

IN THE NEWS

When a Frog's Sound Is Music

By Paul Irish

Call it the frog squad. About 30 volunteers will soon be trampling through the marshy Frenchman's Bay watershed in Pickering, Ontario, hoping to hear the trill of an American toad or the chirp of the spring peeper frog . . . if they're still there. The amphibian population is quickly disappearing from the world—including our own backyards—and this group will spend the next few months near the shores of Lake Ontario attempting to get a fix on what's hopping out there.

Frog and toad monitoring started in the early 1990s, and it didn't take long for results to show the Frenchman's Bay watershed was in trouble. "We know that a number of frog species have disappeared from the wetlands, and those that are left are few in numbers," says Patricia Lowe of the Frenchman's Bay watershed rehabilitation project. "The leopard frogs aren't calling like they used to and there isn't a bullfrog south of the Oak Ridges Moraine."

Lowe blames it on urbanization and the fact that about 60 storm sewer drains—full of pesticides, fertilizers, and salt—empty into the areas' wetlands and creeks. She explains that monitoring frogs is an excellent way to put your finger on the pulse of a wetland. Amphibians depend on clean water and forests throughout their life cycles (they actually breathe through their skin) and are very sensitive to environmental adversities. This sensitivity, along with their ability to make their presence known by singing during the spring breeding season, makes them an excellent indicator of ecosystem health. Simply put, if the environment is toxic, the frogs die out and their songs go with them.

The frog monitors have just finished a crash course in identifying the various croaks and calls with the help of audio tapes, and will soon be taking to the marsh. "It really can be fun," says Lowe, who helped train the spotters. "Sometimes an entire family will come out. It's a learning experience." She says the volunteers, who usually don't see their subjects, will chart the location of the calls as well as their frequency.

Lowe says attempts already undertaken to restore the wetland—with hopes of bringing back the frogs and toads—include the planting of native trees and bushes as well as the installation of bird, toad, and bat houses. An ultimate answer would be the construction of more storm management ponds —artificial ponds that allow the affected water to sit for a period to clean and stabilize before returning it to the wetland, she

Patricia Lowe, of the Frenchman's Bay watershed rehabilitation project, holds a green frog. She's helping volunteers gauge the frog population.

adds. "It may have taken 40 years for the frogs to disappear, so, unfortunately, it may take another 40 years for them to return, if ever."

1. **Give two reasons why working as a volunteer at the Frenchman's Bay watershed project would be a challenging experience.**

2. **What skills that could be transferred to another situation would a person gain by working on the project?**

3. **What strategies do you think the people who support the project should employ to heighten the awareness of the plight of the amphibians in the Frenchman's Bay watershed?**

A c t i v i t y ③ · · · · · · · · ·

Creating a Bulletin Board Display

In a group or individually, create a bulletin board display, under the heading "How Can You Help?" Create a picture for each example of ways to help in the community. Explain each image on the board in an oral presentation to the class. You might wish to invite other classes to the presentation to encourage them to get involved in the activities.

Strengthening the School Community

One place to start getting involved as a volunteer in your community is within your school. You have probably been part of a fund-raising project or a school team. You might also have been a library assistant, a student tutor, a receptionist, or a peer mediator. By participating, you widen your own learning and improve the community in which you spend so much time.

A c t i v i t y ④ · · · · · · · · ·

Creating Volunteer Positions

Work with your teachers and classmates to widen the scope of volunteer positions within your school. Here are some possibilities:
• Preparing the gym for an after-school tournament.
• Being part of the stage crew.
• Delivering information to classrooms.
• Answering the telephone while staff has a break or lunch.
• Going on excursions with younger students from a neighbourhood school.
• Hosting school visitors.
• Establishing new councils for such interests as a music or computer club.
• Writing for the school newspaper.
• Becoming a peer mediator or tutor.
• Serving on the Student Council.
• Becoming a game official, scorekeeper, or timer for school sports.

CASE STUDY

Student Seeks Fresh Ideas to Fix Up St. James Town

By Kristin Rushowy

St. James Town seems particularly bleak at this time of year. Snow blankets the few community gardens and green spaces the residents of this dense downtown Toronto neighbourhood have to enjoy. Piles of snow and slush line the already narrow roadways between the 18 drab highrise buildings crammed into 11 hectares. Even on a warm winter day, not many residents wander about, save for a group of 30 who came together at the behest of a 24-year-old University of Toronto student who's trying to get members of the community thinking about how they can better this concrete jungle.

"Instead of spending my energy on designing a space, I wanted to deal with a space people know, get them together, and go out into the community and improve it," said Yvonne Sze-Man Yuen, who has taken on this project for her thesis in her final year of landscape architecture. "Collective effort can make a difference," she added. "When you get people together, that's where the magic comes in."

Yesterday, the group—comprising St. James Town residents both young and old, U of T landscape architecture students, local landscape architects, and urban planners—did an hour-long "walkabout," critically examining the neighbourhood and writing down suggestions.

"There's nothing for children to do in the winter," said area resident Naheeda Khan, a mother of three. She would like to see more parks —with benches, which would encourage families to go there and socialize—as well as speed bumps in the area to force drivers to slow down. Better lighting at night would also help people feel safer, she added. Taher Chaudry, who works at a local

day-care centre with Khan, said they often take their charges out for walks in strollers, and cars whiz by too close. "It's a bit scary," she said. "The lane ways are too narrow."

Landscape architect Paul Young, who volunteered his time to put residents' ideas on paper, said there's too much parking space. "Highrises, historically, were meant to free up open space so you could have parks," he said. "Here, they've taken the idea of the highrise and forgotten about the park."

After the walkabout, everyone gathered at Rose Avenue Junior Public School to brainstorm. It was the second such meeting. Yuen plans to put all the ideas in a booklet, have it translated into several languages, then get residents to vote for their favourites. The best will be forwarded to the city.

Yuen's thesis is the one thousandth "Our Millenium" project, a national program encouraging Canadians to give to their communities to celebrate 2000. Councillor Pam McConnell said all ideas will help in the city's overall plan for St. James Town, which includes a community centre and more gardens, which have been a big hit. St. James Town is the most densely populated neighbourhood in Canada, with about 20 000 residents.

1. As part of their training, architecture students usually design new buildings or spaces to meet specific criteria. In what ways does Yvonne Sze-Man Yuen's project differ?

2. How does Yuen ensure that she gets maximum input into her project?

3. How do you know that her findings will reach the maximum number of people?

4. Look around your neighbourhood and make a list of possible projects that you and other interested students could become involved in to improve it.

Activity ⑤

Recognizing In-School Volunteer Activities

In-school volunteer activities could be recognized in a number of ways. You might wish to form a committee of students, teachers, and parents who want to enhance the in-school volunteer opportunities. Work together to do some, or all, of the following:

• Create a directory of volunteer opportunities at your school.

• Develop records or a database on which volunteers' activities and hours are kept.

• Develop a certificate to award students who contribute over 50 hours per year.

• Hold sharing sessions for volunteers to discuss what works and what does not.

• At the end of the year, hold a training session for younger students who will be moving into your grade or school.

Creating Your Own Volunteer Experience

Perhaps you do not want to make a long-term, weekly volunteer commitment but you still want to gain experience as a volunteer. Here is an idea that could work for you. Watch the local newspapers for announcements of upcoming events. When you see one that interests you, telephone the organizers of the event and volunteer your services. Make a list of what you can and are willing to do, and let them know. Be sure to discuss your plans with your parents or guardians. Depending on your talents, skills, and available time, the volunteer activities might include those listed at right.

If you do not feel comfortable calling someone you do not know, create a similar list of how you can help and pass it out to family friends. Perhaps they will be involved in an event at which your services could be used.

> **Possible Volunteer Activities**
>
> Before the Event
> • Delivering handbills
> • Making posters
> • Phoning
>
> On the Day of the Event
> • Unloading supplies
> • Setting up tables or displays
> • Giving information
> • Being a guide
>
> After the Event
> • Packing up
> • Dismantling tables or displays
> • Cleaning up

PORTFOLIO

Creating a Thank-You Card

Create a thank-you card for the organizers of the event you helped with. Let them know what you learned by helping. If you really enjoyed it and want to repeat the experience, ask to be a part of the planning for the next event. Ask if a thank-you letter from them could be given to you for your portfolio.

Keep these letters in your portfolio, along with a list of tasks you performed and your reflections on the day. They might help you in the future.

PROFILE

Tree Saviour

By Vesta Giles

Emily Ferguson saved
100-year-old maple trees.

When 12-year-old Emily Ferguson heard that the Royal Inland Hospital in Kamloops, British Columbia, planned to cut down heritage maple trees in order to put in a covered parking lot, she proved that you can never be too young to become a political activist.

Emily and her mother, Pam Ellsay, launched a campaign to save the trees. Braving the sprinkler system, they tied protest signs to the trucks of the endangered trees, got together a petition with 1600 signatures, made presentations to the city council and the Thompson Health Region Board, and held a "Save the Trees" picnic.

Thanks to Emily, protecting green space became a civic election issue. At a candidates' forum, in front of an audience of 700 and TV cameras, Emily demanded that candidates state whether they would support saving the trees. "She did a wonderful job of defining the green space concern," praises Mayor Mel Rothenburger.

In the end, Thompson Health Region officials came up with a compromise plan that spared the 100-year-old maples. Emily is satisfied— almost. Although the new plan calls for the parking lot to be smaller and in a different location, "They need to ensure that the roots and branches are protected during construction," she says.

1. To bring attention to an issue, a successful campaign has to appeal to a wide range of the population. What ways did Emily and her mother use to get their information out?

2. Make a list of at least five issues that have come to the public's attention through the work of political activists in your area.

3. Although Emily is only 12, what career paths might interest her after this experience?

JOURNAL

Reflecting on Your Experience

At the end of a day of volunteering, write about your experience in your journal. Use the following guideline so that you consider all aspects of the day.

Today I worked as a volunteer at . . .
The best part was . . .
One thing I learned was . . .
I think others appreciated the fact that I . . .
The next time I volunteer to help with an event, I will be sure to . . .

Another way of reflecting on your experience is to complete a Response Wheel. Beginning at 1, ask yourself these questions:

1. What did I see and hear?
2. How did I feel?
3. What did it make me think about?
4. What action could I take or what could I do as a result of this?

My Response to Volunteering

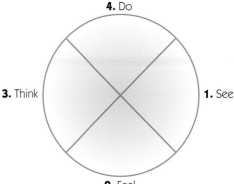

Looking Back

1. List four ways that you can broaden your experience in the world of work.

2. Name three volunteer experiences that interest you. Explain why.

3. Describe what you can do to become involved in your school.

EXPLORATIONS

Reflections

Comment on the following statement: "You never get a second chance to make a first impression." Why is this valuable to remember?

Goals

How have your experiences in the community strengthened, or changed, your goals for the future?

Action!

In groups of three, create skits with the following themes:

• Introducing a friend to a person whom you have met through volunteering.
• Telling your parent or guardian about your community involvement experience.
• Convincing your friend that he or she should join you at your after-school community involvement placement.
• Apologizing for forgetting to inform someone, who was consequently inconvenienced, that you would be absent.

Featuring. . .

Editorial: Write an editorial that outlines the importance of young people finding out more about the people who work in their community. Assume that some of your readers think that the best place for young people to learn is in the classroom.

Advice Column: Write a letter advising a new student who has recently moved into the area about the local opportunities for learning in the community.

Advertisement: Create an advertisement for student volunteer opportunities in your school. Ask school staff members for a description of the help they require and how to get involved.

Personal Story/Interview: Meet with the Advertising Team and interview the staff members who want volunteers about the type of program they run and why a volunteer would enjoy the experience. Try to represent a variety of programs.

Research: Call local agencies and create a Volunteers Wanted column in your magazine that lists opportunities for student volunteers outside of school hours.

P A R T

4

Working in the Community

Now that you know more about what is available in your community and how you can contribute to it by volunteer activities, you will have an opportunity to discover the skills required to be a working member of it. You will see how communication skills are essential when looking for a job or maintaining one you already have. You will learn how to present yourself on paper to create the best impression. Finally, you will explore ways to manage the money that you earn.

Employability Skills 2000+

What You Will Learn

- The skills needed to get, keep, and progress in the world of work.
- How attending school prepares you for the workplace.
- About human rights and the workplace.
- About safety factors in the workplace.

Terms to Remember

employability skills
fundamental skills
personal management skills
teamwork skills
problem solving
decision making
time management
accountability
conflict resolution
human rights
discrimination

workers' compensation
Workplace Safety and
    Health Insurance Board
certification

In this chapter you will learn the **employability skills** that are valued by employers for the years 2000+. School and the workplace have many things in common. The interiors and landscapes of both environments are planned so that people's activities can be carried out in an organized and productive manner. The subjects you learn at school are applied in real situations on the job. Social skills, such as initiating, co-operating, and communicating are an asset wherever you are.

The Conference Board of Canada's Corporate Council on Education developed the Employability Skills 2000+ chart to communicate the changing skills needed to be successful in today's workplace. The Employability Skills 2000+ chart is based on input from employers and is validated by a wide range of organizations and individuals concerned with education and career training in Canada. It a list of foundation skills, that young people need for paid or self-employment and to enhance their citizenship and self-fulfillment—in other words, to become fully participating members of society. Employability skills are transferable skills that are used in all careers, rather than work-specific skills required by certain occupations or levels of responsibility. There are several ways to develop your employability skills:

• Learn them as part of the subject-based curriculum.

• Participate in community involvement and volunteer activities.

• Participate in career preparation, work experience, and co-operative education courses.

• Learn by doing at your part-time or summer job.

The Emloyability Skills 2000+ chart is divided into three categories, but the skills are not organized in order of priority and should receive equal emphasis.

Employability Skills 2000+

The skills you need to get, keep, and progress in the world of work—whether you work on your own or as part of a team. These skills can also be applied and used beyond the workplace in a range of daily activities.

FUNDAMENTAL SKILLS

The skills needed as a basis for further development

You will be ready for growth when you can:

Communicate
- Read and understand information presented in a variety of forms (e.g., words, graphs, charts, diagrams)
- Write and speak so others pay attention and understand
- Listen and ask questions to understand and appreciate others' points of view
- Share information using a range of information and communications technologies (e.g., voice, e-mail, computers)
- Use relevant scientific, technological, and mathematical knowledge and skills to explain or clarify ideas

Manage Information
- Locate, gather, and organize information using appropriate technology and information systems
- Access, analyze, and apply knowledge and skills from various disciplines (e.g., the arts, languages, science, technology, mathematics, social sciences, and the humanities)

Use Numbers
- Decide what needs to be measured or calculated
- Observe and record data using appropriate methods, tools, and technology
- Make estimates and verify calculations

PERSONAL MANAGEMENT SKILLS

The personal skills, attitudes, and behaviours that drive one's potential for growth

You will be able to offer yourself greater possibilities for achievement when you can:

Demonstrate Positive Attitudes and Behaviours
- Feel good about yourself and be confident
- Deal with people, problems, and situations with honesty and integrity
- Recognize good effort
- Take care of your personal health
- Show interest, initiative, and effort
- Be socially responsible and contribute to your community

Be Responsible
- Set goals and priorities, balancing work and personal life
- Plan and manage time, money, and other resources to achieve goals
- Assess, weigh, and manage risk
- Be accountable for your actions and the actions of your group

Be Adaptable
- Be able to work independently or as part of a team
- Carry out multiple tasks or projects
- Be innovative and resourceful: identify and suggest alternative ways to achieve goals and get the job done

TEAMWORK SKILLS

The skills and attributes needed to contribute productively

You will be better prepared to add value to the outcomes of a task, project, or team when you can:

Work with Others
- Understand and work within the dynamics of a group
- Ensure that a team's purpose and objectives are clear
- Be flexible: respect, be open to and supportive of the thoughts, opinions, and contributions of others in the group
- Recognize and respect people's diversity, individual differences, and perspectives
- Accept and provide feedback in a constructive and considerate manner
- Contribute to a team by sharing information and expertise
- Lead or support when appropriate, motivating a group for high performance
- Understand the role of conflict in a group to reach solutions
- Manage and resolve conflict when appropriate

Participate in Projects and Tasks
- Plan, design, or carry out a project or task from start to finish with well-defined objectives and outcomes
- Develop a plan, seek feedback, test, revise, and implement

Think and Solve Problems
- Assess situations and identify problems
- Seek different points of view and evaluate them based on facts
- Recognize the human, interpersonal, technical, scientific, and mathematical dimensions of a problem
- Identify the root cause of a problem
- Be creative and innovative in exploring possible solutions
- Readily use science, technology, and mathematics as ways to think, gain, and share knowledge, solve problems, and make decisions
- Evaluate solutions to make recommendations or decisions
- Implement solutions
- Check to see if a solution works, and act on opportunities for improvement

- Be open and respond constructively to change
- Learn from your mistakes and accept feedback
- Cope with uncertainty

Learn Continuously
- Be willing to continuously learn and grow
- Assess personal strengths and areas for development
- Set your own learning goals
- Identify and access learning sources and opportunities
- Plan for and achieve your learning goals

Work Safely
- Be aware of personal and group health and safety practices and procedures, and act in accordance with these

- Work to agreed quality standards and specifications
- Select and use appropriate technology for a task or project
- Adapt to changing requirements and information
- Continuously monitor the success of a project or task and identify ways to improve

A c t i v i t y ①

Identifying Your Employability Skills

1. Read the Employability Skills 2000+ chart and make a list of the skills that you are already developing at home, school, and in the community. Compare your list with a partner's.

2. Take your list of skills and sort them into the three categories used in the Employability Skills 2000+ chart. Use the diagram at right to do so.

Employability Skills Web

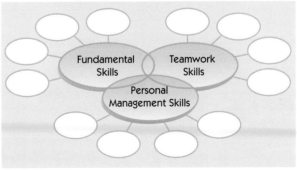

A c t i v i t y ②

Identifying Skills Developed in School

Make a list of the main categories from the Employability Skills 2000+ chart. With a group, brainstorm the ways that these skills are now included in the school curricula as well as the ways that you can seek these skills independently. Make sure that every point in the chart is covered thoroughly.

A c t i v i t y ③

Determining Your Employability Skills

1. List the attributes from the Employability Skills 2000+ chart that you consider to be strengths you have.

2. Using the following scale, rate yourself from 1 to 5 for each category in the chart.
   5 - excellent, 4 - good, 3 - average,
   2 – adequate, 1 - limited

3. Create a chart like the following to categorize your results and outline ways in which to improve.

STRENGTHS	WEAKNESSES	WAYS TO DEVELOP

 You may wish to file this chart in your portfolio.

FOR BETTER OR FOR WORSE © Lynn Johnston Prod., Inc. Reprinted with permission of UNIVERSAL PRESS SYNDICATE. All rights reserved.

CASE STUDY

Workshops Give Girls the Lowdown on High Tech

By Elizabeth Church

Julia Di Poce isn't sure what she wants to be. "Maybe a lawyer or a doctor," the Toronto Grade 10 student speculates. Her classmate Lauren Pasut figures she'll take psychology when she gets to university. "Math is not my strongest subject," she says. But right now, both are talking technology.

The pair are part of a group of close to 200 girls from two Toronto high schools who have been sprung from class on a sunny winter day to get a taste of what work's like in high tech. For half a day, the Grade 10 students—15- and 16-year-olds from Richview and Kipling collegiates in west-end Toronto—huddle in groups around large tables at a Ramada Inn munching on jelly beans while women from IBM Canada Ltd. chat to them about what they do. After a quick quiz on technology, the girls crowd around portable computers to put together graphics for a presentation.

"For girls, there is a misconception about IT (information technology) careers. They think it is a geeky profession," explains IBM Rena Chenoy, head of the one-woman office that arranges these half-day workshops across the country as well as larger day-long events. IBM's program is aiming to reach out to girls and show them that not everyone who works in the field wears a pocket protector. It is being tried out with this group of Grade 10 students who may be tempted to drop math or science in the last years of high school. With tech-savy workers in such high demand, the thinking is that the industry cannot afford to lose out on potential workers just because they hold some misconceptions about the field. "We want to build awareness of the options and show them some female role models," Ms. Chenoy says.

In return, the Canadian subsidiary of Big Blue hopes to bulk up the pool of new hires in the years to come, and foster some good will with its current female work force. We think in terms of filling the pipeline," Ms. Chenoy says. "The fact that IBM is doing this also shows that it is a great place to work."

For the IBM women who volunteer to act as group leaders, Ms. Chenoy says it's a chance to give something back and informally network with colleagues. So far, lots of women are willing to do that. When Ms. Chenoy sends out an e-mail requesting volunteers, she usually has 20 or so replies by the end of the day.

Rukhsana Syed, team leader at IBM's Toronto call centre, is one of the women who often says yes. An IBM employee for two years, Ms. Syed, 32, feels it is important to show girls what they can accomplish, no matter what their gender or background. "You can see diversity in me, big time," says Ms. Syed, who completed a post-graduate degree in computer science in Pakistan before moving to Canada. When it comes to technology, girls "just need a gentle push to say, yes, you can do it," she says. "In every group, there are always two or three who say, 'Wow, I never thought of that. I'll give it a try.' To me, that statement is worth it," she says.

1. Do you agree with the statement "for girls there is a misconception about IT"? State your reasons why or why not.

2. List four reasons why IBM provides this workshop to girls in Grade 10. Do you think these reasons are valid?

3. What motivates Ms. Syed to be involved?

4. As a class, are you interested in organizing a session for your school by contacting IBM?

To assist you in improving your skills we will expand the areas of problem solving, positive attitudes and behaviours, time management, accountability, working with others (teamwork), conflict resolution, respecting diversity, and working safely. The development of communication skills is examined in Chapter 11.

Problem Solving

New situations involve unexpected challenges. To solve problems at the workplace, you need to be able to:
- Define the problem and find a suitable solution.
- Make decisions that are considered carefully and are appropriate for the situation.

Effective **problem solving** and **decision making** are essential for success in the workplace. When a problem occurs, consider it a challenge and work to find a solution. The following problem-solving model might help you.

Problem-Solving Process

Step 1 Define Your Needs and Wants

In your graduating year, you need to work to make a specific amount of money for college and attain a certain percentage in marks at school to gain entrance.

Step 2 Analyze Your Resources

You are a capable student who is well organized and has a reputation for doing well. Your family supports the fact that you work. Your employer also supports your educational goals.

Step 3 Identify Your Choices

Your choices are:
- cutting back on your working hours
- finding a less-demanding job
- taking fewer subjects and returning to school next year
- borrowing money for college
- finding time for more assignments

Step 4 Gather Information

Look at your resources and choices. Add information that might affect your choices. For example, what is the cost of a student loan? Is it possible to cut back on your timetable and return to school next year? Can your parents help you? Could you borrow a computer for home use.?

Step 5 Evaluate Your Choices

Take time to evaluate the effectiveness of each solution. List the pros and cons of each choice.

Step 6 Make a Decision

Decide which of your choices will solve the problem. If the choice does not solve the problem, try something else and repeat steps 2 to 6. Decisions are not usually irreversible.

Step 7 Evaluate Your Decision

Refer back to the problem. Have you achieved a solution?

Activity  4

Following Up on the Decision

Reread the problem-solving process model. Describe what you think the outcome would be if the student borrowed a computer and got up an hour earlier each day to do homework assignments. Consider how the student's resources could affect what happens.

JOURNAL

Assessing Your Problem-Solving Ability

Describe a job- or school-related problem you have had. Then respond to the questions below.

- How did I solve the problem?
- How did I feel about the outcome?
- Would I solve it differently now? If so, how?

Positive Attitude and Behaviour

The first impression you make is important. Some essential aspects of making a good impression are to be enthusiastic, show a positive attitude, have a willingness to learn, portray friendliness, cultivate the ability to remember names, and practise good grooming.

Attitude

Attitude is the beliefs and feelings that cause a person to behave in a certain way. By displaying a positive attitude toward yourself and your workplace, people will respond positively to you. The moment people sense that you have a sincere desire to be with them and a willingness to learn and contribute, you will be on your way to full acceptance.

Willingness to Learn

A willingness to learn involves accepting responsibility and performing duties with enthusiasm. In the workplace, you learn by doing the tasks of your job as well as by observing. Be open to new ideas and tasks, even if they are not what you expected.

Friendliness

To communicate friendliness, try to avoid extreme shyness or aloofness, as well as excessive enthusiasm and non-stop chatter.

Use these guidelines when you first meet someone
- Shake hands firmly.
- Look the person in the eye.
- Smile.
- Say something polite, such as "Pleased to meet you" or simply "Hello."
- Try to remember the person's name and use it in conversation.

Remembering Names

When you start a new job, you will meet many new people in a short period of time. When you make an effort to remember people's names, you demonstrate courtesy and friendliness.

Use these guidelines to help you remember names
- Be interested in every person you meet.
- Listen carefully and concentrate on what the person is saying.
- Repeat the person's name to yourself several times.
- When you get a chance, write down the names of the people you have met.
- Associate a picture, phrase, or character with the name of each person.
- Look around you and say the names of the people to yourself as they come into view.

Dressing for the Workplace

Good grooming is also very important for a successful experience in the workplace. Generally, it is better to err on the side of conservative or low-key attire. Make sure your clothes are clean and pressed and that your shoes are clean and in good repair. Practise good personal hygiene, bathing daily and brushing your teeth regularly. Avoid the use of brilliant nail polish, strong cologne, or unusual hair colouring or styles that will draw attention to your appearance, rather than to what you have to say.

Dressing for Success

Complete the following chart on a sheet of paper, describing what the workers in the left-hand column would wear to work to ensure success, health and safety, and practicality. Three examples are given to get you started.

What to Wear on the Job

JOB	WHAT TO WEAR
receptionist	• conservative dress or suit • comfortable shoes • small jewellery
playground leader	• casual clothes (T-shirts should have no offensive illustrations/sayings) • hat • running shoes • plain watch, no jewellery
plumber's helper	• work clothes • safety boots • leather work gloves
library technician	
race car driver	
cashier	
gas station attendant	
wildlife biologist	
landscape gardener	

PORTFOLIO

Creating a Total Image

Think of yourself in a workplace that would be of interest to you. How will you be dressed? What will you have to be conscious of in terms of personal hygiene? What extra equipment might you need? Write a list that you would make to prepare for the job.

Time Management

Managing your time wisely enables you to get the most out of your work and your leisure time. Good time management means organizing and planning tasks and events for greater efficiency, productivity, and reduction of stress. These skills demonstrate a positive attitude toward your work. Good **time management** also means that your co-workers can rely on you to be on time and to complete tasks on time. Poor time management can result not only in lost productivity but also a great deal of stress. To manage your time effectively, use these guidelines:

- Use an engagement calendar or desk diary to log your professional and personal commitments.
- Create a daily list of things to do. Beside each entry, indicate the priority or level of importance of the task: A means *must do*, B means *hope to do*, and C means *would be good to do if there is time*. Review your list at the end of the day and cross off the tasks you completed. Unfinished tasks become part of tomorrow's list.
- Use a calendar to outline major projects or events. You may need to look at activities in blocks of time—weekly, monthly, three months at a time, or yearly. Plan your other activities around these dates to prevent you from double-booking your time. Pocket-sized computerized calendars are also available to help you keep track of your time.

These hints can help you complete tasks more efficiently on the job:

- Visualize each task. Mentally see yourself performing the task before you actually do it.
- Always leave complete messages when telephoning people. If possible, tell people when you are available to receive calls. If you have to wait on the phone, complete small tasks while you wait. When you return a call, throw away the message or indicate the result and file for reference.
- Have all business-related phone numbers ready for quick access beside your phone.
- Load all business related e-mail addresses onto your computer.
- Keep the notes you made when receiving instructions and the instruction manuals for the equipment you use in an accessible place.
- Make sure your work area is arranged so that you can move easily from one task to another. Organize your tools and equipment and keep your work area neat.
- Complete less important tasks during slack times. Demonstrate initiative and willingness to learn by seeking out new tasks.

Activity 6

How Do You Spend Your Day?

1. Draw a circle to represent a 24-hour day. Divide the circle into parts to show the time you would spend on each activity — all the things you do each day — such as school, time with friends, chores, sleeping, eating, and so on.

2. Draw a second circle to represent a time when you are not in school, such as on holidays or at a co-op or community-based learning placement. In what ways does time management change when school is not the main focus?

PORTFOLIO

Rating Your Time Management

1. Use the questionnaire that follows to determine how well you manage your time. On a sheet of paper, write the number of each statement and respond with *Sometimes, Always,* or *Never.*

Time-Management Questionnaire
1. I am self-disciplined.
2. I can focus on a task without being distracted.
3. I do not procrastinate.
4. I complete all tasks.
5. I order my tasks by priority.
6. My work area is neat and organized.
7. I do not waste time on unimportant tasks.
8. I do one task at a time.
9. I have received the necessary instructions to do each task.
10. I ignore unnecessary details.

2. List the steps you could take to change your *Never* responses to *Sometimes* or *Always* responses. What difference would it make to your life if more of the responses were in the *Always* column?

Accountability

A job involves specific tasks that need to be done by the person appointed to do them. It often involves planning, organizing, decision making, and working with others, besides actually doing the tasks. Along with these responsibilities comes the commitment to complete the tasks in a thorough manner to the best of your ability. Since you expect to receive credit for doing your job well, you should also be prepared to accept responsibility for your mistakes. This is called **accountability**. When you think you have made a mistake that you cannot correct by yourself, be accountable by following these steps:

1. Make sure that what you did is an error.

2. Tell your supervisor or fellow team member immediately. Assume ownership of the error.

3. Offer suggestions for a solution.

4. Ask others for their ideas and listen to them.

5. Find the lesson in the mistake.

6. Learn from it but do not dwell on it. Move on.

In most situations, the person in charge will appreciate your honesty and your eagerness to correct the situation. He or she might also have an immediate solution, since the same error might have been made by other people in the past. You might also discover that the error was not as serious as you thought, and be relieved that you told the supervisor and that a simple solution was found.

JOURNAL

Learning from Mistakes

Everyone makes mistakes, especially in a new situation. Describe a mistake you made as a result of not being familiar with the rules, customs, and/or equipment in a new situation.

After you have described the situation, respond to the questions below.

• What did I learn from my mistake?
• What could I have done to prevent this mistake?
• Could others have done anything to help me?
• In what way could others have done something to help me?

Working with Others

Community members come together to work as a team. In her book, *Games Teams Play*, Leslie Bendaly writes, "A team is a highly effective, cohesive group of individuals who work together with commitment to reach a common goal." It is not enough just to have people working on the same project. They must work together toward a common goal. The following are guidelines for teamwork and the roles within a team.

Guidelines for Brainstorming

Defer Decisions!
Do not use put-downs.
Do not make positive or negative judgements.

Opt for Offbeat!
As a thinker, be original.
Try different ways, seek a new combination.

Vast numbers Are Needed!
Go for quantity.
From quantity comes quality.

Expand!
Piggyback or hitchhike on the ideas of others.

Roles Within the Team

The Timekeeper
Do we agree on what to do?
Are we doing what was asked?
Is everyone helping?

The Checker
Have I written down everyone's ideas?
Does everyone understand?
Can everyone explain the answers?

The Cheerleader
Am I keeping the group on track?
Am I smiling and giving the others a thumbs up?
Am I saying, "Good idea!" "Let's go for it!" "Great job!"?

Developed by the Toronto District School Board.

When working together as a team, it is very important to be supportive of the other team members, to keep the team focussed on the goal, and to be together in your thinking. The following are some suggestions for behaviour that results in good teamwork.

WANT TO BE A GOOD TEAM PLAYER?

Invite others to talk.

Ask for others' opinions.
Make a plan and stick to it.

Participate by sharing your ideas and information.
Accept responsibility for your task.
Respond to new ideas.
Take time to enjoy the experience.

Open up to other people's feelings.
Follow the ideas of others.

Apply yourself.

Talk about new ideas.
Encourage others.
Appreciate your team members.
Make sure to listen without interrupting.

PROFILE

Saturday Night at the Art Gallery

By Sharlene Azam

If you weren't there, you missed a great party. Shocking Vibes, a multi-media show of teen fashion, music, dance, video, and paintings, was the place to be Saturday night. Organized by a group of young people at the Art Gallery of Ontario, the show was delicious. Packages of sweet sound by girl and guy bands, runway designs to rival any in Paris or Milan, break dancers that took your breath away by spinning so fast on those tiny bones in their necks. And then there was a corridor full of art, including seven skateboards painted by 17-year-old Patrick Dunal in the theme of the conflict between man and machine. Enough to make anyone want to learn the art. Painting? Boarding? Both, I think.

The 11 teens who came up with the concept for Shocking Vibes are part of Teens Behind The Scenes, the Art Gallery of Ontario's new committee started in September [1999]. "The purpose (of the committee) is to get young people to come to the gallery, so they understand that art is a living part of their lives," says Jackie Chiu, one of the young organizers. "It isn't just naked women in paintings. It's fashion and music, too."

The teen council of organizers—all between the ages of 14 and 19—were recruited by the AGO through schools, the Web, and posters plastered around the city. "My teacher told me the AGO was looking for teens to get involved," says Joseph Luk, 18. "So, I came to an info meeting, went to an interview, and started volunteering." Luk helped plan the overall look of Shocking Vibes.

And while that included lots of the things young people are doing, because of the way it was set up, the paintings were still far away from the fashions and music and dancers.

A fashion show was only one of the forms of entertainment at Shocking Vibes.

Planning a show is no small job. "We met every week for about four hours, but usually longer, " Chiu says. "Everyone either chose or was given a task to be responsible for. We put out the call for submissions, vetted them, created promotional packages to spread the word about the night."

More than 300 teens showed up and coughed up $4 to see the show, which began at 8 p.m. and ended sometime after midnight. Money raised from ticket sales will go toward security and printing costs.

The Teens Behind The Scenes committee, which is supported by the Toronto Community Foundation, The Toronto Arts Foundation, The George Lunan Foundation, Youth Tour Guides, and the CIBC, is already gearing up for its next event. "We're planning a hip-hop convention in the summer and a skateboard ballet and a film festival after that," Chiu says.

1. Why did **Teens Behind The Scenes** organize this event?

2. What tasks did they have to complete as a team to organize this event?

3. What do you think of their future plans? Can you think of other events that would be interesting?

4. Who would you include on your team if you were a member of their committee?

Creating a Puzzle

Divide into groups. Each group will receive an envelope containing blank puzzle pieces. On each piece, write a rule that will help your group work together as a team. When you are finished, assemble the puzzle.

Team Fitness

It is important that your team "keep fit." As you are working together, ask these questions. (Post them somewhere so that you can all see them.)
• When we work together are we listening to each other?
• Is everyone having a chance to speak?
• Are we feeling proud of our membership on this team?
• Are we focussed?
• Are we sharing the work?
• Are we getting the job done?

PORTFOLIO

Listing Your Teamwork Skills

Read over the Team Fitness questions. For each one, list the skills that are necessary for answering "yes." For example, if everyone on a team has a chance to speak, it means that team members are co-operating, taking turns, listening, observing, sharing. After you have listed the skills, think about which ones you value most.

Activity 8

Observing Your Community

Over a period of about a week, look around your community for examples of people working together to make things better. Also look for areas or opportunities for you to make a difference. Keep a notebook or tape recorder on hand to record your observations and ideas. Leave room to add to it as you observe more examples. At the end of the time period, combine your ideas as a class and make a master list. Post it on the bulletin board for future use.

Conflict

Throughout your life you receive messages about conflict, or a clash of opposing ideas, interests, or activities, from parents, teachers, peers, the media, literature, and your own experiences. These messages build a set of attitudes and beliefs about conflict that affect how you interact with others and how you respond in conflict situations. How you respond will lead to consequences that may be positive or negative. Yelling would be negative. Talking about the problem and coming to an increased understanding of the other person would be positive. Most people are conditioned, however, to think of conflict in a negative way. If you respond negatively by yelling, name-calling, physical violence, or walking away without solving the problem, this usually leads to a continuation of the conflict at a later time.

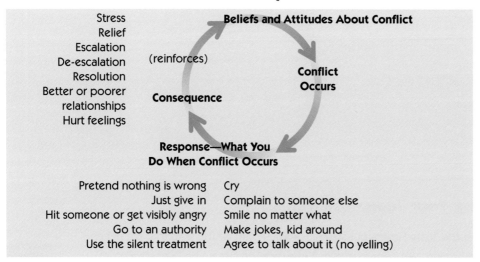

The Conflict Cycle

Stress
Relief
Escalation
De-escalation
Resolution
Better or poorer relationships
Hurt feelings

(reinforces)

Beliefs and Attitudes About Conflict

Conflict Occurs

Consequence

Response—What You Do When Conflict Occurs

Pretend nothing is wrong	Cry
Just give in	Complain to someone else
Hit someone or get visibly angry	Smile no matter what
Go to an authority	Make jokes, kid around
Use the silent treatment	Agree to talk about it (no yelling)

 You might wish to file a copy of The Conflict Cycle diagram in your portfolio.

Activity 9

Examining Attitudes to Conflict

1. The beginning of the conflict cycle is "Beliefs and Attitudes About Conflict." Examine statements made by your parents, by television programs, by movies, and so on. For example:
   - *Don't get mad, get even.*
   - *Turn the other cheek.*
   - *Second place is loser's place.*

2. How do your friends and family react to conflict? How has their behaviour had an impact on your response to conflict?

3. Examine the "Consequence" section of the conflict cycle diagram. Select which items are a positive consequence and which ones are negative and are, therefore, likely to lead to more conflict.

Activity 10

Analyzing a Personal Conflict

1. Analyze the past five conflicts you have had. For each one, describe who it was with, what it was about, and what you did or said. How did you feel before, during, and after the conflict? Do you see a pattern in your response to conflict?

2. From question 1, select a conflict that ended with positive consequences and one that had negative consequences. Complete a conflict cycle diagram for each one.

Conflict Resolution

Even when co-workers practise courtesy and respect and team members are well chosen, it is rare that a workplace does not experience tensions from time to time. Whether two people are working close to each other or are part of a team, conflict can occur. Call it human nature. Resolving conflict can be learned and is a necessary skill for all workers. **Conflict resolution** for the workplace is a problem-solving strategy for settling disputes.

At any time, but particularly in the workplace, the method used for resolving conflict should be one of problem solving. The conflict should end when a solution is developed and implemented. The communication skills featured in Chapter 11 are an integral component of conflict resolution, particularly active listening and speaking. Conflict resolution is a process in which a specific sequence of steps must be followed.

The Informal, Collaborative Process

This process is an informal form of negotiation in which two people in conflict attempt to express and resolve their differences. For the process to work, both people must be willing to co-operate and work together. The process has two major parts:

1. Personal time for each person to reflect and plan.

2. A meeting at which a problem-solving method is used to resolve the conflict.

During the reflecting and planning stage of the process, each individual must define his or her needs and feelings about the situation. By planning in advance, you may be better able to express yourself in a non-threatening way. Planning ahead allows time for both people to calm down, enabling them to listen and to express themselves more effectively.

During the reflecting and planning stage of the process it is important to identify all of the issues related to the conflict. It is rare for conflicts to have a single cause. More often they involve multiple issues. Look beyond the more obvious issues to see what underlying reasons might also be involved. If only the more obvious issues are addressed, the conflict will often re-emerge involving another superficial issue. If a lasting solution to a problem is to be found, it is essential to identify and address all the issues.

These questions can help you in the reflecting and planning stage.
• How does the situation affect me?
• What aspect of the conflict is important to me?
• What are my real needs in the situation?
• Are my personal values being challenged? Which ones?
• How do I view the other person?
• What do I most want this person to understand about me?
• What exactly would make the situation better for me?
• What do I want to change and what do I need for change to occur?
• Who can help bring about this change?

A problem-solving meeting follows the planning and reflection stage. To guide this discussion, it is helpful to follow a sequence of steps known as problem solving.

1. **Set the tone.** Begin by stating your positive intentions for the relationship and the current situation; for example, "I want to resolve this problem." "Our relationship is important." " I want to hear your point of view."

2. **Define and discuss the problem.** If possible, come to a mutual agreement about what the conflict is exactly. Then, both of you outline your concerns and needs from the planning and reflection stage. Express both the surface and the underlying causes of the problem. During this time, do not interrupt the other person.

3. **Summarize the progress.** Take time to confirm that both you and the other person have heard and perceived the same information. Summarize by once again defining the problem and by going over the major points each person stated.

4. **Explore alternative solutions.** Brainstorm a variety of solutions and determine the advantages and disadvantages of each. The solution selected to try first should be:
   • acceptable to both parties,
   • specific, stating exactly what each person will do and how and when it will be done,
   • balanced, so that each person is contributing something to the resolution of the problem.

5. **Follow up.** Before leaving the meeting, agree on a time to meet in the near future. This will enable you to evaluate your solution and make some adjustments, if necessary. The follow-up meeting will also enable you to continue to build a positive relationship.

Activity  11

Applying the Informal, Collaborative Process

Examine the conflict cycle you created in Activity 10. Write a solution, using the five steps of the conflict resolution method described. What could have been done differently? Do you think the result would have been the same?

 You may wish to file your example of the conflict resolution method in your portfolio

Respecting Diversity

Part of Canadian heritage includes the belief that everyone is born free and equal, although this belief is not always reflected in daily life. Canadian law guarantees basic **human rights**, including the right to be respected at all times. Canadians have the right not to be placed at a disadvantage based on factors such as race, place of origin, religion, age, gender, marital or family status, or disability. Everyone has the right to live and work in an environment that is free from such **discrimination**. The Canadian Human Rights Commission administers the Canadian Human Rights Act, which applies to industries under federal jurisdiction, such as air transport, radio and television broadcasting, banking, and telecommunications. Each province and territory also has similar human rights legislation to protect against discrimination for any person not covered under the federal legislation.

Basically, every person in Canada has the right to freedom from discrimination in the areas of services, goods, and facilities; housing; contracts; membership in vocational associations and craft unions; employment.

Every individual has a responsibility to respect the rights of others. Every employer has a responsibility to stop or prevent discrimination in the workplace. Every employee has the right to lodge a complaint of discrimination, and the employer is expected to listen to and act on complaints. Human rights legislation incorporates many other aspects of employment, including recruiting, hiring, training, transferring, promoting, apprenticeship terms, dismissals, and layoffs. Terms and conditions of employment—for example, rates of pay, overtime, hours of work, vacation time, shift work, discipline procedures, and performance evaluations—might also be included in this legislation.

The Canadian Charter of Rights and Freedoms also protects human rights within Canada. Its purpose is to state the rights of every Canadian citizen clearly so that these rights can be understood and protected by the legal system. The Charter is entrenched in the Canadian constitution, which helps to protect these rights from being abolished by federal or provincial legislation. Among the rights included in the Charter are the right to freedom of conscience and religion; freedom of thought, belief, opinion, and expression (including the media); freedom of peaceful assembly; and freedom of association. Discrimination based on race, national or ethnic origin, colour, religion, sex, age, or mental or physical disability is prohibited under the Charter.

J O U R N A L

••••••••••••••••••••••••••••••••••••

Confronting Discrimination

Complete one, several, or all of the following statements.

• I have been a victim of discrimination. Here is my story.
• I have been a victim of harassment. Here is my story.
• I will no longer behave in a discriminating manner. In the past, I have . . .
• I have witnessed acts of discrimination or harassment. Here is my story.

Working Safely

••

Employers and employees both have responsibilities to ensure that everyone is working in a safe environment. Statistics show that young employees are the most at risk.

Most injuries are caused by slips, trips, and falls. Slips usually occur as a result of hidden steps, slippery surfaces (such as waxed, wet, or greasy floors), and loose flooring or carpeting. Trips are caused by clutter and obstacles in hallways or on stairs, improperly placed or secured electrical cords, dropped objects not picked up, and poorly placed furniture. Falls are caused by improper use of ladders, makeshift ladders (such as a stack of boxes) or stools, improper use of safety equipment, and unstable platforms. All of these injuries can be foreseen and prevented.

Employers should ensure that all repairs are completed, anti-slip materials are used, spills are cleaned up, and warning signs are used for wet floors or hidden steps. Employees should be alert and safety-conscious.

A c t i v i t y 12 •••••••••••••••••••••••••••••••••••

Brainstorming Occupations Requiring Safety Equipment

With a partner, brainstorm occupations that require protective equipment and make a list of the safety equipment these occupations might require. Then make an extensive list by combining the class's results. Study the following illustration of safety equipment. Can you add to your list?

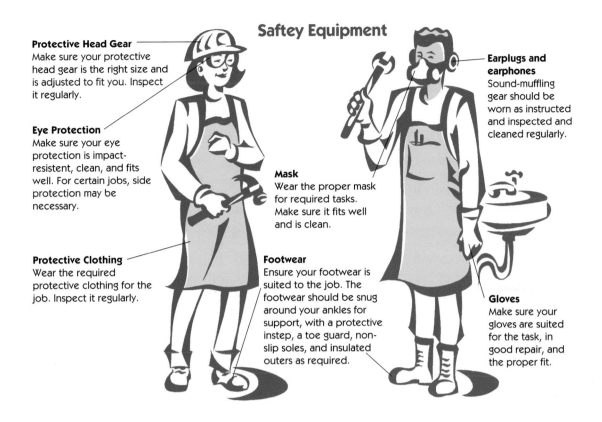

Saftey Equipment

Protective Head Gear
Make sure your protective head gear is the right size and is adjusted to fit you. Inspect it regularly.

Eye Protection
Make sure your eye protection is impact-resistent, clean, and fits well. For certain jobs, side protection may be necessary.

Protective Clothing
Wear the required protective clothing for the job. Inspect it regularly.

Mask
Wear the proper mask for required tasks. Make sure it fits well and is clean.

Footwear
Ensure your footwear is suited to the job. The footwear should be snug around your ankles for support, with a protective instep, a toe guard, non-slip soles, and insulated outers as required.

Earplugs and earphones
Sound-muffling gear should be worn as instructed and inspected and cleaned regularly.

Gloves
Make sure your gloves are suited for the task, in good repair, and the proper fit.

Activity 13

Assessing Your Safety Practices

Use the following safety questionnaire to evaluate how safe you are at a part-time job, at a volunteer position, or at a work experience placement. On a sheet of paper, write the number of each statement and respond with *Never, Occasionally, Almost Always*, or *Always*.

Safety Questionnaire

1. I take time to calm down before acting when I am emotional.
2. I seek information about safe practices and procedures.
3. I focus on my tasks without distraction.
4. I remind others of safe practices.
5. I use equipment for its intended purpose only.
6. I do not cover up other people's unsafe practices.
7. I use the appropriate safety equipment.
8. I inspect my work area for safety hazards.
9. I lift items properly in order to prevent back injuries.
10. I turn off and disconnect from its electrical source all equipment before repairing or adjusting it.
11. I put items in their proper places after using them.

In small groups, compare your answers. Discuss how you can change your *Never* and *Occasionally* responses into *Almost Always* or *Always* responses.

You may wish to file a copy of your completed questionnaire and your resolutions for improving your safety habits in your portfolio.

Activity 14 ●

Comparing Common Causes of Injury

Compare the list of the Top Five Causes of Injury to the Five Most Common Injuries to young workers. List the reasons why you think these injuries are common to young workers and give solutions for preventing these injuries.

TOP FIVE CAUSES OF INJURY TO YOUNG WORKERS	FIVE MOST COMMON INJURIES TO YOUNG WORKERS
1. Slips and falls	1. Sprains and strains (including back injuries)
2. Overexertion	2. Soft tissue injuries (cuts, punctures, bruises)
3. Struck by, or against, an object	3. Bone fractures
4. Bodily reaction (toxic effects from chemicals)	4. Inflammation of the joints
5. Burns	5. Burns or scalds

Employees' basic safety rights are outlined in the Canada Labour Code.

Basic Rights in the Canada Labour Code

The three basic rights outlined in the code are:
• the right to know.
• the right to participate.
• and the right to refuse dangerous work.

The right to know means that employers must inform employees of foreseeable hazards in the workplace as well as prevention measures. Employers are also responsible for displaying the Canada Labour Code in the workplace, details of the company safety program, and other health and safety information.

The right to participate means that employees may assist in identifying health and safety issues and in resolving these issues through a health and safety committee.

The right to refuse dangerous work means that if an employee has reason to believe that a situation presents a danger to herself or himself, she or he can refuse to work without disciplinary action from the employer, providing that proper reporting procedures are followed.

Legal Procedure for Unsafe Work Refusal

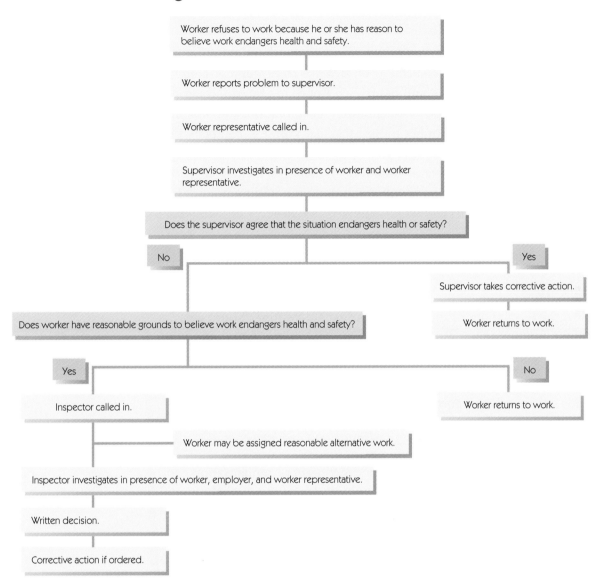

Worker refuses to work because he or she has reason to believe work endangers health and safety.

Worker reports problem to supervisor.

Worker representative called in.

Supervisor investigates in presence of worker and worker representative.

Does the supervisor agree that the situation endangers health or safety?

No

Yes

Supervisor takes corrective action.

Worker returns to work.

Does worker have reasonable grounds to believe work endangers health and safety?

Yes

No

Inspector called in.

Worker returns to work.

Worker may be assigned reasonable alternative work.

Inspector investigates in presence of worker, employer, and worker representative.

Written decision.

Corrective action if ordered.

Activity 15

Role-Playing Refusal to Work

1. In groups of five, think of a situation in which a refusal to work may be necessary.

2. Role-play the situation, including an employee, an employer, a co-worker, a supervisor, and a government inspector. In your role-play, find a solution for the situation and consider these questions:
   - Was the supervisor told about the danger?
   - How did the employer respond to the situation?

   - Was the co-worker knowingly working in unsafe conditions?
   - Was the co-worker concerned or did he or she choose to ignore the situation?
   - Did the co-worker and employee work together to improve the situation?

3. After each group performs for the class, discuss the effectiveness of the solutions presented.

Workers' Compensation

When a work-related injury or illness occurs, provincial **workers' compensation** legislation assists the employee and employer. Benefits from workers' compensation (or the **Workplace Safety and Insurance Board** in Ontario) cover the injured employee's medical costs, hospitalization, rehabilitation, and disability pension, and compensates him or her for lost income. Workers' compensation protects employers from long, expensive court cases since compensation benefits replace a worker's right to sue an employer for damages. Employers pay premiums to support the program based on the number of their employees; employees do not pay at all.

If You Get Injured

The employer must . . .	The employee must . . .
• Follow the regulations of the Workers' Compensation Board or the Workplace Safety and Insurance Board. • Give first aid immediately. • Provide emergency transportation to the doctor, hospital, or home of the injured worker if required. • Pay the employee's full wages for the day of the injury or illness. • Notify the Workers' Compensation Board or the Workplace Safety and Insurance Board of the injury or illness within a specific period of time using a special form. • Offer to re-employ a seriously injured worker, perhaps in an alternative job if the damage from the injury to the employee prevents him or her from doing the original job. • Modify the workplace to accommodate the worker's needs, if necessary.	• Get first aid treatment right away. • Tell your supervisor about any injury. • Tell your supervisor about any illness or condition that you believe happened because of work. • Choose your own doctor. Once chosen, you may not change doctors without the permission of the Workers' Compensation Board or the Workplace Safety and Insurance Board. • Fill out and return all Workers' Compensation Board or Workplace Safety and Insurance Board forms right away. You can get the forms you need from your supervisor.

IN THE NEWS

Serious Safety

Eager to make a good impression at a new job, we might not want to bother the boss by asking about safety training. But we wouldn't play our favourite sports without the proper training and equipment, so why ignore safety at work? After working hard for our opportunities, it's important not to let a workplace injury turn a dream job into a nightmare. Accidents can happen in any industry. Workplace hazards can include spills, contamination, and equipment. Statistics show that most workplace injuries happen within the first two weeks of employment and workers under the age of 24 have the greatest risk for injury or death.

"Safety is one of the most important things you can learn on the job," says Beryl Kirk of Human Resources Development Canada, the federal agency responsible for the Canada Labour Code. "In school you studied hard and as a result landed your first job. Now learning to do it safely may help you keep it."

At age 21, Mel Camilli lost both his legs in a logging truck accident. Now an employee with the Workers' Compensation Board of British Columbia, he urges people to be aware of hazards, ask safety questions, and report dangerous situations to help prevent occupational accidents. "It's a hard thing to do as a young person. You never think anything bad is going to happen to you," he says. "But don't be afraid to ask questions. The boss is there to help and is not going to fire you for asking."

Under the Canada Labour Code you have the right to a safe workplace, training, proper equipment and practices, and to refuse to do unsafe work. It's important to recognize risky situations in your work environment and find out how to avoid them. "Insist on training," says Bryan Collett, Education-Outreach Co-ordinator with Workers' Compensation Board. "Lack of experience in the workforce and lack of training can put workers at risk."

Almost every accident is preventable with the right training, procedures, and gear. When starting a new job, take some time to talk about safety. Ask about hazards, training, procedures, and first aid. Get familiar with the site and equipment and learn to recognize dangerous situations.

This landscaper is wearing protective gloves, ear muffs, and a hard hat with a visor.

Reprinted with permission from *Career Paths* 1996, published by YES Canada-BC and funded by Human Resources Development Canada and the BC Ministry of Education, Skills and Training.

1. **Why should safety knowledge be a priority with new employees?**

2. **Contact your local Workers' Safety and Insurance Board and ask them to send you materials on workplace safety.**

3. **Make safety posters for your school. Focus on potential hazards in and around your school building.**

Certification Courses

You can extend your health and safety knowledge by participating in a training or **certification** course offered by many local organizations, such as:

• Cardiopulmonary Resuscitation (CPR)

• First aid courses (sponsored by St. John Ambulance)

• Red Cross swimming qualifications

• Workplace Hazardous Materials Information Systems (WHMIS) workplace safety

When you can add these courses to your résumé or fact sheet, or add the certificates from them to your fact folder, it indicates that you are a responsible individual who is interested in planning now for the future.

Looking Back

1. List the ways you can develop employability skills.

2. List and define the three major skill areas in the Employability Skills 2000+ chart. Under each heading, list the subheadings.

3. Which of your school skills are transferable to the workplace?

4. Explain the seven steps for problem solving.

5. Explain the two major components of the five steps for the informal, collaborative process of conflict resolution.

6. What are your responsibilities if you are in an unsafe working environment? What are your employer's responsibilities?

7. Address the key features of the Canadian laws outlined in this chapter.

EXPLORATIONS

Reflections

Reflect on the positive attitudes and behaviours you currently possess. How will/do these help you at the workplace? Can you make improvements? How will you do this?

Goals

What can you do to be a safe worker?

Action!

Create skits to perform for your class. Use ideas from this chapter, such as:

• Teamwork
• Injury prevention
• Attitudes and behaviours
• Employee rights and responsibilities

Featuring. . .

Editorial: Write an editorial on the value of Canada's Human Rights Act and the Canadian Chart of Rights and Freedoms.

Advice Column: What advice would you give to a student who wants to improve his or her time management skills?

Advertisement: Create an advertisement for safety clothing or special safety equipment.

Personal Story/Interview: Interview the chief custodian of your school. What are his or her responsibilities concerning safety in the school?

Research: Conduct research into the Conference Board of Canada; for example, who belongs to it, what it does, where its headquarters are located, what they have published.

Communication Skills

....

What You Will Learn

....

- To exchange verbal, non-verbal, and written messages.
- To recognize common barriers to effective communication.
- To improve your active listening and speaking skills.
- To speak on the telephone and use e-mail effectively.

Terms to Remember

....

communication barrier
active listening
non-verbal communication
voice mail
fax
e-mail

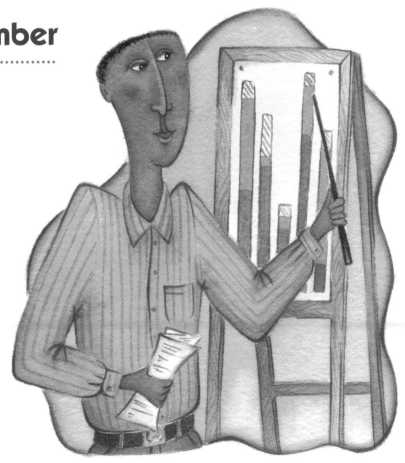

The Importance of Communication

Communication is the process of exchanging information. Effective communication is basic to every successful business and to every successful employee. When you are searching for a job, you will communicate your skills and abilities to a potential employer. When you are on the job, you will communicate with many people, such as supervisors, co-workers, and the public. Every day you will send, receive, and respond to messages when you practise listening, speaking, reading, writing, and non-verbal communication skills. It is important to be aware of the value of these skills and the need to improve them continually.

In any communication, each person is a responsible and active part of the process. The sender is the person who originates the message. He or she communicates in a medium, such as speech, writing, or visual display. The message is the information that the sender wishes to communicate. For example, a message about an upcoming town fair can be communicated in a variety of ways. Town merchants can remind people verbally about the fair, posters can encourage people to attend it, and advertisements can convey the message through radio and television media. The receiver is the person who acquires the message by listening, reading, or viewing. Feedback is the receiver's response to the message and can take many forms, such as gestures, facial expressions, and spoken or written responses. Feedback can occur at any time during the process of exchanging information.

Fall Fair

Avoiding Communication Barriers

Frequently, messages are misunderstood, even when the sender and receiver are standing right next to each other. A **communication barrier** occurs when the true intent of a message is blocked in some way. The following are common barriers to effective communication and ways to avoid these problems.

- **Distractions.** Sounds and movement may distract a receiver from concentrating on a sender's message. Also, the receiver may have a preconceived idea about the message that blocks understanding. To avoid distractions when you are the receiver, focus on the message, regardless of interruptions.

- **Lack of concentration.** Understanding a message is difficult if either the sender or the receiver is not interested in the topic. Concentrate on the message and show an interest in it, whether you are the sender or the receiver.

- **Amount of information.** Too much information can bore or overwhelm a receiver and too little information can cause frustration and misunderstanding. As a sender, adjust the amount of information you give according to the situation and the receiver. For example, if someone asks you how your day was, you might respond by providing a few highlights. If someone asks you how to operate a piece of equipment, you are more likely to respond with detailed step-by-step instructions.

- **Use of jargon.** Language that is too technical or contains jargon can cause a communication barrier. These words should be used carefully and only when all receivers involved understand them.

- **Disorganized message.** A disorganized message can result in a communication barrier. Consider your purpose before you communicate a message, and express your message in a sequential, organized manner.

- **Unsuitable language.** Using an inappropriate language level in a situation is another common communication barrier. When speaking or writing, consider your audience in terms of personality, age, level of ability, and experience with the language.

- **Emotional response.** It is often difficult to receive a message accurately if you disagree with the message or if there is a personality conflict between you and the sender. Try not to let personal feelings interfere with communication. Respond to the message, not the person sending it.

- **Thinking of a response.** When receiving a message, people are often too busy planning a response to receive the complete message. To avoid a misinterpretation, make sure you understand the entire message before responding.

- **Lack of feedback.** If no feedback is offered, a sender may assume a message is understood. A receiver should provide feedback and ask for clarification when necessary. A sender should seek confirmation that the receiver understood the message.

- **Mixed message.** When speaking, a person may send a mixed message by saying one thing and implying another through tone of voice, gesture, or facial expression. Be aware of the subtle messages you send.

 **A c t i v i t y 1** •

Creating a Communication Poster

After you have read the hints for avoiding communication barriers, make a poster illustrating one or more of the barriers, to help others improve their communication skills.

 **A c t i v i t y 2** •

Creating Classroom Communication Barriers

1. Create classroom or workplace scenarios with the following communication barriers:
    - Lack of feedback
    - Disorganized message
    - Lack of concentration

    Here is a sample to get you started.

Consequences of Communication Barriers

SITUATION	BARRIER	CONSEQUENCE
A customer service supervisor (sender) is giving a new employee (receiver) too many instructions at once on how to use the telephone.	Disorganized message.	New employee is frustrated.

2. Add a "Removing the Barrier" column to the right-hand side of the chart. Complete it with an appropriate action for improving communication. For example, to remove the barrier in the sample, the supervisor could have provided written instructions or sat with the new employee while he or she answered the phone calls to make sure the instructions were understood completely.

• •

PROFILE

Making a Difference

by Nicholas Keung

When Ismael Cala Lopez was looking to board a Toronto subway train the first time, he walked into a building with a huge neon sign that said "Subway." But all the 30-year-old Cuban immigrant could find there were beverages and sandwiches—and baffling sneers that embarrassed him. "People told me I could find the stations where the signs were, so I entered the restaurant and asked the clerk, 'Where's the door to the train?'" recalled Cala, who came to Toronto as a refugee in June, 1998. "I had very little English and I thought I would never restart my life in this country."

Today, three months short of his second anniversary in Canada, Cala is a York University frosh working toward an honours bachelor degree in mass communication. He is one of six winners of the eighth New Pioneers awards. "It's so sweet and nice to be recognized for what you have done in a foreign country. It's an amazing feeling," said Cala, who will be honoured with the graduate award for courses he has already completed, at a banquet. The awards, to be presented by Skills for Change, a Toronto non-profit immigration and settlement agency, acknowledge contributions and achievements by immigrants and refugees who overcome tremendous difficulties.

An outspoken radio and television broadcaster in Santiago, Cala started his career job shadowing in a studio at the age of eight but eventually fled Cuba for the freedom of the West. "I was trained in language and speeches, but here I was, couldn't understand a word in English and express myself in English. I felt totally lost in the new world," said Cala, who hosted a radio talk show in Cuba and often challenged the government on social and political issues.

Ismael Cala Lopez, a York University frosh working on an honours bachelor degree in mass communication, could not speak English when he came to Toronto from Cuba two years ago. He experienced embarrassing situations because of communication barriers.

Cala spent his first year as a migrant studying English with the refugee group Costi and taking keyboarding, computer, and career training skills at the Skills for Change.

1. Reading Ismael Cala Lopez's story makes us all think of an embarrassing moment. What is yours?

2. Lopez is called a "new pioneer." In what ways could he be compared to the Canadian pioneers of the 1800s?

3. Is Lopez really in a "foreign country?" It seems that his accomplishments show that he is quite "at home." List them.

4. What three words would you use to describe Ismael Cala Lopez?

5. How does this profile illustrate the importance of communication?

Assessing Your Communication Skills

1. Use the communication inventory that follows to evaluate your communication skills. On a sheet of paper, write the number of each statement and respond with *Never, Occasionally, Almost Always,* or *Always.*

2. In groups of four, discuss your responses. How are you going to change your *Never* and *Occasionally* responses into *Almost Always* or *Always* responses?

3. Make a list of class strategies that will help everyone to improve their communication skills.

Communication Inventory

1. I let others finish speaking before I speak.

2. When I listen, I look at the speaker and express interest in the message.

3. I speak clearly and directly.

4. When I speak, I look at the listener with encouragement.

5. I read carefully and review the content of a written piece.

6. I write thoughtfully and consider the structure of what I am writing.

7. I am more concerned about understanding others than about convincing them that I am right.

8. I ask questions to clarify my understanding of a message.

9. I make sure that others know I understand them.

10. I pay attention to how messages are expressed to help me understand them.

11. I am open to new ideas.

Identifying Communication Challenges

Communication with others is not always easy. Reflect on your communication strengths and weaknesses and, in your journal, complete the statements below:

• Sometimes when I am communicating with someone I get impatient because . . .

• I deal with my frustration over a misunderstanding by . . .

• When I try to put myself in the other person's place, I realize that . . .

Active Listening

Surveys have shown that people spend more time listening than on any other communication activity. After all, there is no communication unless a message is received. The average person is only 25 percent efficient in using his or her listening skills, which means that up to 75 percent of the information contained in a message may be lost. The average person, therefore, can greatly increase his or her listening and retention skills with practice. On the job, being able to listen accurately to supervisors, customers, and co-workers is very important. Effective listening can help you to increase your knowledge, broaden your experience, improve your job performance, and develop better language skills. Some people think that listening and hearing are the same. Listening is actively participating in the communication process by attentively receiving and retaining messages, while hearing is passively sensing sounds. Research indicates that people use less than 25 percent of their listening potential. That is, they are hearing the message but not listening to the intent. **Active listening** requires energy, concentration, and discipline. It means focusing on the message, observing **non-verbal communication,** or physical gestures that send a message, and seeking to understand the message.

Active Listening Strategies

Use the guidelines that follow to help improve your listening skills.

- **Keep an open mind.** Listen to the message with an open mind. Try to listen to the whole message without jumping to any conclusions.

- **Listen, do not talk.** Really listen until the sender is finished. Do not interrupt to ask questions or ask for clarification. Never interrupt.

- **Be alert.** A person's listening capacity ranges from 400 to 600 words per minute. The average speaking rate is 125 words per minute. The result is that receivers often start thinking about other things rather than listening to a message. Listen to both the words and the significance of the words.

- **Show interest.** When someone is speaking to you, stop whatever you are doing and look at the person's face. Think about what the person is saying, and ask questions to clarify points.

- **Take notes.** Recording the speaker's main points or instructions is often useful in some situations. If it is not possible to write, make mental notes. Repeat the message in your own words after the speaker has finished talking to make sure you understand it. Relate the message to your own experience and knowledge.

- **Listen critically.** Listen to determine motives and biases and to distinguish fact from opinion. Listen to what the speaker is not saying. In other words, listen "between the lines" to what is implied.

- **Give feedback.** As a listener, you can improve understanding by sending signals back to the speaker. For example, you can acknowledge that you are listening by nodding your head, and you can encourage further clarification with a quizzical look.

• **Listen with empathy.** Empathetic listeners learn to just listen with understanding and support without taking on a speaker's problems. Try to put yourself in the speaker's place and make an extra effort to understand his or her point of view.

I want to get to the dentist on time but I feel guilty about leaving.

You sound like you feel anxious about having me finish the assignment.

Activity ③ ●●●●●●●●●●●●●●●●●●●●●●●●●●●●●●●●●●●●

Role-Playing Ineffective Active Listening

1. With a partner, outline your views on one of the following issues or a topic of your own choice:
   • Eating in class (or at your desk in the workplace) is acceptable behaviour.
   • All students should work for a year before going to college.
   • Active listening is as important as speaking well.
     One of you should try to keep the conversation focussed on the topic (and use the suggestions above), while the other responds with totally unrelated statements and unfocussed behaviour.

2. As a class, discuss how it feels to make a statement and receive no supportive response from your listener and how it feels when a listener ignores what you are saying.

3. With your partner, continue your discussion with both of you listening carefully and giving positive feedback to each other.

4. As a class, discuss the differences between the two conversations.

Activity 4

Evaluating Your Listening Habits

The following is a list of listening habits that people exhibit. Divide a sheet of paper into two columns. On the left, list the listening habits to which speakers will probably respond positively. On the right, list the ones to which they will respond negatively. For each habit, on the left-hand column, rate yourself using a scale from 1 to 5, with 1 as the lowest score. If you have a score lower than 20, be sure to complete the journal entry that follows the list.

1. Repeats some of the things said.

2. Attempts to complete the speaker's sentences.

3. Looks impatient.

4. Jumps to conclusions and starts to answer before speaker is finished.

5. Reacts with a smile, raised eyebrows, a nod of the head.

6. Keeps looking beyond the speaker.

7. Tries to change the subject.

8. Interrupts.

9. Asks clarification questions when the speaker is finished.

10. Looks at the speaker.

11. Shows sympathy.

12. Looks bored.

JOURNAL

Forming Active Listening Resolutions

In your journal, write the following introductory sentence and complete the statements.

Now that I have discovered how to improve my listening skills, I will change some of my listening habits.

I will continue to . . .

I will try to . . .

I will try not to . . .

Speaking Effectively

Speaking effectively is an important communication skill. It is the verbal part of a message. Although some jobs require more speaking than others, in many jobs you will need to be able to express yourself verbally to your supervisor, co-workers, customers, and others. How well you communicate is decided by:

• The words you use.

• The ways in which you put words together.

- The sound of your voice (in terms of tone, pitch, volume, and tempo).
- Your pronunciation.
- Your enunciation.

Before speaking, organize your thoughts and think carefully about your choice of words. You should be aware of how to use proper grammar. Avoid inappropriate language, such as slang, at work.

Research shows that the impact of a spoken message is 7 percent verbal (word meanings), 38 percent vocal (tone of voice), and 55 percent physical (facial expression and body position). That means that how you say something is much more important than what you say.

Effective Speaking Strategies

Use the guidelines that follow to help improve your speaking skills.

- **Tone** of voice reveals your attitudes and feelings. In the workplace, use a pleasant and cheerful tone.

- **Pitch** refers to how high or low your voice is. A moderately low voice is ideal in the workplace.

- Appropriate **volume** involves making yourself heard without projecting undue force and intensity into your voice.

- **Tempo** is the speed of your speech. When speaking, use pauses to stress major points and to add variety to your tempo. Speak important words more slowly and unimportant words more quickly to contribute to understanding.

- Try to vary your tone, pitch, volume, and tempo to add interest. Avoid speaking in a monotone.

- **Pronunciation** refers to speaking words correctly. Pronunciation is affected by social, cultural, and regional influences. Use a dictionary to learn the most common pronunciations of words. Sound out people's names or ask for the proper pronunciation of their names.

- **Enunciation** refers to speaking words distinctly. Poor enunciation results from running words together, leaving out letters and syllables, adding letters and syllables, or mumbling. Speak clearly by enunciating each letter, syllable, and word.

A major part of speaking is being aware of the receiver. Look at your listener while you speak and avoid distracting mannerisms, such as clearing your throat repeatedly or playing with objects. Look at your listener to ensure the level of language you are using is being understood. Remember to give the listener an opportunity to respond to your message. Watch for signs of disinterest, and try to alleviate boredom by using effective speaking strategies. Use people's names or titles (Mr., Mrs., Miss, Ms., Dr., and so on) in formal speaking situations.

Activity 5

Role-Playing Difficult Situations

With a partner, role-play these challenging communication situations. Try to determine the best way to convey your message in speech.

- A person who works at your volunteer placement and who has been very helpful and friendly to you approaches and asks you to help with unpacking a shipment of office supplies. You are in the middle of writing a participant list for your supervisor and unpacking supplies is not your job.

- At the last minute, your supervisor has asked you to fill in for two hours for another volunteer who has not shown up. You have another commitment that you really do not want to change.

- You are late for your placement at the breakfast program because you forgot to set your alarm before you went to bed last night. The first person you see as you walk in, late, is the person who spoke up on your behalf to get you into the program.

- You are new to the school and ask a student for help in finding the history classroom.

- You arrive home past your curfew and a parent is waiting up for you.

- It is your first day at a placement. The supervisor is showing you around and explaining the daily routine.

- You have locked your key in the house and need help from a neighbour.

Non-Verbal Communication

Learning to use and interpret non-verbal communication can help you to send and receive verbal messages more effectively. Watching a receiver's non-verbal communication can help you better adapt your message to suit the receiver. This is why eye contact is so important.

Non-verbal communication greatly contributes to the meaning of messages through
- facial expressions
- gestures and posture
- body movements
- attire
- grooming

For example, slouching in your chair and yawning may indicate that you have lost interest in a subject. An upright posture may indicate that you are confident and in control. Frowning at someone while you are being introduced and saying, "I am pleased to meet you" may indicate that you would rather not. Furthermore, if you dress inappropriately for an occasion, a negative message is also sent. It makes those around you uncomfortable.

Activity 6

Using Non-Verbal Behaviour

1. On a sheet of paper, divide the following list of non-verbal behaviours into positive and negative.

Smiling	Nodding your head
Sitting forward	Looking away
Maintaining eye contact	Frowning
Looking at your watch	Rolling your eyes
Fiddling with something	Scowling
Folding your arms	Sighing
Narrowing your eyes	Puffing your cheeks
Looking delighted	Tapping your fingers
Bouncing your leg	Slouching in your seat

2. Beside each behaviour, indicate a situation when the behaviour is most helpful or most inhibiting. For example, if you are helping your reading buddy with a difficult passage and you roll your eyes, your reading buddy will lose confidence and think that you think she is stupid. But if you nod your head, she will feel encouraged and try harder.

JOURNAL

Improving Your Non-Verbal Behaviour

Complete the following resolutions in your journal.

- From now on when I am speaking, I am going to follow these three practices . . .
- When I greet someone who is late, I am going to show my feelings by the following non-verbal actions . . .
- Above all, I am going to . . .

Activity 7

Recognizing the Impact of Non-Verbal Communication

1. With a partner, role-play a conversation based on one of the following situations or make up a situation of your own. Your words should not be heard (as if the sound on the television is turned down) and the conversation should be supported by non-verbal behaviours. One person should take a positive stance and the other, a negative one.
   - You are new to the school and ask a student for help in finding the social studies classroom.

- You arrive home past your curfew and a parent is waiting up for you.
- It is your first day at a new job. The supervisor is showing you around and explaining the daily routine.
- You have locked your key in your car and need help from a nearby storekeeper.

2. Repeat the role-play, with each person playing the same roles but switching behaviours.

3. Perform your silent role-play for the class.

JOURNAL

Describing Your Non-Verbal Communication

Other people are unaware of the impact their non-verbal communication has on others. Ralph Waldo Emerson said, "What you are speaks so loudly I cannot hear what you say." With this in mind, complete the following sentences in your journal.

- When I feel bored with a discussion, I usually . . .
- When I feel annoyed with someone, I usually . . .
- When I am excited and try to communicate my thoughts, I always . . .
- When a stranger asks me for directions, I . . .
- When I am trying to convince someone that I am right, I . . .

IN THE NEWS

Prof Tries to Put Finger on What Gestures Mean

by Barbara Mahany

You do it all the time.

You do it, wildly, at cocktail parties. You might even do it in the shower. You certainly do it on the phone. And you absolutely do it whenever you explain to someone how to get from there to here.

You flail. You point. You curl and uncurl your fingers.

You twirl your hand this way and that.

You gesture.

Ah, you think, nothing to it. Just random fly-swatting. Something to do with your paws while your jaw flaps up and down. Wrist exercise.

Wrong.

This flip-floppy hand work is, in fact, deeply tied to how you think, as much a part of your language as the words spewing from your mouth.

For his study of gesture, David McNeill, professor of

psychology and linguistics at the University of Chicago, has variously been called "the father of the field" or just plain "loopy." He has spent some long, lonely years out in the academic wilderness when no other psycholinguist would so much as lift a finger toward the study of non-verbal communication.

"When most people think of gesture, they think of what people do (when they are behind the wheel of a car)," says McNeill, his own fingertips forming a polite cage, fleshy pad touching fleshy pad, left hand to right, even as he launches into the history of the ancient Roman gesture *digitus impudicus,* or impudent finger, the extended middle digit.

"Flipping somebody off is 2000 years old and would have been understood by a Roman legionnaire." But this is not the kind of gesture McNeill has studied so arduously since 1980.

What he's passionate about is the very stuff you would do if you put this paper down and started to explain to someone nearby what you were reading about—in other words, "the spontaneous, ephemeral, made-up-on-the-fly" gesturing you do all day. You probably never give it a second's thought, but to McNeill it is a window to your mind, the best way—without neurosurgery—of getting a peek inside the language centre of your brain.

What he has seen is this. At least half of language is imagery, and the gesturing—the way we move our hands—plays out that image more spontaneously than the spoken words, which are by definition part of a constrained, rule-laden code.

"When we're speaking we're thinking in two forms simultaneously," says McNeill. "Speech and gesture are one system. Our hands evolved for manipulating

tools but language has co-opted the hands to create images."

To study language by listening only to utterances, says McNeill, is to miss as much as 75 percent of the meaning.

Here's a simple experiment to prove the point: Tape-record a meeting. Listen to the tape. You might later find yourself saying, "But I know I heard something that's not on the tape."

Chances are the information was conveyed through a gesture someone made and you didn't even remember the gesture. You only knew that you got the information and figured somone must have said it.

In their cramped lab, huddled in front of a video screen, McNeill and a knot of graduate students watch unwitting folks recount, in languages from Swahili to Mandarin, the antics of Sylvester, the cat who won't give up, and Tweety Bird, the winged one who won't be lunch.

The researchers scrutinize how the cartoon watchers lift arms. Bang fist into palm. Wiggle fingers. Put hands to eyes then drop palms to lap.

They've shown the film to everyone from a two-and-a-half-year-old to a professor of radiology in China. Over and over, the irrepressible cat tries to make a morsel of the puny bird.

McNeill's crew asks the viewer to tell the story to someone else who hasn't seen it, clearly and completely. The average narration takes eight minutes, rife with gesture. McNeill is a man who can wax poetic about gesture. He talks about seeing the "dawn of an idea" in the upstroke of someone's hand.

And in what amounts to a big thumb to the nose to whatever grade-school teacher in your past told you to keep your hands still, McNeill issues the following dictum: "The more articulate and well-educated a person is, the more likely (one is) to see gesture."

1. What is a psycholinguist?

2. Why does language need gestures?

3. In what way do McNeill and his students use Sylvester and Tweety Bird cartoons?

4. Ask a friend to observe your gestures over a period of time and write down the most frequent ones. Give this list to someone else and ask him or her to put a check mark beside each gesture over a longer time period of time. How do gestures help you?

Telephone Interaction

Using the telephone to contact businesses or volunteer organizations is not the same as talking on the phone with a friend. It is recommended that you plan your conversation and the questions you want to ask before you start to dial. When placing a call, you must speak clearly, demonstrate a positive attitude through your tone of voice, and make sure you do not use words such as *um*, *uh*, *you know*, and so on. If you have to leave your name and telephone number, speak slowly, spell your name if necessary, and include your area code with your phone number.

Often when you make a business call today, you will be answered by a recording on a company answering machine or **voice mail,** a person's private business line. Leaving a complete and accurate message is even more important in this case. For this purpose, include the following information:

- Name of the person for whom the message is intended (if it is not a personal voice mail).
- Your full name and your company's name.
- Your phone number, including the area code.
- The date, time of the call, and a brief message.

Be sure to state your message clearly and at the appropriate volume and tempo, so the person receiving it can understand it easily and has enough time to write down any pertinent information.

Activity 8

Role-Playing Telephone Conversations

Refer to the Telephone Response Checklist on page 218 to evaluate each role-play in this activity

1. With a partner, role-play telephone conversations that may occur in the following situations.
   - Making a dentist appointment.
   - Ordering concert tickets by telephone.
   - Responding to a job advertisement.

2. With a partner, role-play telephone conversations that involve one of you taking a message for a third person. Use a notepad to record the messages. Suggested situations are:
   - Making a date for a committee meeting.
   - Reminding someone of an appointment.
   - Informing the school office of an absence.

3. On your own, role-play the message which you would leave on an answering machine or voice mail in the following situations:
   - You have left your bank card at the coffee shop and it is closed.
   - You have heard about a placement that is available at an agency near your home. When you call the agency about it, no one answers.
   - You cannot go to your volunteer placement to teach young children to skate.

Telephone Response Checklist

❏   Answered call promptly.
❏   Answered by identifying the company and self.
❏   Greeted caller pleasantly.
❏   Spoke clearly and confidently.
❏   Treated caller with respect and courtesy.
❏   Obtained needed information.
❏   Wrote down necessary information, asking for proper spelling of name.
❏   Did not make the caller wait unnecessarily.
❏   Answered questions discreetly.
❏   Helped the caller as much as possible.
❏   Kept any caller who was on hold informed.
❏   Spoke clearly and at an appropriate volume.
❏   Spoke at an appropriate pace.
❏   Used appropriate language.

 You may wish to file a copy of the Telephone Response Checklist in your portfolio for future reference.

Written Communication

It is difficult to think of a job that does not involve some reading and writing. A wide variety of written documents are necessary for the successful daily operation of an organization. Ineffective written messages often cause confusion, lost business, and frustration. Workers may be required to complete forms and write memos, letters, directions, and announcements.

Sending a facsimile or **fax,** which means copy or replica, is also a fast, efficient way to communicate. A fax machine sends documents, reports, letters, and illustrative material electronically. A fax saves the time it would take to mail the material. The message that accompanies the material is often less formal than a business letter.

Electronic mail or **e-mail** is a popular form of communication in the workplace today. Messages can be sent from one computer to another in seconds. It is important to recognize the privacy of e-mail messages. Treat electronic communication as you would treat private mail. Do not read it unless it is addressed to you.

Activity 9

Locating a Company's Web Site

Seventy-five percent of large Canadian companies have a home page because it is a relatively inexpensive method of connecting to a potentially wide audience. If you are having trouble finding a local company's web site, call them and ask if they have one. Try at least three or four search engines first (for example, Alta Vista, Excite, Info Seek, and Maple Square). As a class, make a reference list of local companies and agencies.

Writing for the Workplace

Follow these guidelines when writing for the workplace.

1. **Consider the purpose for writing.** These purposes include informing, making or responding to a request, confirming, inquiring, complaining, selling, or promoting. Make sure that the purpose is readily apparent to the reader.

2. **Select a format.** There are so many forms of written communication, but, in business, most written messages are in the form of memos, letters, and reports.

3. **Consider the audience.** Before writing, consider who will be reading the message, why they will be reading it, and what they already know about the topic.

4. **Consider the structure.** Outline the content of your message by listing the main points. Then arrange the points in logical order. Any message should have an introduction, a body, and a conclusion.

5. **Write clearly.** Avoid unnecessary expressions, such as "due to the fact that," "all things considered," and "in spite of everything." Include only the information that is necessary and relevant to the reader.

6. **Check for accuracy.** Proofread your written messages for spelling, grammar, and content errors.

Activity 10

Writing Workplace Messages

1. Assume you are a supervisor. Write an e-mail memo to your employees announcing the appointment of a new volunteer employee. Be sure to include all the details that they will want to know, such as the person's name, school, his or her general responsibilities, and his or her starting date.

2. Assume you want to know about a company's product or service. Write a letter outlining what you want to know.

3. Write a report about the dangerous condition of the parking lot at your school.

CASE STUDY

· ·

Rule, Freedonia

by Sarah Elton

A visit to the Principality of Freedonia couldn't be easier. The trip is short, the weather never changes, you don't need a passport, and it costs nothing to get there. That's because Freedonia doesn't really exist. It is a make-believe country that has been online since 1997.

Freedonia is only one of many so-called "Micronations" that exist on the World Wide Web today—tiny, self-declared states (of mind) run by people (usually their rulers) who invented them and keep them running with varying degrees of verisimilitude. There are so many of these Internet nations these days that 22 of them (including Freedonia) have linked up in a United Micronations organization.

A whirl around Freedonia's well-articulated web site reveals a pretty complex cyber-state of affairs. The web site is so chock-full of realistic details that it's hard to tell how seriously its founders are taking this stuff. According to the history books (or rather, Freedonia's online history page), the country was born back in the early 1990s when the self-declared monarch, Prince John (then known as John Alexander Kyle), got together with his friends and declared their own houses to be independent of the United States. The enterprise went online in 1997, after Prince John was surfing the web and noticed that others had declared their own independent nations.

Today, the principality's web page proudly displays Freedonia's constitution, its national coat of arms, its green-and-yellow flag (plus a black standard for times of strife and mourning), and its very own currency (which bears the national motto: *Superibimus*). There are also photographs of the monarch and some members of his government. Prince John's photo reveals him to be a skinny, clean-cut guy who looks about 16 years old. He is shown standing in front of a gilded fireplace and ornate mirror, looking regal in a preppie kind of way—sort of like Prince William.

Prince John and his pals have even written a three-verse national anthem, complete with the familiar-sounding chorus: "Oh, Freedonia, Freedonia the land that saves. Freedonians never shall be slaves." Freedonians adhere to the principles of libertarianism and their cry is for maximum freedom and low taxation. But, then where else would a bunch of libertarians hang out? The Internet is the bastion of individual freedom.

1. Why is the name Freedonia suitable for this make-believe country?

2. What is the United Micronations?

3. What characteristics does Freedonia have that make it seem like a real place?

4. Why might you want to be a member of Freedonia?

5. In what ways has the Internet changed people's perceptions of what is real and what is imaginary?

6. What lesson does web sites like Freedonia teach users of the World Wide Web?

Looking Back

1. Give three reasons effective communication is important at school and in the workplace.

2. Describe a situation you have observed in which a communication barrier prevented a message from being received.
   a) Which barrier caused the message to be interrupted?
   b) How could this communication barrier have been overcome?

3. How is e-mail changing how we communicate with friends and in the business world?

EXPLORATIONS

Reflections

Write a paragraph describing yourself as a communicator in school, with your friends, and at your part-time job or volunteer placement. Are you better at speaking or writing?

Goals

Think of a person who you think is a good listener. Create an action plan to become a better listener.

Action!

You are in a position where you have to convince your employer that you need time off from your part-time job. The employer doesn't want to give you the time. With a partner, role-play this scenario.

Featuring. . .

Editorial: Write an editorial on the advantages and disadvantages of instant communication (cell phones, faxes, e-mail, the Internet).

Advertisement: Prepare an advertisement for the latest communication tool. Use your imagination.

Advice Column: Write a column outlining proper etiquette when using e-mail to research information about a company, product, or service.

Personal Story/Interview: Interview one or more adults over the age of 50 and ask them to outline the advances in communication that have been made since they were in elementary school. What is their reaction to all these changes?

Research: Survey fellow students to find out how they spend the majority of their time—speaking, writing, listening, or reading? Which communication tools do they use regularly?

CHAPTER
12

Job Search Tools

What You Will Learn

- To identify various ways to find employment.
- To gather and organize information required to complete a résumé and forms for community service and employment.
- To create a résumé.
- To complete an application form.
- To write a covering letter and other business letters.
- To learn how to participate in an interview.

Key Terms

job lead
search engine
content index
reference
résumé
application form
bondable

covering letter
occupational research interview
job interview
human resources department
personnel department
letter of recommendation

Finding Information About Employment

There are many ways to get information about possible jobs. Finding the right job begins with a **job lead**—a tip or information abut an available job. It can be a lead from a friend, information from the Internet, or an ad in a newspaper. The latest statistics in Canada show that people get jobs in the ways shown in the pie graph.

In today's job market, it is essential to be aware of the number of avenues available to you to help you find a job. Do not limit yourself to just one of these suggestions. Explore a variety of opportunities at the same time. Here are some possibilities.

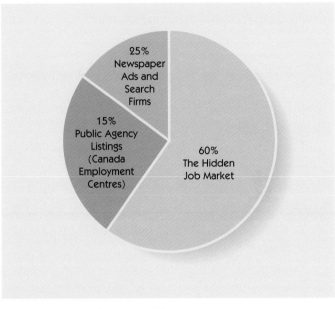

Ways that People Get Jobs

- Develop personal and professional networks.
- Keep in touch with people you meet at your volunteer experiences and co-op placements.
- Explore the Internet.
- Request an information interview at a specific company you are interested in.
- Find unadvertised jobs by researching and contacting companies listed in reference books at the local library and in the telephone directory, and by attending workshops, conventions, and job fairs.
- Visit your school's career centre or guidance office and ask where the job opportunities are listed.
- Visit local, provincial, and federal government employment centres.
- Search through the classified ads in your community and local newspapers.
- Create your own job.

Navigating the Internet for Employment

The Internet covers a worldwide electronic community and gives you career centre information, access to jobs, and opportunities to post your résumé. Some companies have web sites or home pages that profile the company, which are useful to visit when seeking company information or in preparation for an interview at one of the companies. For these, type in the web address, if you know it. Web addresses are often found in a company's traditional print literature or advertising.

Job listings are easy to find. Using a **search engine** such as Hotbot or a **content index** such as Alta Vista, type in search words such as *employment opportunities*, *job listings*, or *careers*. Or, you may want to input words that define your own job search, such as *employment and pharmacy*. These words will provide you with links to a number of web sites. You may want to try different search engines, because each uses different criteria to search through the web.

Many search engines provide outlines on how they access information, so you may want to read about the search engine before you select one for your search. In any case, you should take a look at the link before you follow it to see if it looks relevant to your original search. (It is easy to get sidetracked on the Internet!) You can also go directly to a site by using specific addresses such as those for the Canadian Association of Career Educators and Employers (http://www.cacee.com), CanWorkNet (http://canworknet.ca), and Career Mosaic (http://canada.careermosaic.com).

Five Reasons to Use the World Wide Web in Your Job Search

According to *Career Option Magazine*, these are the main reasons you should use the web to look for employment:
1. The web helps you to find out about employers through their own home pages.
2. A variety of university career centres and commercial sites post job search advice.
3. You can network through online discussion groups, forums, and special-interest web sites.
4. You can post your résumé online or put it on your own home page.
5. The web supplies you with job postings regionally, across Canada, and around the world.

PORTFOLIO

Researching Career Programs

Search the Internet, the Yellow Pages, and the career centre and library of your local educational and training institutions that offer programs in your area of interest. Contact them to find out when they offer information sessions and/or open houses for interested students. Mark the dates in your calendar/organizer. Request written information from each for your areas of interest by e-mail, fax, or letter. File any information that represents future possibilities in your portfolio.

Tap into the Hidden Job Market

Did you know . . .
• that only a small percentage of jobs are advertised in newspapers or employment centres?
• that most jobs are in the "hidden job market"?
• that most employment opportunities get filled by word-of-mouth and by being in the right place at the right time?

Gathering Information

Whether you are looking for a full-time position, a part-time job, a volunteer placement, or a career-related job-shadowing experience, once you begin the job-search process you will need to be able to access certain pieces of information quickly in order to complete a résumé, a covering letter, or an application form. The information you will need is outlined in the following list. You may not need to include it all in your résumé, letter, or application form, but you should have it available at all times.

- **Career goals.** A single-sentence career goal is often included in a résumé or in a covering letter that is sent when applying for a specific position.

- **Personal information.** Include your legal name, current address, telephone number, fax number, and e-mail address, if you have one, on all your documents. These details must be accurate.

- **A Social Insurance Number (SIN).** The federal government uses this nine-digit number to identify people for purposes such as income tax. Everyone in Canada must have an SIN to be employed. Although it is not legally necessary to give your SIN to anyone until you have been hired, make sure that you have one before applying for a job. You can obtain an SIN by visiting your local Canada Employment Centre. Take your birth certificate and one other piece of identification with you.

- **Education.** This category includes your educational background and training in reverse chronological order.

- **Employment.** In reverse chronological order, list the names, addresses, and telephone numbers of all the businesses you have worked for, as well as all volunteer work and work experience gained through school programs. Be prepared to include the supervisors' names, your periods of employment, the types of businesses, your job titles, your reasons for leaving, and the responsibilities you carried out in each position.

- **Skills.** Three types of skills apply to résumés and application forms: technical skills, which are practical skills that you have learned, such as the use of specific equipment, computer programs, and languages; self-management skills, which are personal skills, such as organizing and communicating; and transferable skills, which can be applied to many situations, such as mathematical ability. Both technical and self-management skills can be transferable skills.

- **Activities and interests.** Although your activities and interests allow a potential employer to gain some insight into your personality, they should be included only if they clearly relate to the position for which you are applying. For example, if you are applying for a job as program director of a day camp, you may want to list the sports in which you participate. Often your activities and interests lead to a volunteer position with a local team or club. Be sure to highlight these experiences in this section.

- **References.** A person who agrees to recommend you to a potential employer is a **reference**. People who are acting as references should know something about your skills, personality, experience, and education. You should select references who can be contacted easily and who will respond quickly and positively to inquiries from a potential employer. Your references might include work references, such as former employers and people for whom you have done volunteer work; academic references, such as teachers; and character references, such as friends. Using family members as references is not considered acceptable practice.

Contact people you have in mind in advance and ask them if they are willing to act as references for you. Make them aware of your plans—you might send them supportive material, such as a copy of your résumé and a list of the companies to which you have applied. When contacting potential references, ask them what they would say about you to a potential employer. Obtain the correct spelling of their names and job titles, and make sure you have their correct addresses and telephone and fax numbers. Once all this information has been collected, you are ready to write your résumé or complete an application form.

Transferable Skills

Transferable skills is a term that is being used more and more these days as technology forces people to change careers, as people who have been at home as caregivers return to an altered workplace, and as "retired" people take jobs in new areas. Transferable skills are the skills you already have that can be applied to a new situation. For example, many students exhibit leadership skills in the sports they play. They realize that before they can be a good leader, they must be a good follower. They realize that all team members must be consulted, or have an opportunity to offer their opinion and be listened to. Consulting is a transferable skill that is valuable throughout your lifetime. Another example of a transferable skill is problem solving. If you are a person who approaches the problem of an unco-operative computer or a lost math text calmly and with resolve, you will probably handle the broken fax machine and the lost invoice at the workplace in the same way. The chart that follows shows examples of skills learned at home or school that could be applied at work.

Transferable Skills Chart

SKILL	EXAMPLES AT HOME/SCHOOL	EXAMPLES IN THE WORKPLACE
Communication	• math tutor • reading buddy • newsletter editor	• explain concepts to others • read with understanding • write persuasively

Interpersonal	• community club volunteer • peer mediator • new student welcome wagon volunteer	• express feelings appropriately • withstand and resolve conflict • sensitive to cultural differences
Leadership	• basketball team member • peer mediating co-chair • YMCA camp counsellor	• appreciate/reward peers' efforts • bring reason to a problem • motivate others
Problem Solving	• alter recycled clothing • worked out a scheduling conflict at home	• see all sides of a situation • open-minded
Adaptability	• changed schools twice • created new system of team playoffs	• accept change as a challenge • tackle problems with optimism
Self-management	• use a planner • earn own spending money • prepare meals	• demonstrate the need to achieve • resourceful • creative
Initiative	• found own mentor • started baby-sitting co-op	• identify untried possibilities • carry out ideas

Activity ① ·

Compiling Personal Information

Make a list of all the information that you will need to prepare a résumé and/or complete an application form.

 File the personal information you gathered in your portfolio.

· ·

Résumés
· ·

A **résumé** is a summary of your employment history, education, and accomplishments. The purpose of a résumé is to summarize aspects of your life that are relevant to an employer. It must establish a strong first impression of your background and hiring value. Having a well-constructed, well-designed résumé is vital to finding employment, as well as part- or full-time volunteer placements.

A résumé is only one or two pages in length and should be neat, concise, and complete. When preparing to write a résumé, consider your past experiences and accomplishments in terms of how they can benefit an employer. You should be able to prove every statement by using a specific, recent example. Also consider the unique advantages you can offer an employer. Your résumé must convey to the employer that you have the required knowledge, skills, and attitude to do the job both physically and mentally. Ultimately, the purpose of a résumé, like every aspect of a job search, is to help you find a job you enjoy.

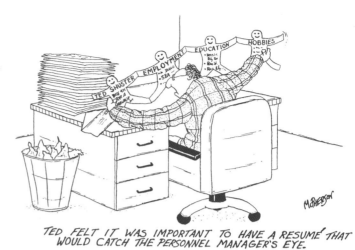

TED FELT IT WAS IMPORTANT TO HAVE A RESUMÉ THAT WOULD CATCH THE PERSONNEL MANAGER'S EYE.

Copyright © 1982 John McPherson. Reprinted from MCPHERSON GOES TO WORK.

A résumé can serve several different functions during the job-search process.

- It is an inventory of your experiences. It can help you to clarify your value as an employee and to prepare yourself for the job-search process.
- It offers a valuable summary to an employer. At a glance, a potential employer can evaluate whether you should be interviewed.
- At a job interview, it can be used as a reference for questions by the interviewer and for comments by the applicant.
- It can be used by a potential employer to review candidates who have been interviewed or it can be filed for future reference.

Employers' Pet Peeves About Résumés

- More than two pages long
- Coloured paper
- Clerical mistakes
- Handwritten corrections
- Old jobs that do not mean anything
- Repetition
- Attempts to inflate responsibilities
- Fancy graphics, unless the person is applying for a graphics position
- Poor quality paper
- A photocopy of a photocopy
- Insufficient information included to contact former employers.

What Is Your Résumé Style?

The challenge of writing a résumé is to include as much relevant information as possible in a readable, attractive format. Remember that an employer will probably spend 15 to 30 seconds reading the résumé that you spent hours putting together! Here are some guidelines for four types of résumés. Choose the one that is most appropriate for you.

- **Chronological:** Lists skills and experiences in reverse chronological order, with emphasis on relevant experiences.

- **Skills-based:** Lists skills and talents in order of importance. This form of résumé is suitable for those with little work experience.

- **Combination:** Combines elements of skills-based and chronological résumés. It begins with a skills summary and follows with a reverse chronological listing of relevant experiences. It is the most commonly used form of résumé.

- **Electronic:** Are organized as in a traditional résumé. These are gaining popularity as more employment opportunities become available on the Internet.

Writing a Résumé

Résumés are a useful part of the job search because they are an easy way to contact many people cheaply and efficiently. But using a résumé to find a job can have certain drawbacks. Consider how many résumés may be sent in response to a single job advertisement in a newspaper. If an employer receives 200 résumés in response to an ad, how much time will he or she spend reading each one? Most employers will only quickly glance at a résumé to determine the appropriateness of a candidate for a job. Therefore, your résumé must be extremely effective and appealing in order to stand out from the crowd.

When writing a résumé keep in mind that studies show that you have 15 to 30 seconds to get the reader's interest. Your goal is to encourage employers to keep reading, so give them the information that they want to know early in the document.

These guidelines will help you write a résumé.

- Use verbs that indicate action and continued growth. For example, use words such as *achieved, developed, enriched, demonstrated,* and *gained* when describing job responsibilities and skills.
- Use adjectives such as *creative, motivated, enthusiastic,* and *self-motivated* when writing about your personal traits.
- Spell out words in full; for example, use "Street" not "St." and "Telephone" not "Phone."
- Avoid using the word "I" where possible.
- Include enough relevant information to clearly demonstrate your skills and abilities without being wordy.
- Present yourself in the best possible way. For example, a job description for a sales clerk might include the following: "Developed an ability to effectively serve the public in a courteous manner."
- Ensure there are no spelling, grammar, or punctuation errors.
- Create a page with a professional, "clean" appearance. Neat margins, adequate "white space" between sections, and indentations make reading easier.
- Avoid highlighting, underlining, and italics as they are distracting. For electronic formats, these may not translate if the receiver stores them on his or her computer or sends them to another person via e-mail.
- Make sure that your address and phone number is clear and prominently placed.

IN THE NEWS

Résumé Tells Your Story, So Make It Stick

by Janis Foord Kirk

When looking for work, you communicate with employers in all sorts of obvious ways. The care you take writing your résumé and covering letters tells a tale about you; for example, the way you answer questions during interviews. But you also communicate with employers in far more subtle ways, as Paula Bass explains.

Bass, president of a Mississauga, Ontario, company, KBC Tools Inc., has been interviewing recently and writes to offer job seekers some advice. Interviews are "expensive, tedious, and time-consuming for both parties," she says. "They are not set up for the discomfort and inconvenience of the applicant, but as an opportunity for both parties to find a match that will work into the future."

Carefully target your written material, Bass advises. "Many of the résumés that deluge me are not appropriate to the position, or the stated objective is not applicable." A better approach, she says, is to offer a fairly general objective on your résumé and then, in your covering letter, discuss specifically your interest and qualifications for the job for which you are applying.

Like many employers, Bass often advertises more than one position at a time. "It would help the sorting process if candidates would specify what position they are applying for," she writes.

Faxed résumés can be difficult to read, so before faxing yours to employers, make sure it is legible by faxing a copy to yourself or a friend, she advises. These tips can help you make a positive first impression.

Yet, your "second impression" is as important, Bass believes. "When I call potential candidates, I find it amazing and disheartening that my calls are often answered by family members and roommates who seem unaware and unprepared to take a simple phone message. It is important to enlist those people answering the telephone for their support and professionalism. Having a pen and paper by the telephone would help, and should members of the household not be conversant in English, it would be more appropriate to leave a pleasant and professional message on an answering machine."

I have heard similar complaints from employers before. The search advice is clear: Once you have gone to the trouble of communicating professionally on paper and in person, make sure the telephone number you leave with employers is answered professionally as well.

1. According to Paula Bass, it is very important to "target your written material" for prospective employers. What information does she offer for the writing of objectives?

2. Write a generic objective that would be suitable for your résumé.

3. What strategies would you use to ensure that the telephone was answered in a professional way if an employer called you for an interview? What information should be recorded regarding the interview?

4. Write a script for the message that you would leave on your answering machine if you were expecting a call from a potential employer and/or a list of instructions you would leave for family members who might answer the phone.

A Combination Résumé

• **Name and Address**
Give your name, full address, and telephone number (with area code), fax number, and e-mail address at the top of your résumé.

• **Career Objective**
Give a brief, general statement about your career goal and experience.

• **Skills**
Identify any business or other skills and abilities you have gained in school, on a job, or in other situations, and any activities you have participated in that relate to the job you want.

• **Work Experience**
List your work experience, beginning with your most recent job. Include volunteer work if it relates to the job you are applying for.

• **Education**
List the schools or colleges you have attended and diplomas or degrees you have received. You may also include any subjects or programs you specialized in and any honours or awards you have received.

• **References**
If your résumé is short, you may include references. If not, say "Available on request" and be sure to bring them on a separate sheet of paper to your interview.

Bryan Wilson
183 Brock Street
North Bay, Ontario
X1X 1X1
Phone: 705-555-3434
Fax: 705-555-3435
e-mail: bwilson@hotmail.com

Career Objective
To work in the service sector with elderly people or people with disabilities.

Skills
Fluent in English, French, and Italian
Knowledgeable computer user (Mac and PC)
Strong organizational and interpersonal skills
Bookkeeping and finance experience

Work Experience

Summer 1999	Day Camp Assistant Counsellor, North Bay Parks and Recreation
Winter 1998-99	Newspaper route, *North Bay Nugget*

Education

1998-2000	Maclean Memorial High School, North Bay, Ontario

References
Available on request.

Activity ② ·

Writing a Résumé

1. Prepare your résumé in response to one of the ads in the margin on page 232 or to an ad from your local newspaper, the Internet, or a career centre.

2. Ask three classmates to assess your résumé, using a copy of the checklist on the following page.

3. Revise your résumé based on the comments you receive.

 File a copy of résumé in your portfolio.

Résumé Checklist

ITEM	CHECK IF YES	SUGGESTIONS FOR IMPROVEMENTS
Is the résumé clear? Does it provide a "picture" of the writer's qualifications?		
Is all personal information relevant to the job?		
Is all the necessary information included?		
Does the résumé include positive self-evaluation?		
Is the language clear and understandable?		
Does the résumé emphasize benefits for a potential employer?		
Does the résumé make the reader want to continue to read it?		
Is the layout appealing? Do strong points stand out?		
Do the sentences begin with action words?		
Is the résumé brief, to the point, and neat?		
Is the length appropriate?		
Is the résumé free of spelling and grammatical errors?		
If you were a potential employer, would you grant an interview based on this résumé?		

PART-TIME SALES REPRESENTATIVE OFFICE SUPPLIES

POS (Palais Office Supplies), a successful office supply company, is expanding into this region. We are seeking motivated, well-spoken young people who want to work as part of a sales team in our new store. Sales experiences not necessary. Training provided. Fax or send your résumé and references to:

POS
Attn: Sales Manager
346 Canal Street
Regina, Saskatchewan
X2X 2X2
Fax: 222-212-5151

TEAMWORK, TALENT, TECHNOLOGY IT PROGRAMMER

As a member of the development team, you thrive in an information-rich and deadline-oriented environment. You are comfortable in a variety of computer programs and are able to modify complex procedures for others. Knowledge of banking/financial/accounting principles is a definite asset.

If you want to forge a new future, we are a growth-oriented company that is prepared to meet the challenges of the 21st century. We offer a friendly and productive environment, comprehensive training, and benefits. Apply in writing to:

Human Resources
Banca Commerciale
130 York Street
Vancouver, BC
Z1Z 1Z1
Fax: 250-222-2121

Activity 3

Listing Key Words for Résumés

Action words that describe the things that you have done, such as *achieved, developed, maintained, initiated, established,* and *operated,* are valued as ways to attract the attention of a potential employer. Use as many different key words as possible to describe your skills. To develop a list of good key words for your areas of interest and expertize, scan the recruitment ads and want ads in your local newspaper. Share your list.

Completing Application Forms

An **application form** provides companies and agencies with educational and job-related information about you that indicates your suitability for employment with them. Many organizations ask you to fill out their application form "on the spot," so make sure you have your personal information with you.

Use the following guidelines to complete application forms:

• Read the whole form first. Note the structure: Do you fill in the blanks above or below the line?

• Follow the instructions carefully. Should you "Print in block form"? Are certain sections "For office use only"?

• In the Personal Data section, First Name is also called Given or Christian Name; Last Name is also called Surname.

• If a question does not apply to you, fill the space after it with a dash or N/A (meaning "not applicable") to indicate that you have read the question, not missed it.

• Be accurate. Facts can be checked.

• Focus your responses on the requirements of the employer. Stress the skills you have developed which are relevant to the job.

• Include volunteer work if it is pertinent to the job for which you are applying.

• You may be asked about Employment Preferences: position, hours, shifts, location. Know what you want ahead of time.

• If the application form asks you to indicate the pay you expect and you do not know the company's pay scale, write "negotiable," "open," or "will discuss." If the form asks you the salary you received at your previous job and you do not want to reveal it, put "going rate."

• "Are you **bondable**?" is a frequently asked question. If you are in a job where you are handling valuables, your employer will buy insurance against the loss or theft of these valuables. You, as an employee, will be bonded.

• If there is a question such as "Comment on aspects of your experience or education especially relevant to the position for which you are applying," keep the employer's needs in mind. List such assets as job-related skills, accomplishments, personal qualities, career-related memberships, workshops, awards, and/or related outside interests.

Activity 4

Completing an Application Form

The following generic application form has all the categories of information for which you will be asked when completing an application form in the workplace, whether you are applying for a paying position or a volunteer experience.

1. Look back at the personal information you collected for Activity 1. Use it to complete this form.

2. Take the completed form with you as a reference when completing an application form at a work site.

Sample Application Form

APPLICATION FOR EMPLOYMENT

Personal Data

Name (last)	(first)	(middle)

Phone No. Home	Phone No. Message

Address (street)

(city)	(province)	(postal code)

Social Insurance Number (to be added if hired)	Date Available

Position Applied For	Salary Expectation

Are you legally entitled to work in Canada?	Yes No

Would you be willing to work?   Full Time   Part Time   Shifts   Weekends   On-Call

Are you willing to relocate?   Yes   No   Are you bondable?   Yes   No

Work History

Present or Last Employer	From	To	Salary

Address	Telephone	Supervisor's Name

Position Held	Supervisor's Title

Duties

Reason for leaving

May we contact the employer?   Yes   No

Previous Employer

Address	Telephone	Supervisor's Name

Position Held	Supervisor's Title

Duties

Reason for leaving

May we contact the employer?   Yes   No

Previous Employer

Address	Telephone	Supervisor's Name

Position Held	Supervisor's Title

Duties

Reason for leaving

May we contact the employer?   Yes   No

Education

	Name and Location	Course/Program	Credits	Diploma/Degree	Dates
Elementary/Secondary					
Vocational/Trade					
College/University					
Postgraduate/Other					
Special Courses					

If you are a licensed professional or trade worker, give details:

Province Issued	Year	

Skills Profile

Word Processing	wpm	Data Entry	Shorthand	Speedwriting	Other

Do you have a valid driver's licence?   Yes   No   Class

Comment on the aspects of your experience or education especially relevant to the position for which you are applying:

References

Give names of three persons not related to you.

Name	Phone Number	Occupation/Business	Address

I hereby declare that the foregoing information is true and complete to my knowledge. I understand that a false statement may disqualify me from employment, or cause dismissal.

Signature _____   Date _____

You might wish to file a copy of this information in your portfolio.

Covering Letters

A **covering letter** is a letter that accompanies your résumé when you respond to an advertisement, follow up a job lead, or just want to indicate interest in a company. The purpose of the covering letter is to introduce yourself and your résumé and to get an interview.

A covering letter should be addressed to a specific person. If necessary, phone the company to which you are applying to find the appropriate person, such as the manager of a particular department, the manager of the human resources department, or the owner of a small business. The receptionist or the human resources department can usually give you the person's name, title, correct mailing address, and any other information you may need. If you cannot discover the name of the contact person or if you are unsure of the person's gender, begin your letter with "To Whom It May Concern" or "Dear Sir/Madam."

A covering letter should also be neatly typed, free of errors, and follow standard format. Be sure to include your name and full address, the date, the name and title of your contact person, and the full address of the company.

In the first paragraph, clearly explain your purpose for writing, which is to apply for a job. State the job for which you are applying and how you learned about the position. If you are replying to a job advertisement, explain where you saw the ad.

In the second paragraph, explain why the person should want you as an employee. Refer to your résumé, highlighting the major qualifications that relate to the position for which you are applying and how they can benefit the employer. Include any of your special experience or training.

In the concluding paragraph, express your enthusiasm and appreciation for the person's attention to your application, and request a personal interview.

Three sample covering letters appear on this and the following pages. Each is for a different situation and each will be sent with a résumé.

February 20, 20—

Mr. Chris Kavoukian
Ontario Water Research Centre
23 Lakeside Drive
Pickering, Ontario
X0X 0X0

Dear Mr. Kavoukian:

Please accept this letter and résumé as an indication of my interest in working with the Ontario Water Research Centre as a field technician.

I am very impressed with the work your division has been doing in the area of ground water management. The article that appeared in the September 18 *Valley View Herald* about your success in controlling the erosion in the Rouge River Delta area was most interesting. As a recent graduate of Valley View Collegiate Institute who has experience in field work (data collection for our local conservation authority) and an interest in pursuing environmental science as a career, I would welcome the opportunity to join your team.

Next month, I will be visiting Ontario and would be pleased to arrange a meeting with you to discuss my suitability for the position. I will call you on Tuesday, March 4 to see what date would be convenient for you. I can be reached at 519-555-1726 during the day.

Thank you for taking the time to consider my application. I look forward to speaking with you.

Sincerely,

Letter from applicant with no job lead.

June 7, 20—

Ms. Barbara Booth
New Way Book Sales
Unit 10
336 Landover Road
Cambridge, Ontario
X0X 0X0

Dear Ms. Booth:

I am writing to apply for the position of Sales Representative as advertised in the June 6 edition of *The Cambridge Chronicle*.

Your advertisement states that you are looking for someone with strong communication skills who is self-motivated and interested in learning more about the publishing business. I have recently graduated from secondary school where I specialized in entrepreneurial studies and took several business courses. As part of my school experience, I participated in a work experience program with a local publishing firm where I had a variety of responsibilities in the accounting department. I am familiar with several computer programs, including book ordering and record keeping. I am confident that both my technical and personal skills would be an asset to your company.

I look forward to hearing from you so that we may arrange a convenient time to meet and discuss my qualifications further. Thank you for your consideration.

Sincerely,

Letter in response to a job advertisement.

December 3, 20—

Ms. Fahima Virji
Customer Services Division
Computers Unlimited
2221 Shore Drive
Kingston, Ontario
X0X 0X0

Dear Ms. Virji:

Recently, I heard through William James of your department that a change in the products you are carrying has created a need for more trainers to update your customers. I would like to be considered for one of the positions and have enclosed my résumé for your consideration.

Since graduating from university, I have worked with the companies Home Office Computer Services and Computer Office Wares as a sales representative and software installation trouble shooter. My communication skills and knowledge of computer equipment and software are excellent. I am confident that the knowledge that I have gained will be of value to me at Computers Unlimited.

I would appreciate a personal interview at your earliest convenience to discuss how my skills can benefit your organization. I will call you on Monday, December 7 to arrange a suitable date. Thank you for taking the time to read my résumé.

Sincerely,

Letter from an applicant with a job lead.

Activity 5

Writing Covering Letters

1. Look through the newspaper and choose a job advertisement that appeals to you or use the samples from Activity 1 on page 232.

2. Write a covering letter to apply for this job, outlining your suitability for the position.

3. Exchange advertisements with a partner and write a covering letter for his or her advertisement.

4. Compare the similarities and differences between your covering letters.

Activity  6

Evaluating Your Covering Letter

Use the following checklist to evaluate your covering letter.

• Is it addressed to a specific person?
• Is it no more than one page long?
• Is it typed?
• Does it show pride in what you have done and what you want to do?
• Does it demonstrate energy and enthusiasm?
• Does it maintain a balance between professionalism and friendliness?
• Does it indicate where you can be reached?
• Does it refer to the requirements of the job listing (if there was one)?

Other Business Letters

You will have other letter-writing opportunities during the job search. Some examples are:

• **To people who are your references**. Outline your job search strategies, attach a copy of your résumé for their information, and thank them in advance for their help.
• **To interviewer(s) after an interview**. Thank them for their time.
• **To an employer who interviewed but did not hire you**. Request to be considered in the future.
• **To an employer who hired you**. Thank him or her.
• **To an employer who gave you an information interview**. Thank him or her and tell the person how the interview increased your knowledge and benefited you in other ways.

These letters should be written in a business-like but personal manner. Hand-writing is acceptable, but stationery should be plain.

In this sample, Chris Hood is writing to thank the YMCA Volunteer Co-ordinator for a portfolio conference and his placement experience.

Chris Hood
19 Stoney Road
Barrie, Ontario
X0X 0X0

September 7, 20—

Ms. Jodi Jackson
Volunteer Co-ordinator, YMCA
143 Main Street
Bracebridge, Ontario
0X0 X0X

Dear Ms. Jackson,

Thank you for reviewing my Career Studies Portfolio with me yesterday. Discussing the contents with you certainly has prepared me for the portfolio conference with my teacher on Tuesday. I appreciate the time you spent. I know how busy you are.

I have enjoyed my ten-week placement on the phones at the Volunteer Connection. It was an excellent opportunity for me to sharpen my communication and problem-solving skills. I also enjoyed working with the "Y" staff. I found them to be co-operative and willing to help me at all times.

I look forward to hearing from you when a part-time position becomes available. As you know, I am planning to pursue a career in public relations. "Y" experiences will be invaluable. Contact me at any time at 403-555-1234 or fax me at 403-555-1213. My e-mail address is chood@ilap.ca.

Sincerely,

Chris Hood

Chris Hood

Activity 7

Writing to an Employer

Write a letter to an employer after one of the following situations:

• You went for an interview for a part-time position with ABC Playschool. You believed that the interview went well but the employer phones you to say that she could not hire you because she has no position at a time suited to your schedule. She promises to keep your résumé, application, and interview results on file. How do you ensure this? What does your letter say?

• You have been granted an interview in a business in which one of your references is well known and respected. What could you say in a letter to this person before the interview?

• One of your neighbours not only spent time telling you about his career as a social worker but also let you visit his workplace for a day. How will you thank him?

How Employers Evaluate If You Are Right for the Job

FACT	PERCENTAGE
Find reference checks with previous bosses useful	99%
Find one-to-one interviews to be useful or very useful	98%
Held panel interviews less often	29% (always)
	55% (sometimes)
Verify education, licenses, and designations	30% (always)
	52% (sometimes)
Check character references	17% (always)
	53% (sometimes)
Use psychological vocational tests on candidates	10%
Use assessment exercises to test situational behaviour	7%
Utilize pre-employment medicals	51%
Check credit worthiness	9%
Analyze handwriting of applicants	2%

What Is an Interview?

An interview is a meeting between two or more people. Interviews can have different purposes, including occupational research interviews and job interviews. The purpose of an **occupational research interview** is to gain information about a particular job or occupation. The goal of a **job interview** is to match a job seeker to a particular job. The interviewer may consist of a single person, a few people, or even a panel of people.

A **job interview** requires an applicant to be prepared for anything, to respond to any tactic, and to cope with the outcome. Both the interviewer and the applicant influence the interaction; however, interviews do not have to be controlled by the interviewer alone. The interviewer has influence since he or she decides whether to offer the job to the applicant. But the applicant, as a potential job candidate, may have skills, experience, and attitudes that are highly desirable to the employer.

Besides assessing the applicant's suitability for the job, the interviewer also assesses how well the person handles pressure, since an interview can be quite stressful. A good interviewer will prepare an agenda for the interview in order to address concerns such as the following.
• Does the candidate have the necessary skills and experience for the position?
• Why did the candidate apply for this job at this company?
• What are the candidate's self-concept, personality, and values?
• Would the candidate be able to relate well to other employees?
The interviewer may be the owner of the organization, the manager or supervisor to whom the candidate would report if hired, or a member of the **human resources department**. In smaller companies, which create about two-thirds of all new jobs, the owner or a supervisor will likely conduct the interview. In large companies, a member of the human resources department or **personnel department**—which assists with staff concerns such as hiring, company benefits, and labour negotiations—may screen job candidates for a supervisor. In the screening process, a member of the human resources department assesses job candidates in a first round of interviews and then asks the most appropriate candidates to return for a second interview with the job supervisor.

Preparing for an Interview

Interviews can be obtained in may ways: by networking, through a co-op placement or volunteer position, by contacting people who may have positions available, or by responding to a job advertisement. Once you have obtained an interview, you must prepare for it. This preparation should include the following:

1. **Prepare a script.** Prepare a two-minute oral summary of your career goals, skills, experience, education, and strengths to present at the interview. Include examples from your past experience to back up your statements about your qualifications and suitability for the position.

2. **Know where you are going.** Be sure you know where the interview is, how long it takes to get there, and what route to take. You may even want to do a trial run in advance, especially if you are using public transit. Ideally, arrive about ten minutes early for the interview. *Never* be late.

3. **Prepare a clean copy of your résumé.** Keeping an up-to-date résumé by adding new experiences, certificates, and educational data is a practice that most people follow. For each interview, bring a clean, current copy of your résumé.

4. **Compile a list of references.** It is also important to keep a list of references ready for interviews. Inform your references of your job search progress and the company and interviewers to whom you have given their name(s). To each interview, take two or three names of relevant references.

5. **Bring a folder or briefcase and/or your portfolio.** Taking a small folder or briefcase to an interview offers you the opportunity to look professional and businesslike as well as giving you something to do with your hands if you are nervous. Some items of value from your Career Studies Portfolio could be personal information, a fresh copy of your résumé, a **letter of recommendation** from a former employer or work-experience placement supervisor, and your list of relevant references. Also include a calendar, notepad, and pen to record information or to set a date for another interview.

6. **Dress appropriately.** Your clothes should be appropriate to the work environment. For example, in a business office people typically wear more formal clothing than people who work in an automobile repair shop. Your clothes should always be clean and neat. If you are not sure what to wear, ask someone in the industry or go to a similar place of business and observe what people are wearing. You should be well-groomed, freshly bathed, and neatly dressed.

Body Language for a Job Interview

At a job interview, make sure your body language — what your body expresses about your attitude — says that you are a positive, confident person who is just right for the job.
- Walk in confidently, shake the interviewer's hand firmly, smile warmly.
- Sit down carefully, placing both feet flat on the floor.
- During the discussion, lean forward slightly, look at the interviewer, and nod appropriately.
- Look alert.

PROFILE

First Impressions Count Most

by Fiona McNair

In less than 30 seconds it is all over. A prospective employer has already decided if you are the right person for the job, warns Joanne Blake, a professional image consultant. "You have to communicate the right message and it is really serious business," she says. "After all, you invest a lot in your education but you also need to invest in the tools which will actually help you get jobs."

The information can be found in a recent study completed by the Harvard School of Business. It validates Blake's belief that personal presentation is just as important as a stellar work record or an impressive résumé. For the past few years, her company, Style for Success, has been providing image enhancement workshops for students from local colleges, individuals, and corporations. A former fashion co-ordinator with a national clothing retailer, Blake says image is the one thing that can set a job-hunter above the competition.

Additional studies have proven that 55 percent of that first impression is based on appearance and 38 percent on body language, she says. Only seven percent is based on words. She says she has even heard of a person who was eliminated from a prospective job opportunity because of poor table manners.

A tight job market and increasingly tough consumers motivated Kim Blair, a local massage therapist, to seek Blake's help one spring. No matter what outfit she wore, the former florist says she did not feel comfortable and worried it might be affecting the number of clients drawn to her home-based business. "Massage therapy often has kind of a stigma attached to it so it is better if we dress more professionally and show that we fit into the business world more," says Blair.

Blair had been introduced to Blake at a luncheon sponsored by Connecting Women, a business networking group. Immediately impressed by Blake's own appearance and polished look, Blair decided to buy an individual consultation. "My wardrobe was going in so many different directions. Nothing I had matched at all. I was dressed for business but I did not feel comfortable," says Blair.

The session began with a raid of her closet, with Blake analyzing Blair's figure type, finding her best colours, and demonstrating how to update five of her favourite outfits. It proved to be so productive that Blair decided to also hire Blake for a personal shopping trip. "Now I don't waste money. I have a list of what I need and I stay focussed. Running from this rack to that rack is a thing of the past." Cool wools, knit tops, and rayon/cotton blends that do not require ironing now fill her closet.

And the change in Blair's appearance has not gone unnoticed. She still fields many compliments about her outfits and has seen an increase in business and the number of people asking for her card. Focussing on appearance has almost become a politically incorrect thing to do, but Blair says it is still important. "It is unfortunate it is this way, but that is just the way life is. Unconsciously, people look at you and if you are not dressed up-to-date, they might worry your skills are not, either."

Barbara Thrasher, the executive director of Communicating Power, a marketing company that helps new entrepreneurs put their best foot forward, agrees that image is extremely important. "The way they represent themselves as they mature and grow as a company is vital to their success," she says.

1. What message should your appearance communicate to a prospective employer?

2. Why does image consultant Joanne Blake say that "In less than 30 seconds it is all over"?

3. List three possible job positions that could be available to you. What would you wear to each interview?

The Stages of an Interview

An interview consists of four stages—the greeting, exchange, conclusion, and parting. The greeting is the initial contact between you and the interviewer. Since first impressions can be lasting impressions, this initial contact is important. The exchange is the longest part of an interview, during which the job, the company or organization, and your experience and skills are discussed. During the exchange, practise effective non-verbal communication as well as effective listening and speaking. Remember that you are determining whether the job is right for you, just as they are determining if you are right for the job. Avoid speaking for more than two minutes when responding to a question. Try to create a feeling of trust, and express confidence in the fact that you will be hired.

The parting, or way in which you leave an interview, can affect your image as much as the greeting. Leave in a confident, positive manner. Once again, smile, make direct eye contact, and appear self-assured and friendly. Your parting statement is the last opportunity you have to promote yourself. You may say, "Thank you for your time. The position sounds very interesting, and I hope that I will be able to offer you the benefit of my skills and experience." Offer to shake hands again, and remember to say goodbye to the receptionist.

The follow-up is also an important stage in the interview process. Immediately after the interview, send a thank-you letter expressing your appreciation of the interviewer's time, and emphasizing your interest in the position.

Interview Questions

The questions asked during an interview offer you an opportunity to illustrate your ability to think clearly and to provide a picture of what you are like. The more frequently asked questions can be divided into five main types.

Get Aquainted
- Tell me about yourself.
- Describe a leadership opportunity you have had at school, in the community, or at a job.

Previous Work Experience
- How did you get along with your former co-workers?
- What three points would your fellow workers make about you?
- What would your employer say?
- Were you often absent from your last job?
- What traits do you appreciate in a supervisor?
- Describe a time when you experienced pressure on a job. How did you handle it?
- What have you done that shows initiative and willingness to work?

Education
- Which course did you like best in school? Why?
- What future educational plans do you have?

Suitability and Work Style
- Why should you be our choice to fill this position?
- What is it about this job that interests you?
- Why did you choose this career path?
- What kind of working environment do you prefer? Why?

Personality/Human Relations
- What is your greatest weakness? Strength?
- What five words describe you best?
- Describe the kind of people you like to work with.
- What would your last employer say about you?

Activity 8

Role-playing Interview Questions

1. Write your answers to the interview questions on pages 242-243.
2. Role-play an interview using the same questions.

Look back at these questions. What do they indicate about the concerns of the employer? What opportunities do they offer you to profile yourself as a future valued employee for the organization? When asked about your relationships with others, you could discuss your flexibility and your respect for the rights of others as well as your ability to work as part of a team or independently. Absenteeism is a major concern of employers. Stress your good attendance record and the importance you place on always being at work. If you were often absent from a previous job, briefly explain why and indicate that it is no longer an issue. Don't lie—a reference check to your former employer will turn up a poor attendance record or a poor working relationship with others.

When asked about strengths and weaknesses, talk about your strengths. Briefly mention a weakness, but stress its positive aspect. For example, "At times I may not respond well to too much supervision because I have lots of ideas and like to take initiative."

Find an opportunity to respond with a summary you prepared. Begin with a brief personal history and then outline your career goals, skills, experience, education, and strengths. Conclude with a positive statement about your attitude toward work.

Treat education questions with care. Perhaps the job offers an opportunity to put previous training into practice in a new setting, allows you to expand your knowledge, or presents new educational demands.

As the interview draws to a close, you will want to know when a hiring decision will be made or when a second interview may occur. Ask something like, "What is the next step in the hiring process and when do you expect to make a decision?"

Behaviour-Based Interviewing

Behaviour-based interviewing is a new interviewing trend that asks people about their past job-related behaviour and bases hiring decisions on their responses. This approach to interviewing predicts future behaviour based on past behaviour. Interviewers listen to the itnerviewee's "stories." Therefore, the more success stories you have, the more likely you are to be able to support your claims.

Companies using behaviour-based interviewing to identify the behaviours that are a part of the position they are trying to fill and then design questions to identify these behaviours. For example, if the position requires the ability to think quickly, the behaviour-based question could be "Tell me about the last time you had to think quickly to resolve a problem without your supervisor's input" or "Describe a situation that illustrates you can think quickly under pressure." All candidates are asked the same questions. You will know that you have been asked a behaviour-based question when you are asked to describe something you have done in the past. For example, "Think back to a time when . . ." or "Give me an example of a situation when . . ."

Hints for Responding to Behaviour-Based Questions

- Before the interview, think of success stories that illustrate common traits, such as leadership, initiative, goals, work ethic, teamwork, and commitment to task.
- Use real-life success stories. If you do not have work experience, refer to class projects and extra-curricular activities.
- Remember that the interviewer is interested in the process you used more than the details of your success story.

Activity 9

Practising Storytelling

Behaviour-based interviewing relies on story-telling. Practise your storytelling using the following questions. Remember to profile one of your strong traits in your answer.

- Tell me about a time when you turned a bad day into a good one.
- Give me an example of your skills in the area of time management.

- Describe a situation in which you had to give something up to help a fellow employee or classmate.
- Describe a risk you have taken.
- Tell me about a time when you proved the customer is always right.

 You may wish to file a video or audio recording of your responses in your portfolio.

JOURNAL

Reflecting on Your Past

In his book *What Color Is Your Parachute?* Richard N. Bolles says that no employer cares about your past and that what appears to be a question about your past is really about your future. Write about how the following memories from your past reflect your future.

- Your early school days
- The best advice you ever received
- Your first hero or heroine

IN THE NEWS

Competency the Key Factor in Skills Assessment

By Salem Alaton

Once upon a time, the corporate recruiter saw something in your face or manner that looked promising, and shortly thereafter you had a job. Nowadays, your expression, demeanor, and even your résumé itself hardly even comprise a starting point.

Skills assessment in corporate life has become an elaborate, considered process featuring not only a strong return to various forms of psychological testing but a host of new software programs to aid the analysis. And this screening applies, incidentally, not only to new recruits but people seeking mobility from within the corporation.

Formerly, your experience and facility with a specific function was your selling point. Now, if that function still exists, it may not within six months of your being hired.

"The big emphasis today is on competencies," says Dwight Willett, an organizational-development specialist and partner at Ernst & Young in Toronto. "Believing in the company vision is nice but ultimately the issue is how people act. The measuring stick is behaviours."

Indeed, "behavioural interviewing" is something of a buzz phrase. Like the notion of competence, this looks for an underlying fit with the needed abilities rather than a categorical match of job description. For example, a veteran manager from a sector that formerly called for quick, individual decisions may not do well in a company where teamwork and consensus are highlighted, even though the technical skills on the résumé look fine.

Rather than simply targeting the person as a senior manager in some department, the question, says Willett, becomes, "Give us a specific example of something you have done in the past that would lead you to believe you would be successful in our organization."

Willet identifies three main competency levels:

- **Skills-job competency.** The old model was to figure out how long it took to do a very specific task. Now, the person is asked things like what makes customers happy. The challenge, says Willett, is that such testing is often going on for jobs that have never been done before.
- **Organizational competency.** The current upswing in personality tests, including newly interactive-software versions where the questions branch out in certain directions according to the answers, is because at the managerial level "companies are saying they want to see a predictor of success," Willett says. "But one thing those tools cannot predict is the ability for people to interrelate."
- **Universal competence.** This is largely about a fit with the organization's values. "When senior people do not fit, it often revolves around the corporate culture they have come from, the universal competence level," Willett says. This competence is still largely looked for in the interview process, where the object is to find that the person has worked well in a similar context at some point.

Interviews and tests will only go so far, of course. For lower-level positions, some companies opt to give the candidate some training and then allow them a set amount of time in the job to show how they can handle the tasks. If they do not work out, they are let go. Willett notes, however, that this is an approach that will not work in a union context or where a senior position is involved.

There are important incentives to hire right the first time, believes Rebecca Richards, company director and manager in human resources for the Fifth Option Outsourcing Inc. in Vancouver. Like Willett and many professionals in the field, Richards also puts some emphasis on the use of "behaviour description" questions that focus on getting information about actual events in which the candidate did the kinds of tasks he or she is now being potentially hired to fill.

The bottom line is to get somebody great in several senses and to move fast in doing it. "The change [in business life] is so rapid today you really do need multifunctional people," says Richards, currently immersed in preparing training programs for small-business clients. "We just grab the [new recruits at the] top of the bell curve if we can for a junior spot."

1. What is behavioural interviewing?

2. Give a specific example of how you would respond to Dwight Willett's interview question.

3. Why is it important to hire the right person for the job the first time?

4. Is it possible to use your past performance to predict your future performance? Support your answer.

PORTFOLIO

Completing an Interview Checklist

After an interview, use this checklist to evaluate your progress.

Before the interview, I . . .
❑ arrived slightly early.
❑ was courteous to the receptionist.
❑ had my résumé and other necessary items.
❑ dressed appropriately and was well-groomed.

During the greeting, I . . .
❑ used the interviewer's name.
❑ shook hands firmly.
❑ waited to be invited to sit.

During the interview, I . . .
❑ sat up straight and appeared self-assured.
❑ maintained eye contact.
❑ used a pleasant tone of voice.

❑ used expressive, fluent speech.
❑ showed knowledge of, and interest in, the company.
❑ explained my work experience briefly and clearly.
❑ asked pertinent questions about the company.
❑ asked for clarification about the job.
❑ demonstrated a confident, positive attitude.

Following the interview, I . . .
❑ left suitable paperwork (résumé, reference list, and/or application form).
❑ hanked the interviewer and shook hands firmly.
❑ was courteous to the receptionist.

Following Up on an Interview

Following up on details is critical in the job search. It is important to keep all the participants (former employers, references, and family) informed of the progress of your job search. It is also important to write a follow-up letter. It reminds the interviewer about you, and offers you an opportunity to make a positive comment about the job opening and the company. Taking care of the details demonstrates that your are organized.

Looking Back

1. List the details that are important in the job-search process.

2. List the ways in which letters are used during the job-search process.

3. What is the role of an S.I.N.?

4. Outline the three suggestions that you think are most useful to keep in mind during an interview.

EXPLORATIONS

Reflections

Think about the part of the job-search process that is most challenging for you. Record this aspect and list three ways that you can respond to the challenge.

Goals

How could the contents of this chapter help you to move toward your goal of finding a part-time job?

Action!

Create a scenario in which you are interviewing three of your classmates for a volunteer placement as an after-school receptionist at the local recreation centre.

Featuring. . .

Editorial: Write an editorial that proposes finding a job is easy and requires no skill and/or organization on the job seeker's part.

Advice Column: Keeping calm and focussed during an interview is not easy. Write a letter of advice for a friend to read just before an important interview.

Advertisement: Create an advertisement for a student support group that will meet to help one another with their summer job search.

Research: Look in the help wanted ads in the business section of your local newspaper for key words that would guide readers in the job-search process. Clip ads that give valuable information.

Personal Story/Interview: Interview three adults about their job-search process as young people. Find out which of the job-search tools they used and which ones they found valuable.

Managing Your Money

What You Will Learn

- How to set up a personal budget.
- How to set financial goals.
- How to save and invest money.
- About financial institutions.

Key Terms

budget	The Rule of 72
income	compound interest
expenses	savings account
net income	interest
the ten percent rule	stock market
taxes	General Investment Certificate (GIC)
inflation	shares
real rate of return	shareholders
	Canada Savings Bond (CSB)

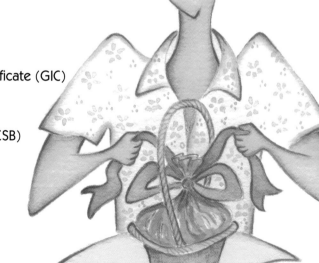

Budgeting

Your behaviours and experiences in the past influence the present. Developing goals and action plans today will impact tremendously on your future lifestyle or standard of living. This is true for personal growth, education, career success, and financial security.

Planning how to spend, save, and invest your money directly affects your lifestyle. Planning is done to ensure that the amount of money you have goes as far as possible. Investing for your future can reduce worry as you get older and wonder what your lifestyle will be like when you stop working. People who handle money wisely usually feel less stress than those who do not. Setting goals concerning how you would like to live is directly linked to your financial situation and how you handle it. Being realistic about what you can afford will keep you out of debt, which is a stressful situation if it gets out of control. If you like to travel, then you can plan how to save enough money to allow you to do that.

© Lynn Johnston Productions Inc./Dist. by United Feature Syndicate, Inc.

Setting a **budget** is more than listing your **income**— how much money you earn in a month from such sources as part-time work, allowance, or special projects (cutting the lawn, babysitting, delivering flyers)— and **expenses**—how much money you spend each month. It involves planning. For example, if you would like more money to spend each month, you have to examine which expenses are essential and which ones could be adjusted. The following is a list of expenses to consider:

• food (lunches, snacks, dinners)
• transportation (bus, car, car insurance, gas, repairs)
• clothing
• entertainment
• books, magazines, CDs, videos
• prescriptions, vitamins, shampoo, hair gel or mousse, razor blades
• school supplies, excursions

For example, you have to spend money to get to school, but you may not need to buy your lunch every day.

You also have to decide what you want to do with your **net income**— the money left over after you have subtracted your expenses. Are you saving for clothing, a car, or a trip? Are you responsible for all your expenses or does your family pay for some? You must decide what you need compared to what you want.

Below is a sample budget that shows how a student named Gillian noted her income, expenses, and net income.

Gillian's Personal Budget for January

INCOME	ESTIMATED INCOME	ACTUAL INCOME
Part-time job	$ 300	$ 300
Snow shovelling	$ 50	$ 75
Total Income	**$350**	**$375**
EXPENSES	**ESTIMATED EXPENSES**	**ACTUAL EXPENSES**
Bus tickets	$ 25	$ 20
School lunches	$ 40	$ 45
Entertainment		
Movies	$ 17	0
Dance clubs	$ 20	$ 30
Concert tickets	$ 60	$ 60
Clothes	$ 75	$ 75
Personal hygiene	$ 20	$ 10
Haircut	0	0
Birthday gifts	$ 15	$ 15
Total Expenses	**$272**	**$255**
Net Income	**$ 78**	**$120**

Activity 1

Creating a Budget

Find out what you earn, what you spend, and what you have left over. If you have already set up a budget, examine it in case changes have to be made. To create a budget, follow this formula.

Total (Gross) Income – Total Expenses = Net Income

To determine your total income, list all your sources of income on a weekly or monthly basis.

To arrive at your total expenses, list all the expenses you incurred in an average week or month. Subtract your total expenses from you total income to find you net income. To test the accuracy of your budget, keep a daily log for several weeks in which you list everything you spend your money on as well as every source of income. Are you satisfied with your net income?

 You may wish to file a copy of your budget and daily log in your portfolio.

Activity 2

Increasing Your Net Income

Examine your income and expenses from Activity 1. With a partner, compare your budgets. Share you ideas on how to increase your net income. Rework your budgets to try and increase your net income.

PROFILE

● ●

Researcher Probes Attitudes of Today's Free-Spending Teens

By Paul Brent

They number an impressive 2.4 million, spend an estimated $14 billion annually, and nobody claims to understand them. Not even their parents. On a Tuesday night, a group of researchers brought four teenagers together to out-do their parents and fathom the unfathomable, a few kids at a time. The teens: Ryan, 17, a host of a YTV program; Kathryn, 18, thin, stylish, and quickly identified as a "java junkie"; Zack, 18, quiet and decidedly non-trendy; and Sydney, 17, a "raver" from her hooded jacket to her *de rigeur* "fat pants." They had assembled to discuss everything from fashion, music, and fast food to banks.

The four nibble on candy and chips and gulp Pepsi as a moderator encourages them to talk about their lifestyles, likes, and dislikes. Asked about CDs, Kathryn says she uses Internet music exchanger, Napster, and no longer buys CDs—"a record company executive's nightmare," an executive with Toronto research firm Youth Culture explains from the client viewing room.

Getting inside the heads of today's teens, those at the forefront of the huge Echo Generation and the offspring of that other famous demographic bulge, the Baby Boom Generation, is a must for advertisers today. While the setup here is typical—four kids in front of a tripod-mounted camera while the researchers lurk in another room—ßthe situation is not. The whole exercise is being done for a reporter's benefit, not a client's. And the Toronto research firm Youth Culture admits the four were selected because they are bright and articulate "early adopters," rather than for any suitability for the topics at hand.

Early in the session it becomes clear the group isn't perfect. The girls quickly dominate the discussion on fashion and their favourite

Youth Culture conducts research on-teens for corporations.

brands—Nike, Tommy Hilfiger, the Gap chain, and Paracuso jeans are cool, Levis are not. The boys slouch. Zack, peering from beneath a well-worn baseball cap, proclaims he doesn't believe in fashion. He tugs at a plaid shirt he says he wears most of the week.

Ryan says he has traded in bell bottoms and an Afro for the preppy look, then claims he shops at the Bay and Eddie Bauer and isn't much into clothes either. "Look at those shoes!" scoffs Patrick Thoburn, a Youth Culture partner, noting Ryan's Clark loafers sell for about $150 a pair.

Kathryn takes off her ten-centimetre soled shoes/moon boots to tuck her feet under her legs. When the talk turns to her, she holds one up and states they cost her $180. "It's really hard to walk," she admits, adding she has fallen over in them a number of times. Sydney wears $126 running/walking shoes that are part of the all-night rave uniform.

When the talk turns to banks, it seems the chartered money changers are as unpopular with teens as with adults, if for different reasons. "I don't like banks," says Sydney. "They ignore me and give me dirty looks. Just give me attitude."

Such statements, captured on videotape, are golden for Doug Steward, Youth Culture founder and main owner. "This is a standard response," he said, noting 86 percent of kids have a bank account by the age of 17 and most of the banks are doing little, if anything, to develop loyalty among this group.

The pitfalls of neglecting the youth market can be seen by the falling sales of Levi Strauss, tagged as a maker of clothes for moms and dads by Echo kids. "We're trying to help them rebuild the brand," says Mr. Thoburn of the jean maker. "Levi didn't begin to re-invest in youth quickly enough, essentially."

While there are a number of companies conducting research on teens and their younger Echo cohorts, Youth Culture claims it is different because it focusses exclusively on the under-20 group. Certainly the young staff have more in common with the kids they investigate than Canada's aging executive class. Mr. Stewart, 31, started the firm as a teen magazine at the age of 24 after dropping out of university. That quickly turned into a research-focussed business as corporations demanded insights into the mysterious

youth market. Now the 14-person firm is opening an office in Montréal and has plans for sites in New York and Los Angeles within a year.

1. **State your reaction to the following statements about teenagers:**

- **"Nobody claims to understand them. Not even their parents."**

- **They spend "$14 billion annually."**

- **Banks "ignore me and give me dirty looks. Just give me attitude."**

2. **What does the company Youth Culture do? Why is it considered to be unique?**

3. **What happened to Levi Strauss when it neglected the youth market?**

4. **How do you contribute to the Echo Generation's profile?**

Planning to Save

Have you heard of **the ten percent rule**? Sound financial management includes saving ten percent of your income for both short-term and long-term goals. Short-term goals could include saving for clothing, CDs, presents for others, school supplies, and trips. Long-term goals could include saving for post-secondary education, and/or for money to enable you to live away from home.

A c t i v i t y ③

Planning for Short-Term Savings

1. Examine your budget from Activity 2. From your gross income, subtract ten percent, then subtract your expenses.

2. List your short-term savings goals. How long will it take you to save up for each item?

3. Develop an action plan to attain your goal. To do this, find out the cost of the item, then

divide it by how much you want to save every month for that item. For example, you want to buy a computer. It will cost you $2000. You are able to save $200 a month. In ten months, you will be able to purchase a computer!

 You may wish to file a copy of your budget in your portfolio.

CASE STUDY

Money Mentality

By Jade Hemeon

Do you know your personality type when it comes to money? Take a look at your deepest feelings and whether you regard money as filthy or clean. The way you feel will have a big impact on your life and relationships. That is the opinion of Olivia Mellan, a Washington, D.C. psychotherapist and author, whose views are part of a booklet published by mutual fund firm Trimark Investment Management.

Mellan has defined a handful of money types, including hoarder, spender, monk, avoider, amasser, and worrier. Most of us will lean toward one of these money types, she says. But if your feelings about money do not bother you or others, you are probably reasonably well-balanced.

Below is a description of the money types and ways to change this personality, according to Mellan.

Changing Your Money Personality

MONEY TYPE	SOLUTION
Hoarder You like to save money, prioritize your goals, have a budget, and review it periodically. You have a hard time spending money on yourself and view spending money on entertainment, vacations, and clothing as unnecessary expenses. You invest money for future security.	• Spend money on some frivolous gift for yourself. • Refrain from looking at or reworking your budget for a week and see how that feels.
Spender You buy yourself goods and services for your immediate pleasure and like buying gifts for others. It is difficult for you to save enough money for future purchases and long-term financial goals. You spend most or all the money you earn and might be in debt. You hate making budgets and sticking to them.	• Put $20 into your savings account. • Refrain from going on shopping binges.
Monk You view money as dirty and bad. You think having too much money will corrupt you. You identify with people who have little money. You would avoid investing money as it might make you wealthier, and prefer socially responsible investments.	• Buy something you have wanted for a while and notice how you feel about that act of "selfish pleasure." • Make a list of ways to use money that include giving to others and to yourself.
Avoider You avoid making a budget or keeping any kind of financial record. You do not know how much money you have, owe, or spend. You avoid investing money because it seems like too much trouble. You feel incompetent or overwhelmed when faced with money tasks.	• Keep track of where you spend your money. • Pay any outstanding debts and balance your chequebook.
Amasser You are happiest when you have large amounts of money to spend, save, and/or invest. You equate money with self-worth and power, so lack of money might lead to feelings of failure or depression. You look for investments with high rates of return to make as much money as soon as possible. You enjoy making your own financial decisions.	• Engage in activities that do not involve money at all, such as going to a museum or packing a lunch and eating it in the park.

Attitudes to money are formed early and influenced by childhood experiences, psychologists say. While growing up, you see how family members relate to money, and form an opinion about what it may be like to be rich or poor and the link between success and money.

Toronto-based therapist Rhonda Katz says we are bombarded by media messages on saving, investing, and getting rich, and money is a big part of our consciousness. "People have become more anxious about money, but at the same time they have more wisdom," she says. "People today, including young people, have more information. I wish I had understood compound interest when I was young."

Your generosity, fear, and guilt about money can be learned young. Most people have also absorbed negative messages about not having money. Emotions, however, can impede a well-thought-out financial strategy. "By acknowledging and understanding the emotions you associate with money, you can set clearer goals and make better financial decisions," Katz says.

1. What money type are you?

2. What is your first reaction to the solution(s) suggested?

3. Devise some strategies to enable you to follow the recommended solution(s).

4. What other solutions could be used? Share your strategies with other members of the class to broaden the possibilities.

Using Technology Wisely

When you opened your bank account, the bank probably issued you a bank card to be used with automatic teller machines (ATMs). You are given or select a personal identification number (PIN) that enables you to withdraw or deposit money into your account or to transfer funds from one account to another. You are not limited to using only your bank's machine but you can access your money from any automatic teller machine. The accessibility you have to your money has both advantages and disadvantages.

Activity 4

Using Bank Technology

1. Create a chart that outlines the advantages and disadvantages of ATMs.

2. Where can your card be used, other than at an ATM?

Maximizing Your Savings

You work hard for your money and it is only right that you should expect your money to work hard for you! You want your saved money to earn the highest rate of interest.

Before you examine the variety of ways in which you can save money, you need to briefly explore the affect of **taxes** and **inflation**. Taxes are money deducted from paycheques and given to the provincial and federal governments to pay for the cost of running the governments. Inflation is the rate at which the price of items, and thus the cost of living, increases. Inflation cuts into and reduces your buying power on an ongoing basis. It generates comments like "Money does not go as far as it used to" or "I remember when ice-cream cones cost ten cents!"

Canadians are among the most heavily taxed people in the world. There is a trend that shows personal income is consumed by an increasing percentage of tax. You have to save more to have enough money after taxes. The following diagram demonstrates that taxes have increased dramatically since 1961. This means having less money to spend on the other items. Taxes decrease your ability to spend more money on shelter, clothing, and other essentials. In other words, it affects your buying power.

Expenses Paid by Average Canadian Home Per Dollar

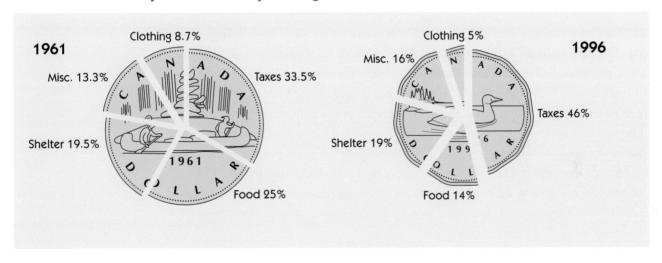

With taxes and inflation increasing, it becomes extremely important that the ten percent you save should be put where it earns the most money possible. Your **real rate of return** is what you make after taxes and inflation. You must take into account that the money you invest is taxed and that the money you put away for saving loses its buying power on an annual basis due to inflation.

Comparing Real Rates of Return

MONEY SAVED IS INVESTED AT 4%		MONEY SAVED IS INVESTED AT 16%	
Taxes (at 50%)	–2%	Taxes (at 50%)	–8%
Inflation (current)	–2%	Inflation (current)	–2%
Real rate of return	0%	Real rate of return	6%

Another way to demonstrate the importance of getting your money to work hard on your behalf is **The Rule of 72.**

The Rule of 72
Do you want to know how long it will take to double your money? Just divide 72 by your investment rate of return. For example, if your money is earning a real rate of return of 12 percent, you will double your money in $72 \div 12\% = 6$ years.

Applying The Rule of 72

Calculate how long it will take to double your money using the following rates of return: 4, 6, and 16 percent. Obviously, the higher the rate of return, the more dramatic the impact is on your savings.

The Magic of Compounding

Another money-saving tool available to you is the magic of compounding, or the effect **compound interest** has on the growth of your money. If you choose a **savings account** in which to save your money, the **interest** is the percentage of money your bank pays you for letting them use or invest your money while it is in their bank. The amount you earn is added to your original investment. The interest is then calculated on the new amount. This is the compound component of compound interest. This will also impact the growth of your money.

To see the effects of compound interest, study the following graph. The longer you are able to keep your money in a savings program, the greater the benefits from compound interest. Once again, the higher the rate of interest, the more your money earns for you.

The Magic of Compounding

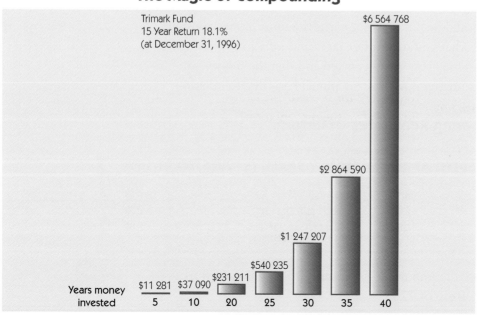

Trimark Fund
15 Year Return 18.1%
(at December 31, 1996)

IN THE NEWS

There's Something About Money: Teens Love It

By Ellen Roseman

It's not often I tell bankers they're dong a great job. But I have to compliment the Canadian Bankers Association on its cleverly conceived new educational program for teenagers, There's Something About Money.

Launched [in April 1999], There's Something About Money is aimed at students in the last years of high school. The program is intended to help the students understand the financial basics, such as savings, budgeting, and credit, before embarking on post-secondary education and working life.

Charles [my 18-year-old son], who's taking an economics course at Northern Secondary School, feels he learned more about the economy by going through the web site. In particular, he liked a section called What Impacts The Loonie, which helped him understand that currency fluctuations are not completely random. He also enjoyed the Pop Quiz, though he scored a middling 5 out of 10.

"I thought I knew about money, but I learned all about compound interest and how if you take a cash advance on your credit card, the interest accumulates right away. I also learned about RRSPs," he said. "They don't talk down to you, but talk to your level. And there are no big words to complicate things."

To improve the site, he suggests the bankers association build in more interactivity and put up a message board for comments. And, please, he asks, give us some information on the U.S. economy and how it differs from the Canadian economy.

Charles didn't see the 75-minute presentation and slide show that is given free on request to high school classes. About 800 bankers are trained to give the seminars as a voluntary effort on their own time. When asked to evaluate the presentation, 87 percent of students at high schools in Woodbridge, King City, Stouffville, Richmond Hill, Hamilton, and Sarnia said the content was very good to excellent.

Were they preparing for their financial futures before the presentation? Half said no. Did the students feel better equipped to prepare for their financial futures after the presentation? The vast majority (95 percent) said yes. What was the most important information the students walked away with? Most said it was learning how credit works and how easily you can destroy your credit rating.

An interesting result: 36 percent of students said they saw themselves starting their own business in ten years.

To lighten up an often dull subject, the bankers use clips from popular Canadian TV shows such as *Street Cents* and *Dawson's Creek* in the presentations. Students often mention the clips as a highlight. About 3000 youths have seen the seminars since they began in October. The web site has had 1.2 million hits and the average user stays for 22 minutes. "We're very pleased," says Anne Wettlaufer, director of public affairs for the bankers association.

1. Do you think the web site, There's Something About Money, was a good idea? Why or why not?

2. Would you use the web site? What would you like to find out?

3. Were you surprised by any of the student responses to the Canadian Bankers Association's school presentation? Which ones and why?

4. Are you interested in having the Canadian Bankers Association come to your school for a presentation? What steps will you take to make this happen?

Investment and Saving Options

There are many ways to save money and to earn interest on that money. The rate of interest your money earns can vary depending on which option you choose. You may choose a savings account at a bank that earns 4 percent. This option is very safe, since you are guaranteed that percentage rate. Investing your money in the **stock market** could earn you an interest rate of 30 percent, but there is no guarantee the stock would earn that. It is riskier than a savings account, but the difference in interest rate will dramatically impact on your money! Here are a variety of options.

Financial Institutions

All banks, trust companies, and credit unions have a wide variety of ways to help you earn interest on your money. They vary from simple savings accounts to Guaranteed Investment Certificates (GICs) and Canada Savings Bonds (CSBs) to investment portfolios.

A **General Investment Certificate** pays a higher interest rate than a savings account. You purchase a GIC for a specific length of time and cannot touch the money until that time is up. With a savings account you can withdraw your money at any time. Like a savings account, however, the rate of return is guaranteed by the financial institution.

Canada Savings Bonds (CSBs) can also be purchased at financial institutions. A CSB is issued by the Federal Government. Each bond costs a certain amount of money. The government guarantees the interest you will earn. The money you invest in bonds is used by the federal government to help them operate.

Activity 6

Researching Financial Institutions

1. Divide into groups of three or four. Select one financial institution for each group to research. By talking to the managers or by visiting the banks' web sites on the Internet, make a thorough list of what they offer their customers—types of accounts, GICs, CSBs, and Investment Portfolios. Collect any published materials, brochures, and software programs available. Give a description of each plan. Specifically, compare the rates of interest for each option. Are there additional charges the client must pay for participating? Outline the level of risk involved.

2. As a class, do a comparison of each institution. Compare the variety of plans offered, rates of interest, and the service costs. The business section of your local newspaper may have a comparison chart that you can use.

3. From the work the class has done, which institution would you prefer to use? Why?

 You may wish to file a copy of the class comparison in your portfolio.

The Stock Market

To raise money, a corporation sells **shares** to individuals. A share represents a piece of ownership of that corporation. The public can buy these shares and thus become partial owners, called **shareholders**, of the company. With bank accounts and bonds, you are a lender of money. A bank or government borrows your money. Because you are a lender, you are promised your money back at a guaranteed rate of interest. With shares, you become an owner. This enables you to share in the profits and success of the company. It also means that you share in its losses.

Prices for a share vary. You want the shares you purchase today to continuously increase in value, enabling you to make money on the shares if you decide to sell them later at a higher price than the purchase price. You may have heard the phrase "buy low and sell high." The expertise in "playing the stock market" depends on knowing what and when to buy and then when to sell. You have to study the companies who are selling shares and predict which companies will do well and thus increase the value of your share(s).

People who predict well and sell at the right time are known to "make a killing" and those who do not are often known to "lose their shirt." Before you decide to invest your money in stocks, you have to determine how great a risk-taker you are. You could lose all your money or you could earn a lot of money!

Mutual Funds

To reduce the risk involved in playing the stock market individually, many people contribute their money to a mutual fund that is managed by professional financial planners—experts on where to invest the money in the mutual fund. A **mutual fund** is a pool of money from different people that is invested in a variety of ways. The diagram at right demonstrates how mutual funds work.

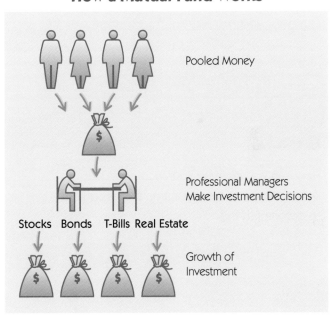

How a Mutual Fund Works

Pooled Money

Professional Managers Make Investment Decisions

Stocks   Bonds   T-Bills   Real Estate

Growth of Investment

A c t i v i t y ⑦ •

Talking With a Financial Planner

Invite a financial planner to speak to your class. Ask the planner about ways to invest money. What is best for your age group? How can you get started? As a class, develop a list of questions you would like to have answered. Also include questions about the career of being a financial planner, such as what education is required or what a typical day is like.

Looking Back

1. Explain the advantages of setting up a budget and sticking to it.

2. What is the Rule of 72?

3. What is the Magic of Compounding?

4. How do mutual funds work?

EXPLORATIONS

Reflections

What is the value of work? Does it change as you grow older?

Goals

How can you increase your income? Determine the goals and action steps required to accomplish this.

Action!

In your group, act out different scenes involving an interview with a bank manager or financial planner. What advice would they give to a young person wanting to save money?

Featuring. . .

Advice Column: Write columns that advise young people on how to earn money, set up a budget, and save money.

Advertisement: Create ads for a financial institution that has a terrific savings plan for students.

Research: Research the spending and saving habits of teenagers across Canada. You might wish to contact the Canadian Bankers' Association or the CBC television program *Street Cents* web site.

Editorial: Write an editorial on "Mutual Funds are the way to save."

Personal Story/Interview: Interview an adult or senior citizen asking them to reflect on how technology has affected doing business with banks and other financial institutions.

Photo Credits

....

page 20 Dick Hemingway; **page 22** Canapress Photo Service; **page 27** *The Toronto Star*/B. Spremo; **pages 28, 29** Dick Hemingway; **Page 30** COMSTOCK; **page 31** Canapress Photo Service/Andrew Vaughan; **page 53** COMSTOCK; **page 58** Photo by Vendula Ralkova, courtesy of *Career Paths* Newspaper; **pages 63, 77,** Dick Hemingway; **page 71** *The Toronto Star*/R. Lautens; **page 75** Jose L. Peláez/First Light; **pages 89, 90** Dick Hemingway; **page 91** Canapress Photo Service; **page 95** *The Toronto Star*/B. Dexter; **page 102** Dick Hemingway (top and bottom left), Sue Ogrocki/Reuters/Archive Photos (top right), Canapress Photo Service (bottom right); **page 113** Photography by Rich Chard; **page 116** Masterfile/Garry Black; **page 129** Chris Schwarz/*Maclean's*; **page 131** *The Toronto Star*/C. McConnell; **page 132** Reprinted by permission of Sara Beaudry, National Native Role Model Program; **page 134** Peter Bregg/*Maclean's*; **page 135** Todd Korol; **page 143** Stuart Davis/*The Province*; **page 144** *The Toronto Star*/S. Russell; **page 144** Courtesy of Jenna Huberty; **page 153** Reprinted by permission of the Pathfinder Learning Centre, Port au Port West, Newfoundland; **page 156** *The Toronto Star*/P. Irish; **page 159** Bayne Stanley; **page 169** *The Toronto Star*/P. Irish; **page 173** COMSTOCK; **page 190** *The Toronto Star*/R. Lautens; **page 201** Dick Hemingway; **page 207** *The Toronto Star*/T. Bock; **page 251** COMSTOCK

Text Credits

....

p. 7	"Personal Profile" The *Career and Life Planning Portfolio* was designed and produced by Junior Achievement of Toronto and York Region in co-operation with the Scarborough Board of Education to assist students to be self-sufficient.
p. 7	"Career Plan Update" Reproduced from the *Career Planning Portfolio* and developed by the North York Board of Education. Copyright © 1995 North York Board of Education. Permission granted.
p. 19	"Teenagers' Values Across Canada" From *The Emerging Generation* by Reginald Bibby and Donald Posterski, 1985. Reprinted by permission of Stoddart Publishing Co. Limited.
p. 24	Reprinted by permission from The Globe and Mail
pp. 32-33, 36-40	"Identifying a Person's Intelligence" and "Learning Styles" Excerpted from *Psychology for Kids* by Jonni Kincher, © 1995, 1990 with permission from Free Spirit Publishing Inc., Minneapolis, MN. Telephone 1-800-735-7323. ALL RIGHTS RESERVED.
pp. 33-35	"Personality Type" True Colors, created by Don Lowry © 1992 and adapted for this book by Diana Ketterman, Ph.D., co-author of ESI's True Colors ClassRunner. True Colors ® is a registered trademark of True Colors Inc. For further information on True Colors and Career Education contact Education Systems International (ESI) at 2875 Sampson Avenue, Corona, CA 91719. Telephone 1-800-422-4686.
pp. 45-46	"Animals of the Workplace" Reprinted by permission of *The Kansas City Star*.
p. 50	"The Phases of Transition" Reprinted by permission of Crisp Publications, Inc., 1200 Hamilton Crt., Menlo Park, CA 94025 USA
p. 58	Reprinted with permission from *Career Paths* 1996, published by YES Canada — BC and funded by Human Resources Development Canada and the BC Ministry of Education, Skills and Training. For more information, Phone: (604) 435-1937, FAX: (604) 435-5548, E-mail: editor@careerpathsonline.com, Website: http://careerpathsonline.com
p. 59	"You're Allowed" From *You're Allowed To Be Happy!* by Barry Davis published by Octopus Publishing

Group (NZ) Ltd. ISBN 0-86863-897-8. Reprinted by permission of the author.

pp. 67-69   "Building Your Work Skills in School"
Adapted from Canada Career Information Partnership and *Canada Prospects*, 1996-97.

p. 79   "Describing Expectations"
Reprinted with permission from *Ages 12 Through 15: The Years of Transition* published by the Ontario Public School Teachers' Federation.

p. 94   "What Is Out There?"
Adapted from Canada Career Information Partnership, *Canada Prospects* and *Ontario Prospects*, 1996.

pp. 95-96   Reprinted with permission – The Toronto Star Syndicate

pp. 103, 104-105   "Career Clusters" and "Playing the Job Trek Game"
Adapted from Canada Career Information Partnership, *Canada Prospects* and *Ontario Prospects*, Spring 1995.

pp. 111-112   "Occupation Summary"
David Chevreau, Magee Secondary School

p. 113   "Personal Career Profile Form"
Adapted from *Succeeding in the World of Work*, 6th Edition, by Grady Kimbrell and Ben Vineyard. Copyright © 1998 Glencoe/ McGraw-Hill. Reprinted by permission.

p. 116   Canada Career Consortium

pp. 117-118   "Today's Facts, Tomorrow's Possibilities"
Adapted from Canada Career Information Partnership, *Canada Prospects* and *Ontario Prospects*, Spring 1995.

pp. 118-119   "One Hundred Best Careers for the Twenty-First Century"
Excerpted with permission of Macmillan General Reference, a Simon & Schuster Macmillan Company, from *100 Best Careers for the 21st Century* by Shelly Field. An Arco Book. Copyright © 1996 by Shelly Field.

pp. 119-120   "New Ways to Work"
Alberta Advanced Education & Career Development.

pp. 120-121   "Normal Workers Are Minority"
Reprinted with permission from *The Globe and Mail*.

p. 121   "Canadian Work Patterns"
Courtesy of Human Resources Development Canada. Reproduced with the permission of the Minister of Public Works and Government Services Canada, 1997.

p. 125   "Job Trends"
Adapted from *Where the Jobs Are: Career Survival for Canadians in the New Global Economy* by Colin Campbell. Published by Macfarlane Walter & Ross, Toronto, 1994.

p. 131   Reprinted by permission – The Toronto Star Syndicate

pp. 135-136   Reprinted with permission from The Globe and Mail

pp. 136-137   *Professionally Speaking* published by the Ontario College of Teachers

p. 144   "The YMCA's Black Achievers"
Reprinted with permission — The Toronto Star Syndicate

p. 169   Reprinted with permission – The Toronto Star Syndicate

p. 171   Reprinted with permission – The Toronto Star Syndicate

p. 173   Reprinted with permission of Vesta Giles

pp. 174-175   "The Know-Want-Learn Chart" and "My Response to Volunteering"
Reprinted with permission from *Ages 12 Through 15: The Years of Transition* published by the Ontario Public School Teachers' Federation.

p. 178   "Employability Skills 2000+ (Ottawa: The Conference Board of Canada, 2000).

p. 181   Reprinted with permission from The Globe and Mail

p. 190   Reprinted with permission – The Toronto Star Syndicate

p. 192   "The Conflict Cycle"
Copyright © 1987 The Community Board Program, Inc.

p. 197   "Occupations Requiring Safety Equipment"
From *Expanding Your Horizons: A Career Guide* by Judi Misener. Copyright © 1993 McGraw-Hill Ryerson.

p. 198   "Top Five Causes of Injury to Young Workers," "Regulating Health and Safety in the

Glossary

Accountability   To accept responsibility for a job done well or a mistake.

Action Plans   Steps to take to achieve goals.

Active Listening   Focussing on the message, observing non-verbal communication, and seeking to understand the message.

Alternative Education Programs   Education programs that differ from traditional schooling, such as enrichment programs, flexible scheduling, and/or schools without formal classes.

Application Form   A form that provides companies and agencies with educational and job-related information about a job applicant.

Apprentice   A person being trained on-the-job by a qualified supervisor.

Aptitudes   Natural talents and abilities.

Assessment   Reflecting on information about your growth and development that you have gathered for your portfolio from a variety of sources.

Attitudes   How a person views things.

Auditory Learners   People who learn best by listening.

Autobiography   The story of a person's life, told by that person.

Bondable   An employee who handles valuables on the job must be able to be insured by the employer against loss or theft.

Budget   Planning what to do with money.

Canada Savings Bond (CSB)   A bond purchased from the government for a certain amount of money that has a guaranteed interest.

Career   A way of making a living, usually in a particular field of work. Can be categorized in four main areas, or clusters, namely Communication and the Arts; Engineering, Industrial, and Scientific Technology; Health, Human, and Public Services; and Business and Marketing.

Career Goals   Goals set once you have determined what occupation you wish to pursue and how to pursue it.

Career Plan   A plan you develop using short-term and long-term goals to attain your career goals.

Certification   A certificate proving that a person has achieved a course of study or a qualification.

Characteristics   Special qualities or features.

Cluster   Group.

Communication Barrier   When the true intent of a message is blocked in some way.

Community   A group of people living in the same place under the same laws.

Community Involvement In Ontario, students must complete forty hours of community volunteer work outside of school hours to graduate from high school.

Compound Interest A percentage of money the bank pays a person for letting them use, or invest, that person's money. It grows, or compounds, monthly.

Compulsory Something that must be completed, such as credits that must be completed to graduate with a high school diploma.

Conflict Resolution A problem-solving strategy for settling disputes.

Content Index A computer search service that looks for search terms in its index then provides the user with web sites containing those search terms.

Co-operative Education An education program that offers, or combines, work experience with regular classes.

Correspondence Courses Study materials for courses are mailed to a student's home, where he or she completes them and mails them back for evaluation.

Covering Letter A letter that introduces you and your résumé to a potential employer so that you will get a job interview.

Creative Visualization A method of focussed daydreaming, picturing something positive in one's mind.

Credits When a student completes a course at high school, he or she receives a credit for it. A certain number of credits are required to earn a diploma.

Decision Making To decide on which choice will solve a problem.

Degree What a student receives when he or she graduates from university.

Demographer A person who studies the population of a country and determines what the future needs and what the actions of the population will be.

Diploma The certificate a student receives when he or she graduates from high school or college.

Discrimination Behaviour that contradicts the human right that all people are born free and equal.

Distance Education Studying at home, using computer connections or long distance telephone calls to communicate with an instructor. For people who live far from available schools or universities.

Downsize To reduce the number of employees in a company.

Economy The management of material resources.

Emotional Quotient (EQ) The ability to handle one's emotions.

E-mail Electronic mail sent from one person to another via computer.

Employability Skills The fundamental, personal management, and teamwork skills needed to be successful in today's workplace.

Evaluation The judgement that is made based on what you have gathered in your portfolio.

Expenses The costs involved in running a business; what the business owner has to pay.

Fax A replica of a document, report, letter, or illustrative material sent electronically.

Full Disclosure In Grades 11 and 12 in Ontario, a student's achievement for all courses taken or attempted is recorded as percentage grades earned, credits granted, or "w" if you withdraw from a course before completing it.

Fundamental Skills   The communication, management, number, thinking, and problem-solving skills needed as a basis for further development.

Futurist   A person who specializes in watching what is happening currently, observing changes, and predicting what will happen in the future.

General Investment Certificate (GIC)   An investment certificate you purchase from a bank for a specific length of time that pays a higher rate of interest than a savings account.

Globalization   When the world is viewed as one large community.

Goals   Where a person wants to get to, or what a person wants to achieve.

Human Resources Department   In large companies, a department that assists with staff concerns, such as hiring, company benefits, and labour negotiations.

Human Rights   People's entitlement to fair treatment and justice.

Income   The amount of money a person earns.

Independent Learning Courses   Study materials for courses are mailed to a student's home, where he or she completes them and mails them back for evaluation.

Inflation   The rate at which the price of items, thus the cost of living, increases.

Initiative   Doing something without being told to do it.

Intelligence Quotient (IQ)   A number that describes a person's intelligence, based on a standard test.

Interest   The percentage of money your bank pays you for letting them use or invest your money while it is in their bank.

Inventory   A list of items.

Job Interview   An interview during which an employer attempts to match a job seeker to a particular job.

Job Lead   A tip or information about an available job.

Job Shadowing   Spending a period of time at work with a person in a particular career, at a particular job.

Journal   A record of events in a person's life and his or her thoughts and feelings about these events.

Kinaesthetic Learners   People who learn best by touching and doing things.

Left-Brained   Logical, analytical thinking.

Letter of Recommendation   A letter from a former employer or work-experience placement supervisor that confirms you are a good employee by highlighting your skills.

Literacy   The ability to read and write.

Long-Term Goals   Goals that a person works toward over a long period of time.

Meaningful Goals   Goals that improve a person or follow his or her values.

Mentor   A trusted counsellor or guide.

Multiple Intelligences   Different forms of intelligences, namely music, body, people, self, picture, word, logic, humour, and emotional.

Mutual Fund   A pool of money from different people that is invested in a variety of ways.

Net Income   The money left over from your earnings after your expenses have been subtracted.

Network   A group of people who have got to know you in a variety of ways, such as personally, professionally, through organizations, or by a chance encounter.

Non-Verbal Communication   Physical gestures that send a message.

Numeracy   The ability to understand numbers.

Occupational Research Interview   An interview with a person in an occupation that you are interested in and would like to learn more about first-hand.

Objective   Seeing something as it is, without personal thoughts and feelings affecting one.

Optional   School courses that a student chooses to take.

Outsourcing   When goods are produced outside the parent country, often in Third World countries, because labour costs are much cheaper.

Peer Pressure   Feeling obligated to follow the wishes of one's peers in spite of one's own wishes.

Personal Management Skills   The personal skills, attitudes, and behaviours that drive one's potential for growth, such as having a positive attitude, being responsible and adaptable, continuously learning, and employing safe work habits.

Personal Work Area   A study or work area at home.

Personality Type   The kind of person one is, according to personality tests.

Personnel Department   Another name for a Human Resources Department.

Portfolio Conference   A presentation of work a student has selected from his or her portfolio at a meeting with the teacher (and other people such as parents/guardians, if the student wishes).

Portfolio Icon   A symbol used to indicate that items from activities in which you have been involved would be suitable to include in your Career Studies Portfolio.

Post Secondary   After high school.

Problem Solving   Different ways to approach problems.

Products   Goods; things that are produced for people to buy.

Profile   A brief description of a person's character and abilities. A personal profile is a brief description of oneself.

Psychology   The study of human nature.

Questionnaire   A set of questions used to gather information.

Reachable Goals   Goals that a person can accomplish.

Real Rate of Return   What you earn after the cost of taxes and inflation have been subtracted.

Reference   A person who agrees to recommend you to a potential employer.

Residents   The people who make up a community.

Responsibility   What is expected of one, what one feels obliged to do.

Résumé   A summary of a person's education and work experience, used when applying for a job.

Retail   Stores that sell products in small amounts directly to the consumer.

Right-Brained   Creative thinking.

Role Model   A person whose part played in life is especially worth copying or imitating.

The Rule of 72   To find out how to double your money, divide 72 by your investment rate of return.

Savings Account   A bank account in which you save money and receive monthly interest from the bank on the amount saved.

Search Engine   A service that enables a computer user to search the World Wide Web for specific information using key words that link to specific web sites.

Secondary (School)   Words used for high school.

Self-Esteem   A person's opinion of himself or herself.

Self-Evaluation   Assessing one's own performance.

Semester   An equal part of a school year.

Services   Work provided that enables homes and businesses to operate efficiently.

Share   A piece of ownership of a corporation that helps raise money for its use.

Shareholder   Partial owners of a company.

Short-Term Goals   Goals that a person can achieve in a short period of time.

Skills   What a person has learned to do well.

Stock Market   A place where stocks and bonds can be bought or sold.

Subjective   The way personal thoughts and feelings affect how a person sees something.

Survey   A method of finding viewpoints about a subject. A number of people are asked the same set of questions about the subject.

Taxes   Money deducted from paycheques and given to the provincial and federal governments to pay for the cost of running the governments.

Teamwork Skills   The way a team acts together to be successful.

The Ten Percent Rule   Saving ten percent of your income for both short-term and long-term goals.

Term   A part of a school year.

Time Line   A chart that records the important dates and events in a person's life.

Time Management   Handling how one spends one's time.

Trade   A job or business involving mechanical ability or buying and selling.

Trends   General directions or movements.

Values   What is important to a person.

Visual Learners   People who learn best by reading or seeing pictures.

Voice Mail   A recording on a company answering machine or a person's private business line.

Volunteer Co-ordinators   People in charge of placing and monitoring volunteers.

Volunteer Training Programs   Courses for teaching volunteers how to help at particular volunteer placements.

Work Experience   Opportunity to learn on the job.

Workers' Compensation   Financial benefits that assist an employer or an employee when a work-related injury or illness occurs.

Workplace Safety and Insurance Board   In Ontario, the name of the workers' compensation agency.

Youth Apprenticeship   Combines in-school learning and on-the-job training, with pay from the employer.

Index